IN FLANDERS FIELDS

POETRY AND PROSE OF THE
FIRST WORLD WAR

IN FLANDERS FIELDS
SCOTTISH POETRY AND PROSE
OF THE FIRST WORLD WAR

Edited by
TREVOR ROYLE

MAINSTREAM
PUBLISHING

To my good friends

Knut and Lioba Mackensen

Copyright Introduction and Biographies © Trevor Royle, 1990

First published in Great Britain 1990 by
MAINSTREAM PUBLISHING COMPANY
(EDINBURGH) LTD
7 Albany Street
Edinburgh EH1 3UG

The publisher acknowledges the financial assistance of the Scottish Arts Council in the production of this volume.

British Library Cataloguing in Publication Data
In Flanders Fields: Scottish poetry and prose of the First World War.
1. English literature. Scottish writers. Special subjects. World war 1
820.80258

ISBN 1 85158 327 0 (cloth)

Typeset in 11/13 Bembo by Bookworm Typesetting Ltd, Edinburgh
Printed in Great Britain by Martins of Berwick

Acknowledgments

The idea for this book was prompted by a radio feature of the same title which I was commissioned to write for BBC Scotland in 1984. I am grateful to the programme's producer John Arnott for his help and enthusiasm and also to the three actors who read the extracts – Sandy Neilson, Tony Roper and Paul Young.

The task of selecting the Gaelic contributions was made easier by the ready help of Ian MacDonald, Editorial Officer of the Gaelic Books Council. I am grateful to him for supplying some of the translations and thanks are also due to Fred Macaulay and Derick Thomson for advice on points of translation.

I am indebted to the following copyright holders for permission to reprint the following:

James Bridie: to Ronald Mavor for *One Way of Living* and *Some Talk of Alexander*

Ian Hamilton: to the Executors of General Sir Ian Hamilton's Will Trust Literary Fund for *Gallipoli Diaries*, Vol. I

Violet Jacob: to Marjorie Lingen Hutton for *More Songs of Angus*

Harry Lauder: to Elizabeth Lauder Hamilton for *A Minstrel in France*

Joseph Lee: to Kathleen Lee Blackwood for *Ballads of Battle* and *Workaday Warriors*

Eric Linklater: to Andro Linklater and Peters Fraser and Dunlop Group Ltd for *The Man on My Back* and *Magnus Merriman*

Hugh MacDiarmid: to Michael Grieve for 'Casualties' and *The Complete Poems of Hugh MacDiarmid*

Donald MacDonald: to Margaret Campbell and Gairm for *Dòmhnall Ruadh Chorùna*.

Naomi Mitchison: to Naomi Mitchison for *All Change Here*

Charles Murray: to the Memorial Trust for Hameworth: *The Complete Poems of Charles Murray*

Murdo Murray: to Mary MacIver and Gairm for *Luach na Saorsa*

John Reith: to Christopher Reith for *Wearing Spurs*

David Rorie: to George Alpine for *A Medico's Luck in the War*

The extract from Ian Hay's *The First Hundred Thousand* is reproduced by permission of Samuel French Ltd as Administrators of the estate of the late Ian Hay.

The historical background of the Introduction first appeared in 1989 in *The Sunday Mail Story of Scotland*.

Every attempt has been made to contact copyright holders and I apologise for any accidental omissions. Due acknowledgment will be made in later editions if the information is forthcoming.

Note on the Text

Much of the Scottish poetry and prose of the First World War was published between 1914 and 1920. Wherever possible reference has been made to the original texts and the source is listed with the biographical information which introduces each writer's work. Where the text is still in print, this information has also been recorded. In place of footnotes, historical information and other pertinent background facts have been included in short introductions to the prose pieces. The writers have been listed alphabetically, by surname.

Contents

PROSE

Introduction
The Historical Background

When Britain went to war with the Central Powers in 1914 she was ill-prepared to fight a prolonged campaign in continental Europe. The Regular Army might have been professional and well-equipped but it was small in number and relied on volunteers for its manpower. Most continental armies were large all-conscript forces. Nevertheless, by virtue of a pre-war understanding, Britain had agreed to provide an expeditionary force of four (later six) divisions which would fight on the left of the French Army in Flanders. British politicians believed that it would only be called upon to play a subsidiary role: they prophesied that the war would be over by Christmas and that Germany would be defeated on land by the armies of France and Russia and on sea by the ships of the Royal Navy.

The one exception was Field Marshal Earl Kitchener of Khartoum, Britain's greatest living soldier, who had been appointed Secretary of State for War by the prime minister Herbert Henry Asquith on 5 August 1914. At his first cabinet meeting Kitchener astonished his colleagues by telling them that the war would last three years and that Britain would require one million men in arms to win it. Kitchener's prestige, personified by his soldierly bearing and his bristling moustache, convinced the politicians and within two days of Britain's declaration of war against Germany on 4 August 1914, the search had begun to raise the first 100,000 recruits. Before long, Kitchener's instantly recognisable features were assisting that campaign as Alfred Leete's famous recruiting poster began to be seen everywhere. Very few young men caught swithering outside the country's recruiting offices found it easy to ignore Kitchener's pointed admonition, 'Your Country Needs You!' By the end of October there were sufficient volunteers to form twelve new divisions and on one day alone 35,000 men enlisted, as many as had been recruited during the whole of 1913.

In Scotland, as in other parts of the country, the call to arms was shrill and insistent. 'I feel certain that Scotsmen have only to know that the country urgently needs their services to offer them with the same splendid patriotism as they have always shown in the past,' Kitchener told Sir Alexander Baird of Urie in a letter which was given considerable prominence in the Scottish press on 19 August. 'Tell them from me, please, that their services were never more needed than they are today, and that I rely confidently on a splendid response to the national appeal.'

Kitchener's request had not fallen on deaf ears. Within a day of the declaration of war the army's recruiting office in Cockburn Street in Edinburgh was reported to be a hive of industry and by the end of the month the *Glasgow Herald* announced that 20,000 men had enlisted at the Glasgow recruiting office in the Gallowgate. From other parts of Scotland came news of equally high figures of enlistment – 1,500 from Coatbridge, 900 from Clydebank, 940 from Dumbarton and 750 from Alloa. In Edinburgh, the entire Watsonian rugby XV joined up together in the 9th Royal Scots, the famous 'Dandy Ninth'. A recruiting booth at the local Derby match between Heart of Midlothian and Hibernian also attracted good business.

Recruits in Inverness rushed to join a special battalion of the Cameron Highlanders that was being formed by D.W. Cameron of Lochiel. He had offered his personal guarantee that 'at the end of the war the battalion will be brought back to Inverness where it will be disbanded with all possible despatch.' Other landowners were less generous. On 29 August the Earl of Wemyss gave notice that every able-bodied man aged between 18 and 30 at present working on his estates would be put on half-pay for the duration of the war, and their jobs kept open, provided they joined up. 'If they do not enlist,' continued the Earl's offer, 'they will be compelled to leave my employment.'

With or without blandishments, Scotland had always provided fertile territory for the army's recruiting sergeants: at the outbreak of war in 1914, 17 out of the Regular Army's 157 infantry battalions were Scots in name and origin and Scots accounted for ten per cent of the manpower of the Territorial Force which had been raised in 1908 out of the old volunteers.

By 1919, six of the 70 divisions of the Kitchener armies were Scottish divisions: two, the 9th (Scottish) and the 15th (Scottish) were New Army divisions, comprising battalions raised by Lord Kitchener's appeal; and the remaining four, the 51st (Highland), 52nd (Lowland), 64th (Highland) and 65th (Lowland) were made up largely of soldiers from the Territorial

Force. In addition to these formations, two battalions of the Scots Guards fought in France as members of the Guards Division and the Royal Scots Greys served throughout the war with the Cavalry Division. Scottish troops also served with expatriate territorial regiments like the London Scottish, the Liverpool Scottish and Tyneside Scottish and in support arms like the artillery, engineers and supply corps. Of the half-million Scots who volunteered to serve their country in the First World War some 125,000 were killed in action or died on active service, one-sixth of the total British and Empire casualty list.

Seventy after years the carnage and destruction of the First World War it is not easy to explain fully the reasons why Scots proved to be such enthusiastic volunteers. In the autumn of 1914 many ordinary people certainly felt ennobled by the exhilaration of war and regarded it as a glorious adventure. Even after the first offensive battles of 1915 – Neuve Chapelle, Aubers Ridge, Loos – during which the British Army sustained heavy casualties, recruiting in Scotland remained higher than in many other parts of the country. It was only when conscription was introduced in May 1916 that the numbers began to level out.

One of the most popular manifestations of the volunteering craze in 1914 and 1915 was the formation of 'pals' battalions – so-called because they kept together volunteers from the same cities or towns, or from working, sporting or social backgrounds. All told, 304 'pals' battalions were formed during the war and although the title was never officially recognised in Scotland, the concept did catch on, especially in Edinburgh and Glasgow.

At the beginning of the war the Glasgow Boys' Brigade, inspired by their treasurer David Laidlaw, had volunteered to form a battalion of the Highland Light Infantry. This offer had been turned down. Laidlaw then approached the Cameron Highlanders which was not a Glasgow regiment but finally achieved success when the Glasgow Corporation gave the go-ahead to the formation of a Highland Light Infantry Glasgow Tramways Battalion. Wearing their green uniforms and marching behind a pipe band, the motormen and conductors paraded through the streets of Glasgow to George Square where they presented themselves for enlistment on 7 September. Approval was given for 1,102 men to enlist and to a man they joined the Highland Light Infantry, becoming its 15th battalion. Under the aegis of James Dalrymple, Glasgow's transport manager, the Coplawhill tramways depot became a giant recruiting hall and it took just 16 hours to enlist the new battalion.

Encouraged by the scheme's success, official approval was given to the Glasgow Boys' Brigade to form a 16th battalion, a move which caused a great deal of public excitement and enthusiasm in the city. A few days later, a third 'pals' battalion, the 17th Highland Light Infantry, was formed at the instigation of the Glasgow Chamber of Commerce, with recruits being enrolled in the Lesser Hall of the Merchants' House. 'Never will it be said that men who were connected with the Boys' Brigade movement throughout the length and breadth of the United Kingdom and Ireland funked in the hour of Britain's need,' noted a zealously patriotic journalist in the *Glasgow Post*.

But that togetherness reaped a bitter harvest. More than 500 ex-members of the Boys' Brigade, all from Glasgow and many from the same street or district, died during the Battle of the Somme in 1916. Many of them fell during the first hours of the battle, attacking a German defensive position known as the Leipzig Redoubt on 1 July; some of those who survived only lived to die on the Hohenzollern Ridge during the last days of the battle in November. The camaraderie they shared in life was also theirs in death, and the monument to the dead of the 51st (Highland) Division, who fought alongside them at the Somme, echoes that sentiment. It looks across to Beaumont Hamel and its inscription would have raised a wry smile from those Boys' Brigade 'pals'. Translated from Gaelic – *Là a' bhlàir's math na càirdean* – it reads simply, 'Friends are good on the day of battle.'

Other regiments have equally heroic, yet tragic, stories to tell for none of the Scottish formations which fought in the First World War escaped high casualties when fighting in the killing grounds of the Western Front, Gallipoli, Palestine or Mesopotamia. The 7th Royal Scots suffered their first losses before they even reached the front line. Of their number, 217 were killed in a terrible railway accident at Quintinshill near Gretna in May 1915 – at that time it was the worst accident in British railway history. At Loos in September 1915 the 15th (Scottish) Division lost many of its men in the opening minutes of the battle when British gas drifted back into their trenches. In spite of this the Scottish regiments pressed home their attacks on the Loos and Lens Redoubts, inspired by the playing of Piper Laidlaw of the King's Own Scottish Borderers. Undaunted by the German barrage he rallied his fellow Scots by marching on the parapet of the trenches in full view of the enemy, playing the pipes for all he was worth. He was awarded the Victoria Cross for this feat; it was well-deserved for the attack might not have gone ahead without his encouragement – many of the survivors admitted later that they had been 'dazed by gas'.

Three battalions of the Royal Scots served in the Gallipoli theatre of operations where it was intended to open a second front: they suffered 40 per cent casualties for no tactical gain. During the Retreat from Mons in 1914 the 1,000-strong 1st Royal Scots Fusiliers was reduced to seventy men commanded by a young subaltern.

At Neuve Chapelle the 2nd Cameronians (Scottish Rifles) had 70 per cent casualties during a frontal attack across open ground on the German lines. A few weeks later, over the same ground, three battalions of the Black Watch took part in the Battle of Aubers Ridge: although the 1st battalion took its objective it was forced to retire with heavy losses due to lack of support. The 2nd Seaforth Highlanders lost 500 men during the attack on Beaumont Hamel on the first day of the Battle of the Somme and on the same sector during the same period the 5th Cameron Highlanders suffered equally high casualties. For the Gordons and the Argyll and Sutherland Highlanders the Somme told the same story: the 2nd Gordons lost 450 men at Mametz on the first day and a fortnight later the 10th Argylls lost 400 casualties during a surprise dawn attack on the German lines at Longueval.

At the war's end it was decided to raise a national monument to commemorate the sacrifice of the Scottish soldiers who had fought in the First World War. The project began as a Scottish protest against a proposal to erect a United Kingdom memorial in Hyde Park in London: one of the supporters of the Scottish scheme was the Duke of Atholl who said that 'if the Scottish nation wanted a memorial they would put it up with their own hands, in their own country, and with their own money.'

And so it turned out. Edinburgh Castle was chosen as the most suitable site for the Scottish National War Memorial and after many controversies the completed structure was inaugurated by the Prince of Wales in 1928. Designed largely by Sir Robert Lorimer and emblazoned by the work of Scotland's leading decorators it is a moving symbol of national sacrifice. Each regiment has its own memorial in the main gallery and there are also memorials to the men and women who gave their lives in other services during the First World War – the Royal Navy, the Royal Flying Corps, the Voluntary Aid Detachment, the Women's Land Army, amongst many others. 'Whatever the final verdict may be,' wrote the novelist and historian Ian Hay in *Their Name Liveth* (1931), 'that vanished generation have left behind them something which neither time can efface nor posterity belittle.'

The Literary Background

At the time of the outbreak of the First World War Scottish literature was in the doldrums. Robert Louis Stevenson, Scotland's greatest writer of the late nineteenth century, had died in 1894, without his promise being completely fulfilled. Much of the poetry that was being published was either sentimental, historical verse or the mystical vapours of the Celtic Twilight. Fiction had been left behind in 'the Kailyard', the catch-all phrase used by J. H. Millar in the April 1895 issue of the *New Review* to describe the novels of J. M. Barrie, S. R. Crockett and Ian Maclaren. Here was a well-defined arcadia of village life, a school of rural sentimentality which ignored the ills of turn-of-the-century Scotland, its industrial development, poverty and high mortality rate. Of Scottish drama there was nothing to be said until the 1920s. Critics like Millar and T. F. Henderson regarded Scottish writing in an overall British literary context and both doubted if Scots as a literary language was capable of survival in the twentieth century. Even Scottish publishing, for so long a vital force, was in decline by 1914. As Cairns Craig has pointed out in the opening sentences of his *History of Scottish Literature* (vol. IV), it was a barren enough period.

> When T. S. Eliot, in a review in 1919, asked, 'Was There a Scottish Literature?' the past tense perspective seemed all too appropriate to the possibilities of Scottish literature surviving into the twentieth century

as an independent cultural force. Scotland, politically more integrated into British society by the efforts of the First World War than it had ever been before, and seemingly culturally absorbed into English values by its participation in the previous century's imperial ambitions, had to look back to the era of Scott for a time when a writer's presentation of Scotland and the Scots had received international attention and literary recognition.

The signs of hope in the territory were few and far between. In 1901 George Douglas Brown had exposed the limitations of the Kailyard school in his novel *The House With The Green Shutters*. Having borrowed many of the features of the Kailyard – the rural setting, the raised expectations and a familiar cast of characters – he had then destroyed them by showing the impact caused by external social change. John MacDougall Hay had employed a similar structure in *Gillespie* (1914) which includes many of the themes explored by Brown. Although neither writer was to produce further fiction, both *The House With The Green Shutters* and *Gillespie* pointed to one direction which could be taken by twentieth century Scottish fiction.

The years before the First World War had also seen a revival of verse written in the vernacular. Much of it was coy or romantic nature poetry but there were exceptions written in the natural idioms of spoken speech. John Buchan, whom MacDiarmid was later to describe as 'the Dean of the Faculty of Contemporary Scottish Letters,' was a vigorous critic of the Kailyard school and in 1907 he had become editor of the *Scottish Review*. Its aim, he told Lord Rosebery, was 'to deal with all interests, literary, political and social, with something Scottish in the point of view. We want to make it the centre of a Scottish school of letters such as Edinburgh had a hundred years ago.' Buchan had also written, without publishing them, a number of passable poems in Scots although he was to admit in his introduction to *Poems, Scots and English* (1917) that 'Scots has never been to me a book-tongue; I could always speak it more easily than I could write it; and I dare to hope that the faults of my verses, great as they are, are not those of an antiquarian exercise.'

Better known to most readers was the poetry of Charles Murray, a poet from the north-east of Scotland who continued to write in the vernacular despite living in South Africa. In his often anthologised poem 'The Whistle', he shows a lively feeling for the language and cadences of the Aberdeenshire farming countryside, and he was to say in later life that it was 'simply inevitable' that he chose to write in his native dialect. Other north-east poets who followed in Murray's steps, both during and after the war, include Marion Angus, Violet Jacob, David Rorie and Mary Symon. (There is a full discussion of the vigorous growth of the vernacular poetry of the north-east before the war in Colin Milton's essay 'Modern Poetry in Scots before MacDiarmid' in *History of Scottish Literature*, vol. IV.)

The first reaction to the declaration of war in Scotland, as in other parts of Britain, was one of excitement and relief. Very few people envisaged that it would be a war of entrenchment and within a day or two of the decision most newspapers were talking about the hostilities being over by Christmas. Indeed, it was an indication of British optimism that volunteers were originally signed on for six months, or for the duration of the war, whichever was the longer.

The smooth mobilisation of the British Expeditionary Force, the best equipped and most professional army to have left Britain's shores, was a further example of the no-nonsense approach that would surely give a sharp riposte to German pretensions in Europe. That sense of enthusiastic conviction gave the early weeks of the war an unreal quality, creating a feeling that war was a glorious adventure and that man had been transformed and liberated from the doldrums of a humdrum existence. It found its truest expression in Rupert Brooke's poem 'Peace' and in Herbert Asquith's equally emotionally charged sonnet 'The Volunteer' but it struck a chord, too, in the actions of ordinary people who felt ennobled by the exhilaration of war. Chivalry, self-sacrifice and heroism were the catchwords of those first weeks and there were very few who did not respond to their call. Neil Munro, for example, was too old to enlist but his poem, 'Hey Jock, are ye glad ye 'listed?' is typical of the tub-thumping patriotism that permeated the last months of 1914. The mood found an echo, too, in the English poems of Pittendreigh MacGillivray which he published under the telling title, *Pro Patria*.

Two Scottish poets spoke out against the glory of war and condemned the gadarene rush to 'hate the Hun': Charles

Hamilton Sorley and Ewart Alan MacKintosh. Both were
similar in that they were born into Scottish families but were
brought up and educated in England and stand, therefore,
somewhat outside the Scottish literary tradition of the time.
Both, though, were aware of their heritage – MacKintosh was
a Gaelic speaker and Sorley admitted that he felt no sense of
patriotism towards England. In fact, Sorley had an ambivalent
attitude towards the war and towards Germany, having spent a
semester at the University of Jena early in 1914. He realised that
he had to serve his country but he refused to take the sentimental
approach of the jingoist: there is a delicate sense of irony in the
refrain of one of his earliest war poems, 'All the hills and dales
along' which he wrote shortly after enlisting.

> Sow your gladness for earth's reaping,
> So you may be glad though sleeping.
> Strew your gladness on earth's bed,
> So be merry, so be dead.

MacKintosh, too, refused to be taken in completely by the spirit
of jingoism. Although some of his early poems exult in the
excitement and glory of battle, his exposure to warfare soon
changed his tune. There is a world of difference between Neil
Munro's romantic view of the volunteer, which is very much
a civilian attitude, and MacKintosh's sarcastic opinion of 'fat
civilians' and 'girls with feathers' ('Recruiting') who push young
men into uniform.

Sorley first saw action in France in 1915 when his battalion
was posted to the Western Front in the Ypres sector, the scene
of some of the first great fighting of the war. It was then that
he had his first experience of violent death when one of his
bombers blew himself up whilst handling a grenade. Unlike
some of the contemporary English war poets like Brooke and
Julian Grenfell, who exulted in the glory of laying down one's
life for one's country, Sorley recognised the absolute otherness
of death.

> . . . we tried
> To live as of your presence unaware.
> But now in every road on every side
> We see your straight and steadfast signpost there.

There is a good deal of moral indignation in the focus of Sorley's poetry, much of which was written while he was in the front line – his poem 'When you see millions of the mouthless dead' was found in his kitbag after his death. By then Sorley had seen through the romantic myth of war but unlike Siegfried Sassoon and Wilfred Owen, for example, he shied away from describing in realistic detail the conditions endured by men in battle. ('One is hardened by now: purged of all false pity,' he wrote to his friend Arthur Watts.) Instead, he saw war as a nightmarish activity, quite separate from the experiences of ordinary day-to-day life. This was a common feeling amongst men who had seen active service – Owen used to keep photographs of casualties to show to those civilians who praised war. Men felt that it was impossible to convey the horrors they had endured and many descriptions have a dreamlike or grotesque quality which distances the reader from the subject.

The obverse was a desire to shock readers out of their complacency. Owen did this to good effect in 'Dulce et decorum est' and after his experiences on the Somme it informs most of Sassoon's poetry. ('Blighters' is a good example.) The idea of the poet as witness was particularly strong among those writers who experienced combat during large-scale infantry battles like the Somme and Third Ypres (Passchendaele). They believed that they had to come to terms with the experience and then record it so that others could understand it, too. For that reason Owen described the effects of a gas attack as realistically as he could.

> Dim, through the misty panes and thick green light,
> As under a green sea, I saw him drowning.

By burning the spongy tissues of the lung, mustard gas really did cause men to 'drown': Owen was not exaggerating. A similar sense of outrage is found in Roderick Watson Kerr's 'From the Line' and no one reading 'A Dead Man' could be left in much doubt about the effects of death on the human frame.

> Did that thing live of late?
> That sodden thing of ebony head
> With empty holes that gape?

In like vein neither Joseph Lee nor W. D. Cocker, both front-line soldiers, could see any glory in killing the enemy. In poems like 'The Sniper' and 'The Bullet' they saw that, in killing, the killer himself was diminished.

By the beginning of 1915 stalemate had come to the Western Front and the war leaders – British, French and German – were at a loss to know how to break it. The spring battles of Aubers and Neuve Chapelle ended in failure, as did the unwanted and unnecessary Battle of Loos in September that same year. With the heavy casualties and the increasing need for more men the numbers of volunteers began to fall and conscription was introduced in May 1916, two months before the costly Battle of the Somme.

War weariness began to infiltrate civilian life and this was noticed especially by the women writers who waited at home. The poetry of Violet Jacob and Mary Symon reveals some of the despair felt by the wives and mothers at the slaughter of so many men on the world's battle-fronts. (This feeling was not confined to women as Harry Lauder's memoirs testify.) In her long poem, 'The Glen's Muster-Roll' Mary Symon extended that sense of personal loss to other rural communities which had been touched by the carnage of war. In that respect, her poem, though rooted in a community which she knew well, attains a universality of feeling through the dominie's articulation of his personal sorrow.

On another level the war revolutionised the position of women in the community by putting them into the industrial work-force. When the war ended women workers demonstrated against their removal from these jobs, a further sign of the radicalism which was one of the war's lasting consequences in Scotland. In 1915 women on Clydeside had started a rent strike in the west of Scotland against the high rents demanded by their landlords. Workers in the shipyards and engineering works stopped work to show their solidarity and the concept of 'Red Clydeside' was born. James D. MacDougall, a socialist leader, said of this time: 'Jingoism was at a discount in Glasgow from the very beginning of the war; it was the sole place in the British empire where there was perfect freedom of speech for international socialists and opponents of the war.' ('Clyde Labour: A Study in Political Change', *Nineteenth Century*, 5 February 1927.) Scotland's emergent radicalism found a hero in the figure of John Maclean who advocated a termination of hostilities and the overthrow of capitalism. He was also an opponent of conscription and was imprisoned on four occasions during the war. Examples of his writing, though not strictly literary, have been included to show that in Scotland there was a vocal body of opposition to the war and that ultimate victory brought economic depression instead of the hoped-for triumph of free enterprise.

In addition to the poetry of war published during the conflict, there was also an outpouring of prose, both fiction and non-fiction. Partly this was in response to the need for an articulate response to the horrors of war; partly, too, the prose pieces in the shape of diaries and letters describe what was happening at the time. The letters of Sorley and MacDiarmid and the diary of Naomi Mitchison fall into this category. Equally significant is the prose which was written after the war and which thus provides a more measured response. James Bridie, Eric Linklater and Compton Mackenzie all continued to be fascinated by the war long after it was over and went back to it to use the raw material in different forms. It would have been surprising had they not done so for all had different experiences of combat. Linklater and Bridie were under fire in front-line positions and Mackenzie experienced the ill-starred campaign in Gallipoli. Naturally, in each case, there is a strong sense of the writer distancing himself from past events, and in the case of Bridie and Linklater of making light of the difficulties, but they still managed to convey the horror, futility and boredom of war.

With the exception of John Buchan's *Mr Standfast* no Scottish fiction of any merit was written during the war. Campbell's *Spud Tamson* and Bell's *Wee MacGreegor Enlists* are off-shoots of the Kailyard school, but extracts from them have been included as a prose counterpart to the poems of Munro and MacGillivray. James Leslie Mitchell was too young to enlist but he was a serviceman in the immediate post-war years and some of the survivors' stories found their way into his novel *The Thirteenth Disciple*. Under the pen-name of Lewis Grassic Gibbon he wrote the *Scots Quair* trilogy whose immediate background is the break up of the already declining crofting communities in the aftermath of the First World War; in turn this led to the disintegration of small-town life and the turmoil of the strike-ridden cities of the 1920s.

Of the poetry written by Scots during the First World War, Sorley's is best remembered and has featured prominently in anthologies of British war poetry. (Parsons, Silkin et al.) W. D. Cocker, Roderick Watson Kerr, Joseph Lee, Ewart Alan MacKintosh and J. B. Salmond, all front-line soldiers, have been largely (and unjustly) forgotten, a poor recompense for all their endeavours. MacKintosh was killed on active service and was unable to fulfil his potential; the other four turned to journalism and their poetry never developed beyond the lightweight verses they had written before the war. It could be claimed for them that they found their true voices fighting in a war that was supposed to end wars. They confronted unimagined degrees of horror, yet discovered on the battlefield a sense of truth, and, in so doing, they have helped us today to understand more completely the endurance and the courage of the men who fought and died during the First World War. When peace came in November 1918, concepts like honour, heroism, patriotism, duty and glory had changed utterly, not just through the experience of a dreadful war, but also through the response of the poets to that experience.

Salmond wrote most of his war poetry in the vernacular and is easily identified as a Scottish writer but there is another aspect of his work which separates it from the English experience. This is the so-called 'reductive idiom' which runs through so much Scottish literature, the 'cocking a snook' at those in authority. Salmond was an establishment figure, the editor of a respected magazine, and later an official of the University of St Andrews, but his poem 'Any Private to Any Private' reveals the antipathy towards the war felt by many ordinary soldiers.

> They'll pester her, and crack a dagoned lot;
> An' Heaven kens, they'll lave her awfu' ticht.
> 'A burden to the State.' Her Wullie's shot.
> I kenna, hoo I canna lauch the nicht.

There are echoes in this poem of the conversational style of Sassoon's 'Base Details' but here Salmond is taking the point of view – and the voice – of a private soldier sickened by the death of his best friend and angered by a newspaper statement that war widows might become a burden to the state. Kerr created the same effect in his poem 'The Corpse'. The speaker introduces the idea of the dead lying on the battlefield after the shooting has stopped – a common First World War image – and then brings the poem to a close with the chilling words: 'Thank God! it had a sack/ Upon its face.' It is also worth comparing the change that had taken place between MacKintosh's early view of the war as expressed in 'Cha Till MacCruimein' and the ironic disgust of 'Ghosts of War', his last poem, written shortly before his death.

Three Gaelic poets deserve mention: Donald MacDonald (Dòmhnall Ruadh Chorùna), John Munro (Iain Rothach) and Murdo Murray (Murchadh Moireach). All three served as front-line soldiers and wrote about their experiences in France. Munro's and Murray's work was published in James Thomson's *An Dileab* in 1930 and Murray's writings appeared in *Luach na Saorsa* in 1970. This extraordinary volume also contains Murray's war diary which was written in both English and Gaelic, a fluctuation which, according to Derick Thomson, was typical of the 'bilingual and bicultural influence' of that period. Murray also translated into Gaelic Charles Murray's poem 'A Sough O' War'.

Twenty years after the outbreak of the First World War, Hugh MacDiarmid addressed Scotland in his poem 'Towards a new Scotland', and asked:

> Was it for little Belgium's sake
> Sae mony thoosand Scotsmen dee'd?
> And never ane for Scotland fegs
> Wi' twenty thoosand mair need!

In a sense MacDiarmid (Grieve) had already answered the question himself. On his demobilisation from the army Grieve had been transfigured, literally and metaphysically. 'With an almost military precision he began putting his plan to transform the Scottish cultural scene into action and within a few years Quartermaster-Sergeant Grieve had metamorphosed into Hugh MacDiarmid, the modern Scottish vernacular poet and leader of what he was optimistically to call the "Scottish Renaissance". (Catherine Kerrigan, 'MacDiarmid's Early Poetry' in *History of Scottish Literature*, vol. IV.)

MacDiarmid's first serious publication was *Northern Numbers* (1920) an anthology based on Edward Marsh's *Georgian Poetry*.

It was followed by two further editions in 1921 and 1922 and the contributors included John Buchan, Violet Jacob, Roderick Watson Kerr, Joseph Lee, Neil Munro, Charles Murray and Mary Symon. He founded a magazine, the *Scottish Chapbook* and began to challenge Scottish literary assumptions in a series of articles for the *Scottish Educational Journal* under the title of 'Contemporary Scottish Studies'. He began writing poetry in Scots and from these efforts he evolved the idea of a Scottish renaissance movement whose aim was to dissociate Scottish writing from the sentimentality of the vernacular based poetry of the late nineteenth century and to bring it into line with contemporary European thinking. His campaign for the revival of Scots letters also had a political aspect: he was one of the founders of the Scottish section of PEN and in 1928 he joined the National Party of Scotland.

During the war Grieve wrote little of any value for publication – one poem 'A Salonikan Storm Song' is faintly embarrassing – but as Alan Bold points out in his critical biography (1988) MacDiarmid had used his time in the military to good effect by developing his literary and political ideas.

> He no longer saw inconsistency as a vice but as an artistic virtue; he was no longer alarmed by his impetuosity. Politically he had become more extreme. Dissatisfied with the parliamentary socialism of the ILP and the Fabian Society he was moving towards a revolutionary faith, one that took account of the failure of the Easter Rising in Ireland and the success of the Bolshevik Revolution in Russia. Having seen men die for 'gallant little Belgium' and the 'honour of England' he now held firmly nationalistic opinions about the economic state and inferior political status of Scotland.

Although Grieve had not seen combat as a soldier, once demobilised he turned his powers of energy and aggression to change the face of Scottish literature. Like Yeats, Eliot and Pound he was aware of the post-war exhaustion of English culture and of the need to explore new means of national self-expression, hence his 'discovery' of Scots as a literary language. MacDiarmid was also aware that the war had changed the cohesion of European civilisation in general. In those circumstances it would be the duty of countries like Scotland to redeem those cultural values; and like many others he realised that the First World War had been fought to protect the rights of small nations. In that respect the First World War hastened the development of Scottish literature, and the men and women who wrote and published poetry and prose influenced by the war can be seen today as harbingers of that change.

POETRY

John Buchan
1875–1940

John Buchan was born in Perth the son of a minister of the Free
Church of Scotland. He was educated at Hutcheson's Grammar
School, Glasgow University and Brasenose College, Oxford.
After a short career as a barrister and journalist he served
with Lord Milner in South Africa between 1901 and 1903;
at the outbreak of the First World War he was a director of
the publishing firm of Thomas Nelson. Physically unfit for
service in the armed forces, Buchan served his country in other
important capacities. In 1915 he visited the Western Front as a
special correspondent of *The Times*; he was attached to Haig's
GHQ as an observer and in 1917 he was appointed Director
of Information and, under Lord Beaverbrook, virtual head of
the British propaganda effort. Many of Buchan's closest friends
were killed during the war – his brother Alistair, Raymond
Asquith, Tommy Nelson – and his poem 'Home Thoughts
from Abroad' was written in response to their deaths. Buchan
also wrote, almost single-handed, the 24 volumes of *Nelson's
History of the War*.

Source: John Buchan, *Poems, Scots and English*, Edinburgh and London:
Thomas Nelson, 1917

On Leave

I had auchteen months o' the war,
   Steel and pouther and reek,
Fitsore, weary and wauf,–
   Syne I got hame for a week.

Daft-like I entered the toun,
   I scarcely kenned for my ain.
I sleepit twae days in my bed,
   The third I buried my wean.

The wife sat greetin' at hame,
   While I wandered oot to the hill,
My hert as cauld as a stane,
   But my heid gaun roond like a mill.

I wasna the man I had been,–
   Juist a gangrel dozin' in fits;–
The pin had faun oot o' the warld,
   And I doddered amang the bits.

I clamb to the Lammerlaw
   And sat me doun on the cairn;–
The best o' my freends were deid,
   And noo I had buried my bairn;–

The stink o' the gas in my nose,
   The colour o' bluid in my ee,
And the biddin' o' Hell in my lug
   To curse my Maker and dee.

But up in that gloamin' hour,
   On the heather and thymy sod,
Wi' the sun gaun doun in the Wast
   I made my peace wi' God.

. . . . .

I saw a thoosand hills,
   Green and gowd i' the licht,
Roond and backit like sheep,
   Huddle into the nicht.

But I kenned they werena hills,
   But the same as the mounds ye see
Doun by the back o' the line
   Whaur they bury oor lads that dee.

They were juist the same as at Loos
   Whaur we happit Andra and Dave.–
There was naething in life but death,
   And a' the warld was a grave.

A' the hills were graves,
   The graves o' the deid langsyne,
And somewhere oot in the Wast
   Was the grummlin' battle-line.

. . . . .

But up frae the howe o' the glen
   Came the wait o' the simmer een.
The stink gaed oot o' my nose,
   And I sniffed it, caller and clean.

The smell o' the simmer hills,
   Thyme and hinny and heather,
Jeniper, birk and fern,
   Rose in the lown June weather.

It minded me o' auld days,
   When I wandered barefit there,
Guddlin' troot in the burns,
   Howkin' the tod frae his lair.

If a' the hills were graves
   There was peace for the folk aneath
And peace for the folk abune,
   And life in the hert o' death.

. . . . .

Up frae the howe o' the glen
  Cam the murmur o' wells that creep
To swell the heids o' the burns,
  And the kindly voices o' sheep.

And the cry o' a whaup on the wing,
  And a plover seekin' its bield. –
And oot o' my crazy lugs
  Went the din o' the battlefield.

. . . . .

I flang me doun on my knees
  And I preyed as my hert wad break,
And I got my answer sune,
  For oot o' the nicht God spake.

As a man that wauks frae a stound
  And kens but a single thocht,
Oot o' the wind and the nicht
  I got the peace that I socht.

Loos and the Lammerlaw,
  The battle was feucht in baith,
Death was roond and abune,
  But life in the hert o' death.

A' the warld was a grave,
  But the grass on the graves was green,
And the stones were bields for hames,
  And the laddies played atween.

Kneelin' aside the cairn
  On the heather and thymy sod,
The place I had kenned as a bairn,
  I made my peace wi' God.

1916

Home Thoughts from Abroad

Aifter the war, says the papers, they'll no be content
  at hame,
The lads that hae feucht wi' death twae 'ear i' the mud and
  the rain and the snaw;
For aifter a sodger's life the shop will be unco tame;
  They'll ettle at fortune and freedom in the new lands far
  awa'.

No me!
By God! No me!
Aince we hae lickit oor faes
And aince I get oot o' this hell,
For the rest o' my leevin' days
I'll mak a pet o' mysel'.
I'll haste me back wi' an eident fit
And settle again in the same auld bit.
And oh! the comfort to snowk again
The reek o' my mither's but-and-ben,
The wee box-bed and the ingle neuk
And the kail-pat hung frae the chimley-heuk!

I'll gang back to the shop like a laddie to play,
Tak doun the shutters at skreigh o' day,
And weigh oot floor wi' a carefu' pride,
And hear the clash o' the countraside.
I'll wear for ordinar' a roond hard hat,
A collar and dicky and black cravat.
If the weather's wat I'll no stir ootbye
Wi'oot an umbrella to keep me dry.
I think I'd better no tak a wife –
I've had a' the adventure I want in life.–
But at nicht, when the doors are steeked, I'll sit,
While the bleeze loups high frae the aiken ruit,
And smoke my pipe aside the crook.
And read in some douce auld-farrant book;
Or crack wi' Davie and mix a rummer,
While the auld wife's pow nid-nods in slum'er;
And hark to the winds gaun tearin' bye
And thank the Lord I'm sae warm and dry.

When simmer brings the lang bricht e'en,
I'll daunder doun to the bowling-green,
Or delve my yaird and my roses tend
For the big floo'er-show in the next back-end.
Whiles, when the sun blinks aifter rain,
I'll tak my rod and gang up the glen;
Me and Davie, we ken the püles
Whaur the troot grow great in the howes o' the hills;
And, wanderin' back when the gloamin' fa's
And the midges dance in the hazel shaws,
We'll stop at the yett ayont the hicht
And drink great wauchts o' the scented nicht,
While the hoose lamps kin'le raw by raw
And a yellow star hings ower the law.
Davie will lauch like a wean at a fair
And nip my airm to mak certain shüre
That we're back frae yon place o' dule and dreid,
To oor ain kind warld–

     But Davie's deid!
Nae mair gude nor ill can betide him.
We happit him doun by Beaumont toun,
And the half o' my hert's in the mools aside him.

1917

The Great Ones

Ae morn aside the road frae Bray
   I wrocht my squad to mend the track;
A feck o' sodgers passed that way
   And garred me often straucht my back.

By cam a General on a horse,
   A jinglin' lad on either side.
I gie'd my best salute of course,
   Weel pleased to see sic honest pride.

And syne twae Frenchmen in a cawr–
   Yon are the lads to speel the braes;
They speldered me inch-deep wi' glaur
   And verra near ran ower my taes.

And last the pipes, and at their tail
   Oor gaucy lads in martial line.
I stopped my wark and cried them hail,
   And wished them weel for auld lang syne.

       . . . . .

An auld chap plooin' on the muir
   Ne'er jee'd his heid nor held his han',
But drave his furrow straucht and fair,–
   Thinks I, 'But ye're the biggest man.'

1916

Fisher Jamie

Puir Jamie's killed. A better lad
  Ye wadna find to busk a flee
Or burn a püle or wield a gad
  Frae Berwick to the Clints o' Dee.

And noo he's in a happier land.–
  It's Gospel truith and Gospel law
That Heaven's yett maun open stand
  To folk that for their country fa'.

But Jamie will be ill to mate;
  He lo'ed nae müsic, kenned nae tünes
Except the sang o' Tweed in spate,
  Or Talla loupin' ower its linns.

I sair misdoot that Jamie's heid
  A croun o' gowd will never please;
He liked a kep o' dacent tweed
  Whaur he could stick his casts o' flees.

If Heaven is a' that man can dream
  And a' that honest herts can wish,
It maun provide some muirland stream,
  For Jamie dreamed o' nocht but fish.

And weel I wot he'll up and speir
  In his bit blate and canty way,
Wi' kind Apostles standin' near
  Whae in their time were fishers tae.

He'll offer back his gowden croun
  And in its place a rod he'll seek,
And bashfu'-like his herp lay doun
  And speir a leister and a cleek.

For Jims had aye a poachin' whim;
  He'll sune grow tired, wi' lawfu' flee
Made frae the wings o' cherubìm,
  O' castin' ower the Crystal Sea. . . .

For Jims had aye a poachin' whim;
   He'll sune grow tired, wi' lawfu' flee
Made frae the wings o' cherubim,
   O' castin' ower the Crystal Sea. . . .

I picter him at gloamin' tide
   Steekin' the backdoor o' his hame
And hastin' to the waterside
   To play again the auld auld game;

And syne wi' saumon on his back,
   Catch't clean against the Heavenly law,
And Heavenly byliffs on his track,
   Gaun linkin' doun some Heavenly shaw.

1916

W. D. Cocker
1882–1970

William Dixon Cocker was born into an old established Glasgow merchant family but he was to take his literary inspiration from the people and countryside of Strathendrick in Stirlingshire, his mother's home. After school Cocker became a journalist and went on to have a distinguished career with the *Daily Record*. During the First World War he served with the Highland Light Infantry and the Royal Scots but was taken prisoner early in 1917. He was incarcerated at Enger near Minden where British and French prisoners of war were forced to work in a nearby factory which manufactured barbed wire. Most of Cocker's poetry at that time was written in English but after the war he turned to Scots and was associated for a while with Hugh MacDiarmid's 'Scottish Renaissance' movement. Cocker also wrote a number of historical romances in the style of Neil Munro.

Source: W. D. Cocker, *Poems, Scots and English*, Glasgow: Brown, Son and Ferguson, 1932

Up the Line to Poelkapelle

Heavy loaded, heavy hearted,
   Up the line to Poelkapelle,
As we trudged we passed a dozen
   Soldiers lying as they fell:
Sprawling in the slime grotesquely,
Left like carrion to rot –
   (Long, long way to Tipperary –)
No one seemed to care a jot!

Transport-waggons splashed upon them,
   Laden limbers clattered by;
Some who saw them vaguely wondered
   When their turn would come to die.
Patient pack-mules plodded past them –
Blast the beasts! why can't they trot? –
   (Long, long way to Tipperary –)
No one seemed to care a jot!

Soldier's wife, or soldier's mother,
   Any nations, north or south,
Could you see your loved one lying
   With the mud upon his mouth,
Such a cry would rise to heaven
God would know you cared a lot.
   (Long, long way to Tipperary –)
Surely God must care a jot!

The Sniper

Two hundred yards away he saw his head;
  He raised his rifle, took quick aim and shot him.
Two hundred yards away the man dropped dead;
With bright exulting eye he turned and said,
  'By Jove, I got him!'
And he was jubilant; had he not won
  The meed of praise his comrades haste to pay?
He smiled; he could not see what he had done;
  The dead man lay two hundred yards away.
He could not see the dead, reproachful eyes,
  The youthful face which Death had not defiled
But had transfigured when he claimed his prize.
  Had he seen this perhaps he had not smiled.
He could not see the woman as she wept
  To hear the news two hundred miles away,
Or through his every dream she would have crept.
  And into all his thoughts by night and day.
Two hundred yards away, and, bending o'er
  A body in a trench, rough men proclaim
Sadly, that Fritz, the merry, is no more.
  (Or shall we call him Jack? *It's all the same.*)

Sonnets in Captivity

I

Like leaves upon a rushing torrent cast,
Toss'd on its troubled bosom towards an ocean,
A wild insatiate water deep and vast,
Then, on their journey stay'd and void of motion,
Held captive in an eddy for a space,
So we, who launched of late on War's red river,
Are swirl'd into this eddy from the race
While the great tide roars on tumultuous ever.
Yet oh! to be in freedom on its waves!
Behind the wire in drear Westphalia
We scan the spacious sky through prison bars.
The sun may flaunt his glorious regalia
The night bring forth her treasury of stars;
We have no pleasure in it — being slaves.

II

As one who sails upon a midnight sea
Beholds behind the phosphorescent wake,
So I, the uncharted future dark to me,
May leave its days to destiny and take
A retrospect, my lost identity
Regain, and in my contemplation find
A solace in my prison, being free
Within the large dominion of the mind.
Thought knows no barriers, the vagrant wind
Hath not more scope. Then let me turn awhile
To these past days, which in their passing seem'd
A dream delirious, a nightmare vile
From which I shuddering wake to know I dream'd
A dream of import could it be divin'd.

III

Endurance! that's the one outstanding wonder!
What finely tempered steel we mortals are!
What man endures! What trials he goes under
When tested in the crucible of War,
And all the unknown strength and hardihood
Latent within him is made manifest!
We had not guess'd that our frail flesh and blood
Contained the metal to withstand such test.
There is an essence of the spirit when
The soul is strong within us which imparts
To wearied bodies something of its blaze;
Strength lies not then in sinews but in hearts.
Comrades, was it not something in those days
To be a man and to endure with men?

IV

Talk not to me of courage as do some
Who speak of valour as a thing unique
Held by the Briton only. Where the drum
Beats for the martial muster you may seek
And find the brave in men of every zone.
Courage is man's distinction o'er the brute.
The brute has courage, but 'tis man alone
Fears and goes forward grimly resolute.
Thus holds he his supremacy and leads.
Who with false pride would scoff at valiant foes
Belittles all his species; let us glory
Not in the deeds we do when nations close
In the mad welter of a grapple gory,
But in the impulse which controls our deeds.

V

O God! that men could love as they can hate!
There is a gospel that is sane and pure,
And we must learn its message soon or late;
Love is the only law that shall endure.
Had all this mighty effort to destroy
Been one united effort to create
An earth to vie with paradise for joy,
What glorious vision could we contemplate!
The world has dreamed it and the world awakes!
Brothers, when Peace, compassionate, hath come,
And the hot-throated cannon silent stands,
Remember those who fell upon the Somme,
Whose bones are bleaching on Assyrian sands,
And build a nobler world for their sakes.

Enger, by Minden, Westphalia
March 1918.

John MacDougall Hay
1881–1919

John MacDougall Hay was born at Tarbert, Loch Fyne, in Argyll. He was educated locally and at Glasgow University where he began writing for journals and newspapers, becoming a reasonably successful journalist. After graduating he turned to the more secure profession of teaching and took posts in Stornoway and Ullapool. While there he contracted rheumatic fever and it was during this period that he decided to follow the calling of the Church of Scotland. In 1905 he returned to Glasgow to study in the university's Divinity Hall, but shortage of funds forced him to return to freelance writing to maintain his family. On his ordination his first parish was in Govan, after which he was transferred to Elderslie, the birthplace of the Scottish patriot Sir William Wallace. The publication of his first, and most successful novel, *Gillespie*, enticed him to give up the ministry but he resisted the temptation and remained in this vocation until his death on 10 December 1919. Towards the end of the war Hay published a volume of free verse commemorating the volunteers who had served in Britain's armed forces. Rich with the language and themes of the Old Testament and the Psalms, the work is at once a lament for the dead and a panegyric for their sacrifice. It is divided into four sections: 'The Call', 'Beyond the Seas', 'Their Mothers' and 'The Consolation of the Cross'.

Source: John MacDougall Hay, *Their Dead Sons*, London: Erskine Macdonald, 1918

from The Call

Do not think of them as soldiers as they pass by,
   the companions of horses, living among steel
   and explosives.
They were men like you.
They had their own burdens, anxieties and cares;
A mother to support; children the leaving of
   whom behind was the first death.
To none is home dearer than to those who go
   forth to fight for home.
They left that sanctuary behind.
Never was war more merciless than then; never
   were they braver than in that hour of
   renunciation.
They, too, had heavy thoughts as they drilled and
   entrenched.
They did not put off humanity when they put on
   a uniform.
They could weep, too.
They also had bad news in letters, and cried
   at night in their dug-out or billet – those
   devoted lads.
They were not soldiers: they were men,
The best God ever created on this war-scarred
   earth.
Not as the world calls soldiers.
Military pomp, pride, pageantry and gorgeousness
   of arms –
It moved them not.
Yet as they marched through the City unarmed,
   unpanoplied,
The world could see they were the prophets of
   their own glorious victories —
They, the spirit of a nation issuing incarnate from
   the humble and high doors of the land
To meet the savagery of tall barbaric thrones.

from *Beyond the Seas*

They were comrades, they were brothers.
Together they learned, ate, worked, suffered and fought,
Walking life abreast,
And out of the fire coming hand in hand.
They knew the need they had of one another.
They were friends – not as the world knows
    friendship, by chance or caste, or common
    interests
In a day they were friends, purified in suffering,
    sanctified in trial together.
Those who were younger in danger got very near
    to those who had come to close quarters with
    the terrifying things
And had passed through the waters.
Whose presence was consolation, whose word was
    guidance,
Whose face relit the fire of courage in the darkest
    hours.
They who had suffered gave to the others the gift
    of enduring.
They who had fought communicated steadfastness
    and quietness of soul.
They were the Big Friends, the big Brothers.

Violet Jacob
1863–1946

Violet Kennedy-Erskine was born in Montrose, the daughter of the 18th Laird of Dun whose family had lived in Angus since the fifteenth century. In 1894 she married Major Arthur Otway Jacob, 25th Hussars, and the first five years of their marriage were spent in Egypt and India. Although much of her life was to be spent in England she was a regular visitor to her native north-east of Scotland. In all her work there is evidence of her deep knowledge of the lore and language of Angus, but she never sentimentalised the lives of the country people. With deceptive ease she was able to echo the rhythms of ordinary speech and her poetry has a song-like quality which makes it particularly easy to read. Like Charles Murray and Helen B. Cruickshank she contributed verse to Hugh MacDiarmid's *Northern Numbers*. Her only son Harry Jacob was killed during the Battle of the Somme in the summer of 1916 and her husband, who survived the war, died in 1936.

Source: Violet Jacob, *More Songs of Angus*, London: Country Life, 1918

Jock, To the First Army

O Rab an' Dave an' rantin' Jim,
  The geans were turnin' reid
When Scotland saw yer line grow dim,
  Wi' the pipers at its heid;
Noo, i' yon warld we dinna ken,
  Like strangers ye maun gang –
'We've sic a wale o' Angus men
  That we canna weary lang.'

And little Wat – my brither Wat,
  Man, are ye aye the same?
Or is yon sma' white hoose forgot
  Doon by the strath at hame?
An' div ye mind foo aft we trod
  The Isla's banks before ? –
'My Place is wi' the Hosts o' God,
  But I mind me o' Strathmore.'

It's deith comes skirlin' through the sky,
  Below there's nocht but pain,
We canna see whaur deid men lie
  For the drivin' o' the rain;
Ye a' hae passed frae fear an' doot,
  Ye're far frae airthly ill –
'We're near, we're here, my wee recruit,
And we fecht for Scotland still!'

The Field by the Lirk o' the Hill

Daytime and nicht,
Sun, wind an' rain
The lang cauld licht
O' the spring months again;
The yaird's a' weed
And the fairm's a' still –
Wha'll sow the seed
I' the field by the lirk o' the hill?

Prood maun ye lie,
Prood did ye gang,
Auld, auld am I
And oh! life's lang!
Ghaists i' the air,
Whaups' voices shrill,
And you nae mair
I' the field by the lirk o' the hill –
Aye, bairn, nae mair, nae mair,
I' the field by the lirk o' the hill.

Glory

I canna see ye, lad, I canna see ye
For a' yon glory that's aboot yer heid,
Yon licht that haps ye and the hosts that's wi ye –
Ayes, but ye live, and it's mysel' that's deid.

They gaed frae mill an' mairt; frae wind-blown places
And grey toon-closes; i' the empty street
Nae mair the bairns ken their steps, their faces,
Nor stand tae listen to the trampin' feet.

Beside the brae, and soughin' through the rashes,
Yer voice comes back tae me at ilka turn,
Amang the whins and whaur the water washes
The arn tree wi' its fit amangst the burn.

Whiles ye come back tae me when day is fleein'
And a' the road oot-by is dim wi' nicht,
But weary een like mine is no for seein',
And, gin they saw, they wad be blind wi' licht.

Deith canna kill. The mools o' France lie o'er ye,
And yet ye live, O sodger o' the Lord.
For Him that focht wi' deith an' dule before ye
He gied the life – 'twas Him that gied the sword.

But gin ye see my face or gin ye hear me,
I daurna ask, I mauna seek tae ken;
Tho' I should dee wi' sic a glory near me
By nicht or day, come ben, my bairn, come ben!

Hallowe'en

The tattie-liftin's nearly through,
They're ploughin' whaur the barley grew,
  And aifter dark, roond ilka stack,
  Ye'll see the horsemen stand an' crack.
O Lachlan, but I mind o' you!

I mind foo often we hae seen
Ten thoosand stars keek doon atween
  The nakit branches, an' below
  Baith fairm an' bothie hae their show,
Alowe wi' lichts o' Hallowe'en.

There's barns wi' guizards at their tail
Clourin' the doors wi runts o' kail,
  And fine ye'll hear the skreichs an' skirls
  O' lassies wi' their droukit curls
Bobbin' for aipples i' the pail.

The bothie fire is loupin' het,
A new heid horseman's kist is set
  Richts o' the lum; whaur by the blaze
  'The auld ane stude that kept yer claes –
I canna thole to see it yet!

But gin the auld fowks' tales are richt
An' ghaists come hame on Hallow nicht,
  O freend o' freends, what wad I gie
  To feel ye rax yer hand to me
Atween the dark an' can'le-licht?

Awa' in France, across the wave,
The wee lichts burn on ilka grave,
  An' you an' me their lowe hae seen –
  Ye'll mebbe hae yer Hallowe'en
Yont, whaur ye're lyin' wi the lave.

There's drink an' daffin', sang an' dance,
And ploys and kisses get their chance,
  But Lachlan, man, the place I see
  Is whaur the auld kist used to be
And the lichts o' Hallowe'en in France!

The Road to Marykirk

To Marykirk ye'll set ye forth
And whustle as ye step alang,
And aye the Grampians i' the north
Are glow'rin' on ye as ye gang.
By Martin's Den, through beech and birk
A breith comes soughin' sweet and strang
 Alang the road tae Marykirk.

Frae mony a field ye'll hear the cry
O' teuchats, skirlin' on the wing,
Noo east, noo west, amang the kye
And smell o' whins the wind'll bring;
Aye, lad, it blaws a thocht to mock
The licht o' day on ilka thing –
For you, that went yon road last spring,
 Are lyin' deid in Flanders, Jock.

Roderick Watson Kerr
1893–1960

Roderick Watson Kerr was born in Edinburgh and educated at Boroughmuir School and Broughton Junior Students Centre. Like his contemporary C. M. Grieve (Hugh MacDiarmid, see p 63) he was much influenced by George Ogilvie and was editor for a time of the *Broughton Magazine*. Shortly after the outbreak of war he enlisted in the army and was commissioned in the 2nd Royal Tank Corps which had been founded in 1916. He was awarded the Military Cross in 1918 for his part in stemming the German breakthrough near Bapaume. (See also John Buchan, *Mr Standfast*, pp 151–3.) While still in the army his war poems were published by John Lane and immediate comparisons were made with the work of Siegfried Sassoon. Kerr returned to Edinburgh on demobilisation with the intention of studying for a degree in English. However, his work as a journalist prevented him from graduating and in 1922 he became a sub-editor with the *Scotsman*. In 1926 he left Scotland to work as a leader writer with the *Liverpool Daily Post*. With George Malcolm Thomson, Kerr was one of the founders of the Porpoise Press, Scotland's principal literary publisher in the years before the Second World War.

Source: R. Watson Kerr, *War Daubs*, London: John Lane, 1919

From the Line

Have you seen men come from the Line,
Tottering, doddering, as if bad wine
Had drugged their very souls;
Their garments rent with holes
And caked with mud
And streaked with blood

Of others, or their own;
Haggard, weary-limbed and chilled to the bone
Trudging aimless, hopeless on,
With listless eyes and faces drawn
Taut with woe?

Have you seen them aimless go
Bowed down with muddy pack
And muddy rifle slung on back,
And soaking overcoat,
Staring on with eyes that note
Nothing but the mire,
Quenched of every fire?

Have you seen men when they come
From shell-holes filled with scum
Of mud and blood and flesh,
Where there's nothing fresh,
Like grass, or trees, or flowers,
And the numbing year-like hours
Lag on – drag on;
And the hopeless dawn
Brings naught but death and rain –
The rain a fiend of pain
That scourges without end,
And death a smiling friend?

Have you seen men when they came from hell?
If not, ah well,
Speak not with easy eloquence,
That seems like sense,
Of 'War and Necessity!'
And do not rant I pray
On 'War's Magnificent Nobility!'

If you've seen men come from the Line
You'll know it's Peace that is divine!
If you've not seen the things I've sung,
Let silence bind your tongue,
But, make all wars to cease;
And work, and work, for Everlasting Peace!

The Corpse

It lay on the hill
A sack on its face,
Collarless,
Stiff and still,
Its two feet bare,
And very white,
Its tunic tossed in sight
And not a button there –
Small trace
Of clothes upon its back –
Thank God! it had a sack
Upon its face!

Sounds by Night

I hear the dull low thunder of the guns
Beyond the hills that doze uneasily,
A sullen doomful growl that ever runs
From end to end of the heavy freighted sky:
A friend of mine writes, squatted on the floor,
And scrapes by yellow spluttering candle light.
'Ah, hush!' he breathes, and gazes at the door,
That creaks on rusty hinge, in pale affright!
(No words spoke he, nor I for well we knew
What rueful things these sounds did tell.)
A pause – I hear the trees sway sighing thro'
The gloom, like dismal moan of hollow knell,
Then out across the dark, and startling me
Burst forth a laugh, a shout of drunken glee!

A Dead Man

A dead man dead for weeks
Is sickening food for lover's eye
That seeks and ever seeks
A fair one's beauty ardently!

Did that thing live of late?
· That sodden thing of ebony head
With empty holes that gape?
Good God! will I be that, when dead?

Perhaps those blackened bones
Were subtly fashioned hand and wrist
That made sweet violin tones,
Or held a face till lips had kissed!

Perhaps – but no! it cannot be,
This thing is but a heap of slime –
A hideous mockery –
The man is safe from rotting time:

Then stick it underground!
It is a thing for spades not tears;
And make no mourning sound,
And finished, have no fears!

For, glowing in some woman's heart,
He lives embalmed, unchanging, and apart!

Then come! let's kill the memory of this place –
O friends! it had a hideous, ebony face!

Joseph Lee
1875–1949

Joseph Lee was born and brought up in Dundee. After leaving school he emigrated to Canada but returned to his native city to join the publishing firm of John Leng. Appointed editor of the *People's Journal*, he built up a local reputation for his humorous verse written in the vernacular, and he was also an accomplished artist. Shortly after the outbreak of war he enlisted in the 4th Black Watch, a local Territorial Army battalion which was composed mainly of Dundee men. Early in 1915 the battalion crossed over to France and took part in the Battles of Aubers Ridge and Neuve Chapelle. In September that year it suffered heavy losses at the badly mismanaged Battle of Loos. Promoted to the rank of sergeant, Lee at first refused a commission and it was not until 1917 that he was gazetted a lieutenant in the King's Royal Rifle Corps. His war ended at the Battle of Cambrai when he was taken prisoner and he was incarcerated in the notorious internment camp at Karlsruhe. As Lee reported later, the camp was situated near the city centre in order to deter allied air attacks on the strategically important railway yards. Lee's first war poems were published in book form in 1916 but he continued to send poems and drawings back to Dundee while he was a prisoner of war. Most of these were published in the *People's Journal* and the *Dundee Advertiser*.

Sources: Joseph Lee, *Ballads of Battle*, London: John Murray, 1917;
Joseph Lee, *Workaday Warriors*, London: John Murray, 1917;
Hilda D. Spear and Bruce Pandrich (eds.), *Sword and Pen: Poems of 1915 from Dundee and Tayside*, Aberdeen: AUP, 1989

Soldier, Soldier

Wastrel, wastrel, standing in the street,
Billy-cock upon your head; boots that show your feet.

Rookie, rookie, not too broad of chest,
But game to do your bloomin' bit with the bloomin' best.

Rookie, rookie, growling at the grub;
Loth to wash behind the ears when you take your tub.

Rookie, rookie, licking into shape –
Thirty-six inch round the buff showing by the tape.

Rookie, rookie, boots and buttons clean;
Mustachios waxing stronger; military mien.

Rookie, rookie, drilling in the square,
Britain's ancient glory in your martial air.

Rookie, rookie, swagger-stick to twirl;
Waving hands to serving-maids; walking out the girl.

Soldier, soldier, ordered to the front,
Marching forward eager-eyed, keen to bear the brunt.

Soldier, soldier, bidding her good-bye –
'When I come back I'll marry you, so, darling, don't you
    cry!'

Soldier, soldier, sailing in the ships,
Cigarettes and curious oaths betwixt your boyish lips.

Soldier, soldier, standing in the trench;
Wading through the mud and mire, stifling in the stench.

Soldier, soldier, 'mid the din and dirt,
More than monastic tortures moving in your shirt.

Soldier, soldier, facing shot and shell;
Jesting as you gaze within the open Gate of Hell.

Soldier, soldier, charging on the foe,
With your comrade's dying cry to urge you as you go.

Soldier, soldier, stilly lying dead,
With a dum-dum bullet through your dunderhead.

Soldier, soldier, with a smile of grace,
Breaking through the grime and grit on your blood-swept
    face.

Soldier, soldier, sound will be your sleep,
You will never waken, though you hear her weep.

Soldier, soldier –
        How I love you!

The Green Grass

The dead spake together last night,
  And one to the other said:
  'Why are we dead?'

They turned them face to face about
  In the place where they were laid:
  'Why are we dead?'

'This is the sweet, sweet month o' May,
  And the grass is green o'erhead –
  Why are we dead?

'The grass grows green on the long, long tracks
  That I shall never tread –
  Why are we dead?

'The lamp shines like the glow-worm spark,
  From the bield where I was bred –
  Why am I dead?'

The other spake: 'I've wife and weans,
  Yet I lie in this waesome bed –
  Why am I dead?

'O, I hae a wife and weans at hame,
  And they clamour loud for bread –
  Why am I dead?'

Quoth the first: 'I have a sweet, sweetheart,
  And this night we should hae wed –
  Why am I dead?

'And I can see another man
  Will mate her in my stead,
  Now I am dead.'

They turned them back to back about
   In the grave where they were laid –
   'Why – are we dead?'

'I mind o' a field, a foughten field,
   Where the bluid ran ruth and red
   Now I am dead.'

'I mind o' a field, a stricken field,
   And a waeful wound that bled –
   Now I am dead.'

They turned them on their backs again,
   As when their souls had sped,
   And nothing further said.

The dead spake together last night,
   And each to the other said,
   'Why are we dead?'

The Bullet

Every bullet has its billet;
  Many bullets more than one:
God! perhaps I killed a mother
  When I killed a mother's son.

German Prisoners

When first I saw you in the curious street,
Like some platoon of soldier ghosts in grey,
My mad impulse was all to smite and slay,
To spit upon you – tread you 'neath my feet.
But when I saw how each sad soul did greet
My gaze with no sign of defiant frown,
How from tired eyes looked spirits broken down,
How each face showed the pale flag of defeat,
And doubt, despair and disillusionment,
And how were grievous wounds on many a head,
And on your garb red-faced was other red;
And how you stooped as men whose strength was spent,
I knew that we had suffered each as other,
And could have grasped your hand and cried, 'My brother.'

Hugh MacDiarmid
1892–1978

The pen-name of Christopher Murray Grieve who was born
in the Borders town of Langholm. In 1908 he became a
pupil-teacher at Broughton Junior Student Centre in Edinburgh
where he came under the influence of his English teacher,
George Ogilvie. Between 1911 and the outbreak of the First
World War he worked as a journalist in various parts of
Scotland and South Wales. A reservist in the Territorial
Army since 1908, Grieve was called up in July 1915 to
serve with the Royal Army Medical Corps (RAMC). In
the following year he was posted to Salonika with the
42nd General Hospital RAMC. Although this was one of
the quieter fronts of the war British casualties were heavy
– 481,000 from malaria and 18,000 from combat. As one
of the former, Grieve was evacuated in May 1918 and the
rest of his war was spent in England and France. After the
armistice he was detached from the RAMC to the Indian
Medical Services – Section Lahore Indian General Hospital
at Marseilles – and was not demobilised until July 1919.
By his own admission Grieve wrote little that he wanted
to publish during the war: according to his biographer, Alan
Bold, MacDiarmid 'was adamant that while in Salonika his
drafts would not be "put into more final shape as long as
I am in khaki".' The poem 'Another Epitaph on an Army
of Mercenaries (MacDiarmid's response to A. E. Housman's
'Epitaph on an Army of Mercenaries' which was written
after press coverage of the First Battle of Ypres, August
1914) made a qualitative distinction between volunteers and
regular soldiers; 'At the Cenotaph' and 'If I was not a
Soldier' emanated from MacDiarmid's experiences during the
First World War.

Sources: Hugh MacDiarmid, *Second Hymn to Lenin and Other Poems*, London:
Stanley Nott, 1935;
Michael Grieve and W. R. Aitken (eds.), *Hugh MacDiarmid: Complete Poems
1920-1976*, vol. I, London: Martin Brian & O'Keeffe, 1978

At the Cenotaph

Are the living so much use
That we need to mourn the dead?
Or would it yield better results
To reverse their roles instead?
The millions slain in the War –
Untimely, the best of our seed? –
Would the world be any the better
If they were still living indeed?
The achievements of such as are
To the notion lend no support;
The whole history of life and death
Yields no scrap of evidence for't. –
Keep going to your wars, you fools, as of yore;
I'm the civilisation you're fighting for.

Another Epitaph on an Army of Mercenaries

It is a God-damned lie to say that these
Saved, or knew, anything worth any man's pride.
They were professional murderers and they took
Their blood money and impious risks and died.
In spite of all their kind some elements of worth
With difficulty persist here and there on earth.

If I Was Not a Soldier

If I wasn't a soldier, a soldier said,
What would I be? – I wouldn't be,
It's hardly likely it seems to me,
A money lord or armament maker,
Territorial magnate or business chief.
I'd probably be just a working man,
   The slave of a licensed thief, –
One of the criminals I'm shielding now!

If I wasn't a soldier, a soldier said,
I'd be down and out as likely as not
And suffering the horrible starving lot
Of hundreds of thousands of my kind,
And that would make me a Red as well
Till I rose with the rest and was batoned or shot
By some cowardly brute – such as I am now!

Donald MacDonald
(Dòmhnall Ruadh Chorùna)
1887-1967

Donald MacDonald, or Dòmhnall Ruadh Chorùna, was born at Corunna near Claddach Baleshare in North Uist and was educated at the village school in Carinish. During the First World War MacDonald served on the Western Front with the Cameron Highlanders and his earliest poems reflect his experiences as a front-line soldier. Later, he transferred to the West Riding Field Regiment, although he continued to wear his Cameron cap badge. Like many other soldier poets of the period MacDonald was repelled by the monstrous war of attrition, yet moved by the comradeship generated amongst the fighting men. In 1919 he returned to North Uist and composed a number of poems and songs of local interest. He is best known as the author of *An Eala Bhàn* ('The White Swan'), which is one of the most popular Gaelic songs of this century. The accomplished craftsman at his traditional trade, MacDonald's most ordinary verse is never less than clean-cut and elegant, while appreciation of his war poems and of those composed in his old age seems likely to increase as time goes by. A new edition of the poems is in preparation.

Source: Dòmhnall Dòmhnallach, *Dòmhnall Ruadh Chorùna*, Glasgow: Gairm, 1969

Oran Arras

Ghillean, march at ease!
Rìgh na sìth bhith mar ruinn
A' dol chun na strì
'S chun na cìll aig Arras.
Ghillean, march at ease!

Tha nochd oidhche Luain
Teannadh suas ri faire,
A' dol chun na h-uaigh
Far nach fhuasg'lear barrall.
Ghillean, march at ease!

Tillidh cuid dhinn slàn,
Cuid fo chràdh lann fala,
'S mar a tha e 'n dàn,
Roinn le bàs a dh'fhanas.
Ghillean, march at ease!

Gus ar tìr a dhìon,
Eadar liath is leanabh,
Mar dhaoin' as an rian
Nì sinn sgian a tharrainn.
Ghillean, march at ease!

'S lìonmhor fear is tè
Tha 'n tìr nan geug 'nan caithris,
Feitheamh ris an sgeul
Bhios aig a' chlèir ri aithris.
Ghillean, march at ease!

Gura lìonmhor sùil
Shileas dlùth 's nach caidil
Nuair thig fios on Chrùn
Nach bi dùil rim balaich.
Ghillean, march at ease!

Arras Song

March at ease, lads!
The King of Peace be with us
As we go to the struggle
And to the grave at Arras.
March at ease, lads!

It is Monday night,
Getting close to watch,
Heading for the grave,
Where boots will not be unlaced.
March at ease, lads!

Some of us will return safely,
Some in pain from bloody weapons,
And, as fate decrees,
A number will stay behind in death.
March at ease, lads!

To defend our country,
Greybeard and infant,
Like men demented
We shall draw our knives.
March at ease, lads!

Many the man and woman
Is awake in the land of heroes
As they wait to hear
What the clerk's news is to be.
March at ease, lads!

Many the eye
Will weep and be sleepless
When word comes from the Crown
That their boys are not expected.
March at ease, lads!

Air an Somme

An oidhche mus deach sinn a-null
  Bha i drùidhteach a' sileadh,
Bha mi fhèin 'nam laighe 'n cùil
  'S thug mi sùil feadh nan gillean.

  Ochan ì, ochan ì,
  Tha sinn sgìth anns an ionad.
  Ochan ì, ochan ì.

Cuid 'nan suidhe 's cuid 'nan suain,
  Cuid a' bruadar 's a' bruidhinn,
Gu robh mhadainn gu bhith cruaidh –
  'Saoil am buannaich sinn tilleadh?'

'Cha dèan biùgaileir le bheul
  Ar pareudadh-ne tuilleadh;
Thèid ar dealachadh bho chèil','
  Thuirt mi fhèin far mo bhilean.

Agus mar a thubhairt b'fhìor,
  Chaidh na ciadan a mhilleadh,
Chaidh an talamh as a rian
  'S chaidh an iarmailt gu mireag.

Dhubh an àird an ear 's an iar,
  Is an sliabh gu robh crith ann,
Is chan fhaighinn m'anail sìos –
  Aileadh cianail an tine.

Is cha chluinninn guth san àm
  Aig commandair gar leigeil,
Bha na balaich 's iad cho trang
  Cumail thall na bha tighinn.

Bha gach fear a' caogadh sùl,
  'S e air cùlaibh a chruinneig,
A' cur peileir glas a-null
  Le uile dhùrachd a chridhe.

On the Somme

The night before we went over
  The soaking rain poured down;
I lay in a corner
  And looked around the lads.

    Ochan ee, ochan ee,
    We are tired in this place.
    Ochan ee, ochan ee.

Some sitting, some slumbering,
  Some dreaming and talking,
Saying the morning would be hard –
  'Do you think we can win back?'

'Never again shall a bugler
  Call us on parade;
We shall be separated one from another,'
  I mumured to myself.

What I said proved true.
  Hundreds were maimed;
The earth erupted
  And the skies went crazy.

The east and the west grew black
  And the hillside shook,
And I couldn't draw in breath –
  The dreadful smell of the fire.

At the time I could hear no commander
  Urging us on;
The boys were fully occupied
  Repelling the attacks upon us.

Each man was cocking an eye
  Behind his sweetheart,*
Sending over a grey bullet
  With his utmost will.

* i.e., his gun

Pittendreigh MacGillivray
1856–1938

James Pittendreigh MacGillivray was a native of Aberdeenshire who achieved fame as the only sculptor member of the 'Glasgow School' of artists. His statues for public places, such as those of Robert Burns in Irvine and John Knox in the High Church of St Giles in Edinburgh, are particularly noteworthy. In 1921 MacGillivray became the King's Sculptor in Ordinary for Scotland. For his poetry he evolved an archaic form of Scots based on the language of the sixteenth century makars, but he was also a contributor to Hugh MacDiarmid's *Northern Numbers*. Because he was associated with poets like Violet Jacob, Mary Symon and Charles Murray, who prefigured MacDiarmid, MacGillivray's work has been largely forgotten, although his poem 'Mercy O' Gode' has been much anthologised. During the early months of the war MacGillivray wrote a series of poems in English, most of which reflected the patriotic and jingoistic mood of the times.

Source: Pittendreigh MacGillivray, *Pro Patria*, Edinburgh: Robert Grant, 1915

Peace and War
From Corstorphine Hill

Again the yellow wealth of August comes
  To crown the rich green land, and be the fair
  Reward of kindly men who gave their care
Through summer's heat, and days when winter numbs.
How dear is such a sight! – what peace it sums,
  Of land, and life, and home! Ah, who could dare
  Deface these precious signs – this gracious air?
And yet the menace nears of war-beat drums.

And far beyond that sunny blue, at bay,
  Our black ships wait athwart a tyrant's fleet,
  While in the womb of Fate the stroke may be,
Shall cleave their battled front and spread dismay –
  Horrors undreamt! where now in kindness sweet
    Lie golden fields of home, and azure sea.

16 August 1914

The Tragedy

Fleeting like shadows vague and phantom led,
   By endless roads, great regiments thousands strong
   Go trooping wearily the whole day long;
Through dust and glaring light, with few words said:
Nearer the firing line – the place of dread –
   The altar where no mass or sacred song
   Shall grace the sacrifice or right the wrong
Of victims guiltless why they should be bled.

Fathers, sons, and brothers – a nation's best;
   From dear familiar haunts by farm and wold –
   From bench and book and all good township ways;
Marching to keep some unknown fate's behest –
   Ever as in rude ages dim and old,
     Lost for a world – spent in a dream-born maze.

15 September 1914

In Memoriam
M.N.F. Serbia, 10th March 1915

Blue-eyed, white-souled; blameless in word
  and deed! –
  How fortunate a thing it is to leave
  This life in such a way that none may grieve,
Or say – 'Alas! but for that little weed
The plot had been so fair.' For her, no need
  To sigh or make lament. She did achieve
  Her sacrifice; and we the garland weave,
Of white and evergreen, by love decreed:

While you, the mother, by the fire alone –
  Dreaming again the happy days forespent,
    Can scarce believe that tragic word the last.
But not for you the dark, unreasoned moan –
  You know she gave herself with high intent,
    And that for hero ways her heart beat fast.

12 March 1915

Ewart Alan MacKintosh
1893–1917

Although his family came from Alness in Easter Ross, Ewart Alan MacKintosh was born in Brighton and much of his short life was spent in England. He was educated at St Paul's School, London and Christ Church, Oxford where he studied Classics and learned Gaelic privately. He was also an accomplished piper. At the outbreak of the war he enlisted immediately and was commissioned into the 5th Seaforth Highlanders, a Territorial Army battalion whose men came mainly from Caithness and Sutherland. During the Battle of the Somme in 1916 he was awarded the Military Cross but after being gassed at High Wood he was invalided home. The opportunity of a safe promotion, instructing cadets at Cambridge, was offered to him but he volunteered for further service in France and was killed while serving with the 4th Seaforths at the Battle of Cambrai in December 1917. Initially, his poems exulted in the excitement and glamour of battle, but this heroic mood quickly gave way to work which reflected his horror and anguish at the high casualties amongst the troops on the Western Front. MacKintosh also wrote a large number of parodies and songs, of which 'Charge of the Light Brigade' and 'High Wood to Waterlot Farm' are examples.

Sources: Ewart Alan MacKintosh, *A Highland Regiment*, London: John Lane, 1917;
Ewart Alan MacKintosh, *War, the Liberator*, London: John Lane, 1918

Cha Till MacCruimein
Departure of the 4th Camerons

The pipes in the street were playing bravely,
    The marching lads went by,
With merry hearts and voices singing
    My friends marched out to die;
But I was hearing a lonely pibroch
    Out of an older war,
'Farewell, farewell, farewell, MacCrimmon,
MacCrimmon comes no more.'

And every lad in his heart was dreaming
    Of honour and wealth to come,
And honour and noble pride were calling
    To the tune of the pipes and drum;
But I was hearing a woman singing
    On dark Dunvegan shore,
'In battle or peace, with wealth or honour,
MacCrimmon comes no more.'

And there in front of the men were marching,
    With feet that made no mark,
The grey old ghosts of the ancient fighters
    Come back again from the dark;
And in front of them all MacCrimmon piping
    A weary tune and sore,
'On the gathering day, for ever and ever,
    MacCrimmon comes no more.'

Bedford, 1915

In Memoriam,
Private D. Sutherland
killed in action in the German trench 16 May 1916,
and the others who died

So you were David's father,
And he was your only son,
And the new-cut peats are rotting
And the work is left undone,
Because of an old man weeping,
Just an old man in pain,
For David, his son David,
That will not come again.

Oh, the letters he wrote you
And I can see them still,
Not a word of the fighting
But just the sheep on the hill
And how you should get the crops in
Ere the year got stormier,
And the Bosches have got his body,
And I was his officer.

You were only David's father,
But I had fifty sons
When we went up in the evening
Under the arch of the guns,
And we came back at twilight –
O God! I heard them call
To me for help and pity
That could not help at all.

Oh, never will I forget you,
My men that trusted me,
More my sons than your fathers',
For they could only see
The little helpless babies
And the young men in their pride.
They could not see you dying,
And hold you when you died.

Happy and young and gallant,
They saw their first-born go,
But not the strong limbs broken
And the beautiful men brought low,
The piteous writhing bodies,
They screamed 'Don't leave me, sir,'
For they were only your fathers
But I was your officer.

On Vimy Ridge

On Vimy Ridge four months ago
We lived and fought, my friends and I,
And watched the kindly dawn come slow,
Peace bringing from the eastern sky.
Now I sit in a quiet town
Remembering how I used to go
Among the dug-outs up and down,
On Vimy Ridge four months ago.

And often sitting here I've seen,
As then I saw them every night,
The friendly faces tired and keen
Across the flickering candle-light,
And heard their laughter gay and clear,
And watched the fires of courage glow
Above the scattered ash of fear,
On Vimy Ridge four months ago.

Oh, friends of mine, where are you now?
Somewhere beneath the troubled sky,
With earth above the quiet brow,
Reader and Stalk for ever lie.
But dead or living out or here
I see the friends I used to know,
And hear the laughter gay and clear,
On Vimy Ridge four months ago.

Recruiting

'Lads, you're wanted, go and help,'
On the railway carriage wall
Stuck the poster, and I thought
Of the hands that penned the call.

Fat civilians wishing they
'Could go out and fight the Hun.'
Can't you see them thanking God
That they're over forty-one?

Girls with feathers, vulgar songs –
Washy verse on England's need –
God – and don't we damned well know
How the message ought to read.

'Lads, you're wanted! over there,'
Shiver in the morning dew,
More poor devils like yourselves
Waiting to be killed by you.

Go and help to swell the names
In the casualty lists.
Help to make a column's stuff
For the blasted journalists.

Help to keep them nice and safe
From the wicked German foe.
Don't let him come over here!
'Lads, you're wanted – out you go.'

. . . . .

There's a better word than that,
Lads, and can't you hear it come
From a million men that call
You to share their martyrdom.

Leave the harlots still to sing
Comic songs about the Hun,
Leave the fat old men to say
Now *we've* got them on the run.

Better twenty honest years
Than their dull three score and ten.
Lads, you're wanted. Come and learn
To live and die with honest men.

You shall learn what men can do
If you will but pay the price,
Learn the gaiety and strength
In the gallant sacrifice.

Take your risk of life and death
Underneath the open sky.
Live clean or go out quick –
Lads, you're wanted. Come and die.

To a Private Soldier

The air is still, the light winds blow
Too quietly to wake you now.
Dreamer, you dream too well to know
Whose hand set death upon your brow.
The shrinking flesh the bullets tore
Will never pulse with fear again;
Sleep on, remembering no more
Your sudden agony of pain.

Oh, poor brave smiling face made naught,
Turned back to dust from whence you came,
You have forgot the men you fought,
The wounds that burnt you like a flame;
With stiff hand crumbling a clod,
And blind eyes staring at the sky,
The awful evidence of God
Against the men who made you die.

You have forgotten, sleeping well,
But what of them? shall they forget
Your body broken with the shell,
Your brow whereon their seal is set?
Does earth for them hold any place
Where they shall never see the flies
Clustered about your empty face
And on your blind, accusing eyes?

Good-night, good sleep to you. But they
Will never know good-night again,
Whose eyes are seeing night and day,
The humble men who died in vain.
Their ears are filled with bitter cries,
Their nostrils with the powder smell,
And shall see your mournful eyes
Across the reeking fires of hell.

Ghosts of War
Sent from France in October 1917

When you and I are buried
With grasses over head,
The memory of our fights will stand
Above this bare and tortured land,
We knew ere we were dead.

Though grasses grow on Vimy,
And poppies at Messines,
And in High Wood the children play,
The craters and the graves will stay
To show what things have been.

Though all be quiet in day-time,
The night shall bring a change,
And peasants walking home shall see
Shell-torn meadow and riven tree,
And their own fields grown strange.

They shall hear live men crying,
They shall see dead men lie,
Shall hear the rattling Maxims fire,
And see by broken twists of wire
Gold flares light up the sky.

And in their new-built houses
The frightened folk will see
Pale bombers coming down the street,
And hear the flurry of charging feet,
And the crash of Victory.

This is our Earth baptizèd
With the red wine of War.
Horror and courage hand in hand
Shall brood upon the stricken land
In silence evermore.

The Charge of the Light Brigade
Brought Up to Date

Half a league, half a league,
Half a league onward –
'That is, unless some damned
Airman has blundered,
If the map isn't right
We'll be a funny sight.'
So as they tramped along
Officers pondered,
While, with equipment hung,
Curses on every tongue,
Forward with rifles slung,
Slouched the six hundred.

Cannon to right of them,
Cannon to left of them,
Cannon in front of them,
Volleyed and thundered,
'And – what was twice as bad –
Our gunners never had
Strafed that machine-gun lad.
I always wondered
If our old barrage could
Be half as bloody good
As the Staff said it would.'
Was there a man dismayed?
Yes, they were damned afraid,
Loathing both shot and shell,
Into the mouth of Hell,
Sticking it pretty well,
Slouched the six hundred.

Through the barrage they passed,
Men falling thick and fast,
Till the machine-gun blast
Smote them to lying
Down in the grass a bit;
Over the roar of it.

Officers yelled, were hit,
Dropped and lay dying.
Then the retreat began,
Every unwounded man
Staggered or crawled or ran
Back to the trench again,
While on the broken plain
Dead and untroubling,
Wounded and wondering,
What help the night would bring,
Lay the six hundred.

High Wood to Waterlot Farm

Tune – 'Chalk Farm to Camberwell Green'

There is a wood at the top of a hill,
If it's not shifted it's standing there still;
There is a farm a short distance away,
But I'd not advise you to go there by day,
For the snipers abound, and the shells are not rare,
And a man's only chance is to run like a hare,
So take my advice if you're chancing your arm
From High Wood to Waterlot Farm.

Chorus – High Wood to Waterlot Farm,
　　　　　All on a summer's day,
　　　　　Up you get to the top of the trench
　　　　　Though you're sniped at all the way.
　　　　　If you've got a smoke helmet there
　　　　　You'd best put it on if you could,
　　　　　For the wood down by Waterlot Farm
　　　　　Is a bloody high wood.

John Munro (Iain Rothach)
1889–1918

John Munro was a native of the island of Lewis and was educated there at the Nicolson Institute, Stornoway. After graduating from the University of Aberdeen he planned to train for the ministry but the outbreak of war interrupted his studies. He was commissioned in the 4th Seaforth Highlanders and served with them throughout the war. In April 1918 he was awarded the Military Cross after his battalion's successful counter-attack on the enemy lines at Wytschaete during the German spring offensive. He was killed in action a few days later. Only two or three of Munro's poems appear to survive. *'Ar Tìr, 's Ar Gaisgeach A Thuit sna Blàir'* appeared in 1930 in *An Dìleab*, edited as two separate poems, by James Thomson but Murdo Murray's *Luach na Saorsa* (see also p 109) gives the unified version which has been translated into English by Derick Thomson. According to Thomson, this poem is 'the finest early burgeoning of the "new" poetry of the century. Its novelty lies in metre and rhythm and construction, and it is clear that it was in some ways influenced by the work of his contemporaries in English poetry' (*An Introduction to Gaelic Poetry*).

Source: Alasdair I. MacAsgaill (ed.), *Luach na Saorsa* (Diary, Poems and Essays by Murdo Murray), Glasgow: Gairm, 1970

Ar Tìr 's Ar Gaisgich A
Thuit sna Blàir

Brat sneachda air mullach nam beann,
Currachd ceòtha mar liath-fhalt man ceann,
Feadain is sruthain mòintich
A' leum 's a' dòirteadh,
'S le torman a' sporghail measg gharbhlach nan gleann,
A' sporghail aig ùrlar nan gleann,
Aig cosan 's mu shàilean nam mòr-bheann;
Fèidh ruadh', fir na cròice,
Air sliosaibh fraoich ruadh-dhonn –
'S i Tìr nan Gaisgeach a th'ann,
Tìr nam Beann, nan Gaisgeach, 's nan Gleann,
'S i Tìr nan Gaisgeach a th'ann!

'S iomadh fear àlinn, òg, sgairteil, deas-làmhach,
Ait-fhaoilt air chinn a bhlàth-chridh',
Tric le ceum daigheann, làidir, ceum aotrom, glan, sàil-ghlan
Dhìrich bràigh nam beann mòra,
Chaidh a choinneimh a' bhàis –
Tric ga fhaireach' roimh-làimh –
Chaidh suas chum a' bhlàir
'S tha feur glas an-diugh 'fàs
Air na dh'fhàg innleachdan nàmh,
Innleachdan dhubh-sgrios an nàmh a chòrr dheth.

Ged bha cuid dhiubh, nuair bu bheò iad,
Tric nach b' mhìn rèidh sinn còmhla,
A! thuit iad air còmhnard na strì,
Fhuair sinn sìnt' iad lem bàs-leòintean
An dusd eudreach' – na bha chòrr dhiubh –
An laighe 'sineadh mar mheòir-shìnt' –
'Smèideadh, 'stiùireadh,
'Sparradh ùr-oidhirpean òirnne,
Strì air 'n adhart, strì còmhla,
An taobh a thuit iads' dol còmhl' ruinn,
Null thar còmhnard na strì.

Our Land, and Our Heroes Who Fell in Battle

(i)

Snow mantle on the mountain peaks,
like white hair lie the mist streaks,
the runnel and the moor-burn
leap and pour
tumbling and rumbling down the rough glens
that skirt and buttress the high bens;
antlered stags and red deer
roam the long slopes, heather-dun –
this is the Land of Brave Men,
a hero's land of hill and glen,
this is the Land of Brave Men.

(ii)

Many a handsome man, young, agile, quick of hand,
with gay mien matching warm heart,
who had often climbed, with strong step, light,
      foot-sure, bright
to the high upland of the great hill,
went to his meeting with death –
often fore-knowing its skaith –
went out to the war:
the green grass grows over
the shreds his enemies' arms
left, when holocaust had had its fill.

With some of them, when they were alive,
we had our differences, did not see eye to eye.
Ah! they have fallen on the battle-field:
We found them lying, wounded to death –
their unsightly dust was all that was left –
five of them lying, like fingers outstretched,
summoning, guiding,
urging fresh effort upon us,
asking us to press on, together,
as when they fell, advancing,
over the plain of the battle-field.

Bi's mo chuideachd geàrr-uin',
Dùin do rosg-sgàilean air d' shùil,
'N seòmar ionmhais do smaoin,
'S caoin sholas òg-mhaidne, ciùin-mhaidne, òg-mhèis,
Ga lìonadh, a' briseadh tre uinneig a' chùil —
'N aite taige, tadhal d' anma,
'Fasgadh cuspairean a' mhùirn,
An sin — tog, taisg dealbh orra
'Nan laighe, mar thuit, san raoin,
    Fairich, cluinn,
      An smèideadh, an cainnt ruinn —
An rùn-gnìomh air an tug iad an deò
    Suas, 'nan càradh
    Air an àr-làr,
Air a ghleidheadh dhuinn beò,
Mar gun snaigheadh fear seòlt'
Cuimhneachan cloiche gun phrìs —
    'Bi'bh deas gu leum an àirde,
    Le ceum gaisgeil, neo-sgàthach, dàna,
    Bi'bh null thar còmhnard na strì,
    Na lagaich ach bi'bh làidir,
    Bi'bh 'nam badaibh is pàidhibh,
    Am fèin-mhuinghin leag gu làr dhaibh,
    Air adhart, air adhart,
    Seo an rathad,
    Cuir a' bhratach an sàs,
    Daigheann, àrd,
    Air sliabh glòrmhor Deagh-sìth!'

Stay with me for a little while,
close your eyelids over your eyes,
and in the treasure-house of your mind,
(with the soft light of early morning, calm June
   morning filling it, dawn at the back window),
in the repository of loved things,
in your soul's shrine,
there, take, cherish a picture of them
lying, as they fell, in the field;
   feel, hear
   their summons, their speech in our ear –
the ideal for which they gave their breath
   lying there
   on the slaughter-floor,
their image kept alive for us
as though a cunning craftsman had carved
a priceless memorial in stone:
   'Be ready to leap up,
   with firm step, bold, fearless,
   crossing the plain of strife,
   do not weaken, be strong,
   attack them, requite,
   destroy their trust in themselves;
   forward, forward,
   this is the road,
   set up the standard,
   firm and high,
   that the glory of Peace may come again.'

trs. Derick Thomson

Neil Munro
1864–1930

Neil Munro was born at Inverary, Argyll, the son of a local farmer. He came from a Gaelic-speaking background and much of his work reflects his love for the history, both real and legendary, of his native county. Many of his most popular novels were written under the pseudonym of 'Hugh Foulis' while he was working as a journalist in Glasgow, but he achieved more lasting fame with the publication of the historical romances *John Splendid* (1898), *Doom Castle* (1901) and *The New Road* (1914). During the First World War Munro contributed a number of poems in Scots to *Blackwood's Magazine*. Published under the title 'Bagpipe Ballads', he claimed in a note to the unpublished collection that these 'were suggested by the names of bagpipe airs, so that some of them take on that spirit of braggadocio which comes so natural to youth: and to races like the Gaels who loiter so much in their past that they are always the youngest and most ardent when it comes to sentiment – the first and last excuse for all poetry.' The 'brattie' was the khaki apron worn over the kilts of Highland soldiers serving on the Western Front.

Source: John Buchan (ed.), *The Poems of Neil Munro*, Edinburgh and London: William Blackwood, 1931

Hey, Jock, are ye glad ye 'listed?

Hey! Jock, are ye glad ye 'listed?
    O Jock, but ye're far frae hame!
What d'ye think o' the fields o' Flanders?
    Jockey lad, are ye glad ye came?
Wet rigs we wrought in the land o' Lennox,
    When Hielan' hills were smeared wi' snaw;
Deer we chased through the seepin' heather,
    But the glaur o' Flanders dings them a'!

This is no' Fair o' Balloch,
    Sunday claes and a penny reel;
It's no' for dancin' at a bridal
    Willie Lawrie's bagpipes squeal.
Men are to kill in the morn's mornin';
    Here we're back to your daddy's trade;
Naething for't but to cock the bonnet,
    Buckle on graith and kiss the maid.

The Cornal's yonder deid in tartan,
    Sinclair's sheuched in Neuve Eglise;
Slipped awa wi' the sodger's fever,
    Kinder than ony auld man's disease.
Scotland! Scotland! little we're due ye,
    Poor employ and skim-milk board.
But youth's a cream that maun be paid for,
    We got it reamin', so here's the sword!

Come awa, Jock, and cock your bonnet,
    Swing your kilt as best ye can;
Auld Dumbarton's Drums are dirlin',
    Come awa, Jock, and kill your man!
Far's the cry to Leven Water
    Where your fore-folks went to war,
They would swap wi' us to-morrow,
    Even in the Flanders glaur!

The Brattie

The brattie for sweepin', the brattie for dirt!
Tie on your brattie and tuck up your shirt!
It's always the case when there's cleanin' to do
That the first for the besom's the Bonnets o' Blue.
Once we were gentry and cleaned in the kilt,
Wi' a braw Hielan' sporran and money 'ntil't;
Now deil to the sporran! and tartan's *napoo*;
It's ower guid for the work and it's put out o' view
Below the brown brattie for sweepin'!

The mothers that bore us – the best ever stept! –
Were up in the mornin' when other folk slept;
Do ye think they were deckin' themsel's in the glass,
Or plannin' diversions to mak' the day pass?
Na, Na! the wee mothers, the dainty and dour,
Were up at revally to fight wi' the stour –
That the hame might be tidy, and children be spruce,
They swept like the winds o' the hill through the hoose,
And bonny they looked in their bratties!

Dirt will come down on ye, dae what ye can,
And cleanin' a steadin's a task for a man,
So we're up like our mothers at screigh o' the dawn,
Sarks up to the elbows and aprons on.
The thing to mak' Europe as clean as a whistle
'S a besom o' heath frae the land o' the thistle,
A besom o' heath and a wash o' the sea;
The breeks for our sailors, for us the bare knee,
And the brattie, the brattie o' Scotland!

If ever we fight wi' true gentry again,
We'll go in full tartan and meet them like men.
Our sporrans 'll glitter, our feathers 'll wave,
To honour a foe that is gallant and brave;
But for mucking a midden and cleanin' out swine
That's needin' a duckin' in water o' Rhine,
It were silly to dress in our Sunday array,
So we'll dress like our work as our mothers would say,
And that's wi' the bonny brown brattie!

Wild Rover Lads

Uncovenanted godless race,
Astray and under spells,
We left for you the promised grace,
  And sought nane for oursels.

Our souls might be in jeopardy,
As lang's our blood ran hot,
But surely we're assoiled and free
  Now that we've paid our shot.

Mickle we missed, be it confessed,
That brings auld age content;
Blaw the wind East, or blaw it West,
  'Twas there wi' a sang we went.

Moon in the glen, youth in the blood,
Sent us stravaigin' far,
Ower late! ower late in the whisperin' wood,
  So we saw nae mornin' star.

Deep, deep we drank in tavern lands,
For the sake o' companie,
And some o' us wrecked on Young Man
    Sands,
  Ere ever we got to sea.

We had nae need for the parish bell,
But still – when the bugle cried,
We went for you to Neuve Chapelle,
We went for you to the yetts o' hell,
  And there for you we died!

Charles Murray
1864–1941

Charles Murray was born in the Aberdeenshire town of Alford and emigrated in 1888 to work as a mining engineer in South Africa. During the Boer War he served as a lieutenant with the Railway Pioneer Regiment and thereafter worked for the Government of South Africa as a civil engineer. By then he had started writing poetry in the dialect of the north-east of Scotland, much of it tinged with nostalgia for his native land. His most popular collection *Hamewith* was first published in 1900 and was reprinted many times thereafter. His later poems demonstrate a more controlled and compressed use of language, especially his best known war poem 'Dockens Afore his Peers', a masterly evocation of the garrulous and insensitive farmer who uses his own standing in the community to gain exemption from war service for his son. Murray served as a lieutenant-colonel in the South African Defence Force during the war and retired to live in Scotland in 1924.

Sources: Charles Murray, *A Sough O' War*, London: Constable, 1917; *Hamewith: The Complete Poems of Charles Murray*, Aberdeen: AUP, for the Charles Murray Memorial Trust, 1979

A Sough O' War

The corn was turnin', hairst was near,
   But lang afore the scythes could start
A sough o'war gaed through the land
   An' stirred it to its benmost heart.
Nae ours the blame, but when it came
   We couldna pass the challenge by,
For credit o' our honest name
   There could be but the ae reply.
     An' buirdly men, fae strath an' glen,
      An' shepherds fae the bucht an' hill,
     Will show them a', whate'er befa',
      Auld Scotland counts for something still.

Half-mast the castle banner droops,
   The Laird's lament was played yestreen,
An' mony a widowed cottar wife
   Is greetin' at her shank aleen.
In Freedom's cause, for ane that fa's,
   We'll glean the glens an' send them three
To clip the reivin' eagle's claws,
   An' drook his feathers i' the sea.
     For gallant loons, in brochs an' toons,
      Are leavin' shop an' yaird an' mill,
     A' keen to show baith friend an' foe
      Auld Scotland counts for something still.

The grim, grey fathers, bent wi' years,
   Come stridin' through the muirland mist,
Wi' beardless lads scarce by wi' school
   But eager as the lave to list.
We've fleshed o' yore the braid claymore
   On mony a bloody field afar,
But ne'er did skirlin pipes afore
   Cry on sae urgently tae war.
     Gin danger's there, we'll thole our share,
      Gie's but the weapons, we've the will,
     Ayont the main, to prove again
      Auld Scotland counts for something still.

Fae France

Dear Jock, – Like some aul' cairter's mear I'm foonert i' the
    feet,
An' oxter-staffs are feckless things fan a' the furth's sae weet,
Sae, till the wee reid-heidit nurse comes roon' to sort my bed,
I'll leave my readin' for a fyle, an' vreet to you instead.

Ye hard the claik hoo Germany gied France the coordy lick,
An' Scotland' preen't her wincey up an' intill't geyan quick –
But fouk wi' better thooms than me can redd the raivell't snorl,
An' tell ye fa begood the ploy that sae upset the worl'.
I ken that I cam' here awa' some aucht days aifter Yeel,
An' never toon nor fee afore has shootit me sae weel;
They gie me maet, an' beets an' claes, wi' fyles an antrin
    dram –
Come term-time lat them flit 'at likes, *I'm* bidin' faur I am.
Tho' noo an' than, wi' dreepin' sark, we've biggit dykes an'
    dell't –
That's orra wark; oor daily darg is fechtin' fan we're tell't.
I full my pipe wi' bogie-rowe, an' birze the dottle doon,
Syne snicher, as I crack the spunk, to think hoo things come
    roon';
There's me, fan but a bairn in cotts, nae big aneuch to herd,
Would seener steek my nieves an' fecht, than dook or ca' my
    gird,
An' mony a yark an' ruggit lug I got to gar me gree,
But here, oonless I'm layin' on, I'm seldom latten be.

As I grew up an' filled my breeks, fyow market days we saw
But me an' some stoot halflin chiel would swap a skelp or twa;
It's three year by come Can'lemas, as I've gweed cause to min',
That Mains's man an' me fell oot, an' focht about a queyn.
We left the inn an' cuist oor quytes ahin' the village crafts,
An' tho' I barely fell't him twice wi' wallops roon' the chafts,
I had to face the Shirra for't. 'Twas byous hard on me,
For fat wi' lawyers, drinks, an' fine, it took a sax months' fee.
I would a had to sell't my verge, or smoke a raith on tick,
But for the fleein' merchant's cairt, my ferrets an' the bick.
Ay, sang! the Shirra had the gift, an' tongued me up an' doon;

But he's a dummy till his sin, fan han'lin' oor platoon;
Gin's fader saw his birkie noo, an' hard the wye he bans,
He michtna be sae sair on some that fyles comes throu' his
    han's.
Ae mochie nicht he creepit ben the trench – it's just a drain –
An' kickit me aneth the quyte an' cursed me braw an' plain –

'Ye eesless, idle, poachin' hurb, ye're lyin' snorin' there,
An' Germans cryin' to be killed, but deil a' hair ye care.
Fatever comes ye're for the lythe, to scrat, an' gant an' drink,
An' dream aboot the raffy days fan ye was i' the clink;
Ye're dubbit to the een, ye slype, he hinna focht the day,
Come on wi' me' an' see, for eence gin ye are worth yer pay.'
Man, fan he spak' sae kindly like, fat was there left for me
But jist to answer back as frank, as furth-the-gait an' free –
'Lead on, my Shirra's offisher, gin summons ye've to ser'
Upon thae billies ower the loan, I'll beet ye I'll be there!'
Syne laden wi' a birn o' bombs we slippit throu' the dark,
An' left upo' the barbit weer gey taits o' breek an' sark;
They bummed an' droned some unco tune as we crap up; it
    raise
Like fae the laft I've hard the quire lift up some paraphrase.
Ae creeshy gurk that led the lave was bessin' lood an' strang,
Fan something hat him i' the kyte that fairly changed his sang;
We henched an' flang, an' killed a curn, an' soosh't them front
    an' flank,
Like loons that's trued the squeel to stane young puddocks i' the
    stank.

The rippit spread, the rockets raise; 'twas time for hiz to skice,
An' tho' we joukit as we ran, an' flappit eence or twice,
Ower aft oor pig gaed to the wall, for noo we strack the day –
Oor brow Lieutenant onywye – fan a' in lames it lay;
A bullet bored him throu' the hochs, it took him like a stane,
An' heelster-gowdie doon he cam' an' brak his shackle-bane:
To hyste him up an' on my back nott a' my pith an' skeel,
For aye he bad' me lat him lie, an' cursed me for a feel.
'Ging on an' leave me here, ye gype, an' mak' yer feet yer
    freen.'
'Na, na,' says I; 'ye brocht me here, I'm nae gyaun hame my
    leen.'

He's little boukit, ay an' licht, an' I'm baith stoot an swak,
Yet I was pechin' sair aneuch afore I got him back.
They thocht him fairly throu' at first, an' threepit he was deid,
But it was naething but a dwaam, brocht on by loss o' bleed.
'Twas months afore he cower'd fae that, an' he was missed a
    lot,
For fan ye meet a hearty breet ye're sorry gin he's shot.
His mither sent a letter till's, a great lang blottit screed.
It wasna easy makin't oot, her vreetin's coorse to read;
She speir't could she dae ocht for me, sae I sent back a line –
'Jist bid yer man, fan neist I'm up, ca' canny wi' the fine.'

But noo to tell hoo I wan aff fae dreelin', dubs, an' din,
An' landit here wi' nocht to dae but fite the idle pin.
Ae foraneen my neiper chap cried – 'Loshtie-goshtie guide's!
The foumarts maun be caul the day, they've startit burnin'
    wydes.'
The reek at first was like ye've seen, fan at the fairmer's
    biddin',
Some frosty mornin' wi' the graip, the baillie turns the midden.
But it grew thick, an' doon the win' straucht for oor lines it
    bore,
Till shortly we were pyoch'rin' sair an' fleyed that we would
    smore;
An' as ye never ken wi' cyaurds faur ye'll be herried neist,
We fixed oor baignets, speel't the trench, and chairged them in
    a breist.
'Twas than I got the skirp o' shell that nail't me i' the queets,
An' here I'm hirplin' roon' the doors, an' canna thole my beets.
Some nichts fan I've been sleepin' ill, an' stouns gyuan doon my
    taes,
Aul' times come reamin' throu' my heid, I'm back amo' the
    braes;
Wi' wirms an' wan' I'm throu' the breem, an' castin' up the
    burn,
Land aye the tither yallow troot, fae ilka rush an' turn:
I hash the neeps an' full the scull, an' bin' the lowin' nowt,
Lythe in the barn lat oot for rapes, or track a fashious cowt;
I watch the leevers o' the mull swing roon for 'oors an' 'oors,
An' see the paps o' Bennachie stan' up atween the shooers;
Lead fae a roup a reistin' stirk, that's like to brak the branks,

Or hearken to the cottar wives lyaug-lyaugin' ower their shanks;
I join the dancers on the buird schottischin' at the games,
An' scutter in the lang forenichts wi' britchin, bit, an' haims;
Or maybe, cockit on the shaft, fan cairtin' corn or bear,
Cry 'Hie' an' 'Wo' an' 'Weesh' again to guide the steppin'
   mear.
An' in the daylicht tee, at times, fan lyin' here sae saft,
I've dream't gin eence the war was by, o' takin' on a craft.
Fan a'thing's settled for the nicht in stable an' in byre,
It's fine to hae yer ain bow-cheer drawn up anent the fire,
An' hear a roch reid-heidit bairn, wi' ferny-tickled nose,
Tired oot an' hungry fae the closs, come yaummerin' for his
   brose;
An' syne a wife – but, weesht! for here's my nurse, the couthy
   ted,
Come cryin' I maun dicht my pen, an' hirsle to my bed.
Gweed nicht! – but bide, or I forget; there's jist ae little thing –
Man, could ye sen' me oot a trumpe? I'm weariet for a spring.
For, Jock, ye winna grudge the stamp to cheer a dweeble frien',
An' dinna back it 'Sandy' noo, but 'Sergeant' Aberdein.

When Will The War Be By?

'This year, neist year, sometime, never,'
  A lanely lass, bringing hame the kye,
  Pu's at a floo'er wi' a weary sigh,
An' laich, laich, she is coontin' ever
'This year, neist year, sometime, never,
  When will the war be by?'

'Weel, wounded, missin', deid,'
  Is there nae news o' oor lads ava?
  Are they hale an' fere that are hine awa'?
A lass raxed oot for the list, to read –
'Weel, wounded, missin', *deid*';
  An' the war was by for twa.

Dockens Afore His Peers
(Exemption tribunal)

Nae sign o' thow yet. Ay, that's me, John Watt o' Dockenhill:
We've had the war throu' han' afore, at markets ower a gill.
O ay, I'll sit, birze ben a bit. Hae, Briggie, pass the snuff;
Ye winna hinner lang wi' me, an' speer a lot o' buff,
For I've to see the saiddler yet, an' Watchie, honest stock,
To gar him sen' his 'prentice up to sort the muckle knock,
Syne cry upo' the banker's wife an' leave some settin' eggs,
An' tell the ferrier o' the quake that's vrang aboot the legs.
It's yafa wedder, Mains, for Mairch, wi' snaw an' frost an'
    win',
The ploos are roustin' i' the fur, an' a' the wark's ahin'.
Ye've grun yersel's an' ken the tyauve it is to wirk a ferm,
An' a' the fash we've had wi' fouk gyaun aff afore the term;
We've nane to spare for sojerin', that's nae oor wark ava',
We've rents to pey, an' beasts to feed, an' corn to sell an' saw;
Oonless we get the seed in seen, faur will we be for meal?
An' faur will London get the beef they leuk for aye at Yeel?
There's men aneuch in sooters' shops, an' chiels in masons'
    yards,
An' coonter-loupers, sklaters, vrichts, an' quarrymen, an'
    cyaurds,
To fill a reg'ment in a week, without gyaun vera far,
Jist shove them in ahin' the pipes, an' tell them that it's 'War';
For gin aul' Scotland's at the bit, there's naethin' for't but'list.
Some mayna like it vera sair, but never heed, insist.
Bit, feich, I'm haverin' on like this, an' a' I need's a line
To say there's men that maun be left, an' ye've exemptit mine.
Fat said ye? Fatna fouk hae I enoo' at Dockenhill?
It's just a wastrie o' your time, to rin them throu', but still –
First there's the wife – 'Pass her,' ye say. Saul! had she been a
    lass
Ye hadna rappit oot sae quick, young laird, to lat her pass,
That may be hoo ye spak' the streen, fan ye was playin' cairds,
But seein' tenants tak' at times their menners fae their lairds,
I'll tell ye this, for sense an' thrift, for skeel wi' hens an'
    caur,

Gin ye'd her marrow for a wife, ye wouldna be the waur.
Oor maiden's neist, ye've herd o' her, new hame fae buirdin'
   squeel,
Faur she saw mair o' beuks than broth, an' noo she's never
   weel,
But fan she's playin' ben the hoose, there's little wird o' dwaams,
For she's the rin o' a' the tunes, strathspeys, an' sangs, an'
   psalms;
O' 'Evan' an' 'Neander' baith, ye seen can hae aneuch,
But 'Hobble Jeanie' gars me loup, an' crack my thooms, an'
   hooch.
Weel, syne we hae the kitchie deem, that milks an' mak's the
   maet,
She disna aft haud doon the deese, she's at it ear' an' late,
She cairries seed, an' braks the muck, an' gies a han' to hyow,
An' churns, an' bakes, an' syes the so'ens, an' fyles there's peats
   to rowe.
An' fan the maiden's frien's cry in, she'll mask a cup o' tay,
An' butter scones, and dicht her face, an' cairry ben the tray,
She's big an' brosy, reid and roch, an' swippert as she's stoot,
Gie her a kilt instead o' cotts, an' thon's the gran' recruit.
There's Francie syne, oor auldest loon, we pat him on for
   grieve,
An', fegs, we would be in a soss, gin he should up an' leave;
He's eident, an' has lots o' can, an' cheery wi' the men,
An' I'm sae muckle oot aboot wi' markets till atten'.
We've twa chaps syne to wirk the horse, as sweir as sweir can
   be,
They fussle better than they ploo, they're aul' an' mairret tee,
An' baith hae hooses on the ferm, an' Francie never kens
Foo muckle corn gyangs hame at nicht, to fatten up their hens.
The baillie syne, a peer-hoose geet, nae better than a feel,
He slivvers, an' has sic a mant, an' ae clog-fit as weel;
He's barely sense to muck the byre, an' cairry in the scull,
An' park the kye, an' cogue the caur, an' scutter wi' the bull.
Weel, that's them a' – I didna hear – the laadie i' the gig?
That's Johnnie, he's a littlan jist, for a' he leuks sae big.
Fy na, he isna twenty yet – ay, weel, he's maybe near't;
Ower young to lippen wi' a gun, the crater would be fear't.
He's hardly throu' his squeelin' yet , an' noo we hae a plan
To lat him simmer i' the toon, an' learn to mizzer lan'.

Fat? Gar him 'list! Oor laadie 'list? 'Twould kill his mither,
  that,
To think o' Johnnie in a trench awa' in fat-ye-ca't;
We would hae sic a miss at hame, gin he was hine awa',
We'd raither lat ye clean the toon o' ony ither twa;
Ay, tak' the wife, the dother, deem, the baillie wi' the mant,
Tak' Francie, an' the mairret men, but John we canna want.
Fat does he dee? Ye micht as weel speir fat I dee mysel',
The things he hisna time to dee is easier to tell;
He dells the yard, an' wi' the scythe cuts tansies on the brae,
An' fan a ruck gyangs throu' the mull, he's thrang at wispin'
  strae,
He sits aside me at the mart, an' fan a feeder's sell't
Tak's doon the wecht, an' leuks the beuk for fat it's worth fan
  fell't;
He helps me to redd up the dask, he tak's a han' at loo,
An' sorts the shalt, an' yokes the gig, an' drives me fan I'm
  fou.
Hoot, Mains, hae mind, I'm doon for you some sma' thing wi'
  the bank:
Aul' Larickleys, I saw you throu', an' this is a' my thank;
An' Gutteryloan, that time ye broke, to Dockenhill ye cam' –
'Total exemption.' Thank ye, sirs. Fat say ye till a dram?

Murdo Murray
(Murchadh Moireach)
1890–1964

Murdo Murray was born at Back in the island of Lewis. He was educated at the Nicolson Institute, Stornoway, where he was a contemporary of John Munro (see p 89) and at the University of Aberdeen. He returned to Lewis to teach in 1913 but enlisted at the outbreak of war and was commissioned in the 4th Seaforth Highlanders. Murray crossed over to France with his battalion in February 1915 and first saw action at the Battle of Neuve Chapelle where the Seaforths fought alongside units of the Indian Expeditionary Force. During the two days of battle his battalion had 150 casualties. Murray returned to teaching after the war and his poetry and miscellaneous writings were published after his death. Of particular interest to students of the First World War is his war diary which is written in Gaelic and English and which combines descriptions of life in the trenches with comments on the war.

Source: Alasdair I. MacAsgaill (ed.), *Luach na Saorsa (Diary, Poems and Essays by Murdo Murray)*, Glasgow: Gairm, 1970

Luach na Saorsa

Stad tamall beag, a pheileir chaoil
Tha dol gu d'uidhe: ged is faoin
Mo cheist – a bheil 'nad shraon
   Ro-ghuileag bàis?
A bheil bith tha beò le anam caoin
   Ro-sgart' o thàmh?

An làmh a stiùir thu air do chùrs',
An robh i 'n dàn do chur air iùil
A dh'fhàgadh dìlleachdain gun chùl
   An tigh a' bhròin,
Is cridhe goirt le osann bhrùit
   Aig mnaoi gun treòir?

An urras math do chloinn nan daoin'
Thu guin a' bhàis, le d'rinn bhig chaoil,
A chur am broilleach fallain laoich
   San àraich fhuair?
'Na eubha bàis a bheil an t-saors'
   O cheartas shuas?

Freagairt
'Nam shraon tha caoin bhith sgart' o thàmh,
   'Nam rinn bhig chaoil ro-ghuileag bàis,
'S an làmh a stiùir bha dhi san Dàn
   Deur ghoirt don truagh;
Ach 's uil' iad ìobairt saors' on Ard,
   Troimhn Bhàs thig Buaidh.

     1915 A' cheud latha san trainnse

The Value of Freedom

Stop a little while, slim bullet
Going to your goal: although foolish
My question – is there in your forward rush
    A foretaste of the death-cry?
Is there a living being with a tender soul
    Already reft from rest?

The hand that directed you in your course,
Was it its fate to guide you on a path
That would leave orphans without support
    In a grieving house,
That would leave a wife without strength,
    Heartsore, sighing heavily?

What surety does it offer mankind,
Your putting the death-wound, with your slim little point,
In the healthy breast of a warrior
    On the cold battlefield?
Does divine justice spell out freedom
    In his death-cry?

Answer
In my forward rush a kindly person is reft from rest,
    In my slim little point is a foretaste of the death-cry,
And the hand that directed was fated to bring
    The wretched a bitter tear;
But they are all a sacrifice to freedom from Above –
    Through Death comes Victory.

1915 The first day in the trench

Na Mairbh san Raoin
(Geàrr-Luinneag)

Bu shunntach iad a' dol thar raoin na strì
  Tha 'n sin 'nan laighe sìnt' an sàmhchair bhuain,
Bu bhlath caoin-aiteal gràidh o mhaoin an cridh'
  Mus d'thaom dubh-dhìle 'bhàis gu shlugadh suas.
Le umhlachd dhaibh a thuit an teas a' bhlàir,
  Gu socair, sàmhach, cladhaich uaigh rin taobh,
'S 'nan èideadh-cogaidh adhlaic iad san àit
  An d'thuit ri làr le bàs don nàmh 'nan glaodh.
Tog tosdach iad, dom b'euchdan òirdhearc cliù,
  'S le mùirn is dàimh leig sìos an ceann san tàmh
Nach crìochnaich tìm troimh shìorraidheachd an iùil;
  Dùin suas an dachaigh 's fàg an neòinean àillt
A' seinn am beus san deothaig mhilis chiùin;
  'S mar chuimhneachan tog crois air laoich a bha.

1917

The Dead in the Field

Eagerly they went across the fields of strife
　　Who lie there stretched in everlasting quiet;
Warm was the tender breath of love from their heart's wealth
　　Before death's black deluge flooded and engulfed it.
In obeisance to those who fell in the battle's heat,
　　Beside them quietly, silently dig a grave
And in their battle attire there bury them
　　Where they fell down, death to the enemy in their cry.
Silently lift them, who won fame for glorious deeds,
　　And with fond regard lay down their heads in the rest
Time will not end through the eternity of their course;
　　Close up the dwelling, and leave the lovely daisy
To sing their virtue in the sweet breath of wind;
　　And raise a cross as a memorial over warriors gone.

1917

(Note: the Gaelic original is in sonnet form.)

J. B. Salmond

1891–1958

James Bell Salmond was born in Arbroath and educated at
Arbroath High School and St Andrews University. After
graduating in 1913 he became a journalist with Amalgamated
Press in London but enlisted in the Inns of Court Regiment on
the outbreak of war. This Territorial Army formation provided
around 12,000 army officers during the First World War and
Salmond was duly commissioned into the 7th Black Watch.
With his battalion he saw service on the Western Front in
the French sector at Arras and he also took part in the
attack on the Beaumont Hamel Ridge during the Battle of
the Somme in 1916. (See also David Rorie, p 256.) After
the war Salmond returned to Scotland to become editor of
the *Scots Magazine*; he was a constant source of encouragement
to younger writers like James Leslie Mitchell (see p 228) and
the novelist Neil M. Gunn and he also wrote pleasing verse
in the vernacular under the pseudonym of 'Wayfarer'. A great
observer of Scottish life, Salmond wrote a standard work on
Wade's military roads and the history of the 51st Highland
Division during the Second World War. Like many other
Scottish soldier-poets he refused to be taken in by the glamour
of battle.

Source: J. B. Salmond ('Wayfarer'), *The Old Stalker and Other Poems*,
Edinburgh and London: The Moray Press, 1936

Pilgrimage
Being the thoughts of an ex-soldier at Ypres, 8/8/28

Me an' Jean an' the bairn,
The wee lad spierin' an' starin';
Daunderin' quiet an' douce-like doun
The Menin road into Ypres toun.
'Did ye kill ony Germans here?'
Man, it's sair what a laddie'll spier.
An' Jean whispers 'Wheesht!' – an' there comes
The band wi' its trumpets an' drums.
There's a glower in the wee laddie's e'e.
Ay, he's ettlin' ti sojer like me.
An' Jean whispers low in her pain:
'Lord, Ye'll no' lat it happen again!'
Syne the Gate whaur the weary feet trod
Like a white kind o' promise fae God.
An' in silence we're spierin' an' starin'
– Me, an' Jean, an' the bairn.

Me an' Jean,
Her wi' a saft warm licht in her een,
Thankfu' that I am come through,
But trimlin' a wee at the mou',
Prood o' the medals I wear –
The same as the Prince stan'in' there;
Her hand grippin' hard in mine here
– Oh Jeannie! Oh Jeannie, my dear!
An' ken a' the things she wud say
– An Geordie was fond o' her tae.
We saw Geordie's bivvie yestreen,
Me an' Jean.

Me,
Lookin' yont ower the years juist tae see
Yon War like the ploy o' a loon;
But a queer kind o' shiver rins doon
My back as the things dribble in
– A halliket lauch i' the din,
The sangs, an' the mud, an' the claes,
An' my buits, an' yon glint through the haze
O' anither lad's bayonet, an' lichts
Makin' day o' the darkest o' nichts,
An' the drinkin' our tea fae *ae* can.
– Oh Geordie! Oh Geordie, my man!
An' – deil tak' this dust i' my e'e,
Me!

Any Private to Any Private
July 1917

(The speaker pointed out that owing to the number of young married men who were being killed, the widows were becoming a great burden to the State - Daily Paper.)
(Our boys are wonderful. They are always able to laugh – Daily Paper.)

Ay, gie's ma rum. I'm needin't sair, by God!
We've juist been bringin' Wullie doun the line –
Wullie, that used tae be sae smairt an' snod.
Hell, what a mess! Saft–nosed ane. Damn the swine!
They micht kill clean. I kent his auld folk fine.
Ay, he was mairrit. Man, she's spared a sicht.
Here, Dave, gie's ower that blanket. Ay, that's mine.
I kenna, hoo I canna lauch the nicht.

We gaed tae Tamson' schule. A clever loon
Was Wullie. He was makin' money tae.
A'body liked him round about the toun.
Fitba? Losh ay! He was a de'il tae play.
We joined thegither for a bob a day;
An' noo he's deid. Here, Dave, gie's licht.
They'll pit it in the papers. Weel they may!
I kenna, hoo I canna lauch the nicht.

I canna mak' it oot. It fair beats a',
That Wullie has tae dee for God kens what.
An' Wullie's wife'll get a bob or twa,
Aifter they interfere wi' what she's got.
They'll pester her, and crack a dagoned lot;
An' Heaven kens, they'll lave her awfu' ticht.
'A burden to the State.' Her Wullie's shot.
I kenna, hoo I canna lauch the nicht.

Envoi

What's that? Anither workin' pairtie, noo,
At six? Ay, sergeant, I'll be there a' richt.
Well, Wullie lad, they winna wauken you.
I kenna, hoo I canna lauch the nicht.

Charles Hamilton Sorley
1895–1915

Charles Hamilton Sorley was born in Aberdeen where his father was Professor of Moral Philosophy. In 1900 his family moved to Cambridge and Sorley was educated at King's College Choir School and at Marlborough. In December 1913, having won a place at University College, Oxford, he spent some time in Germany and was attending the University of Jena when war broke out. After his return to Britain he was commissioned in the 7th Suffolk Regiment and moved across to France with them in March 1915. He served mainly in the Plogsteert ('Plug Street') sector and was killed by a sniper during the Battle of Loos in October 1915. His collection *Marlborough and Other Poems* was published posthumously in January 1916 and although it contained much of his juvenilia it became an instant success, owing to the inclusion of the war poems. Sorley had an ambivalent attitude towards the war and towards Germany. Although he was one of the first volunteer officers in Kitchener's army, his decision was fired neither by jingoistic patriotism nor by hatred of Germany. In his sonnet 'To Germany' he shows a subtle understanding of the brutalisation of war. S.C.W. is Sidney Clayton Woodroffe who was at Marlborough with Sorley. He was awarded the Victoria Cross posthumously after being killed at Hooge near Ypres in July 1915.

Sources: Charles Hamilton Sorley, *Marlborough and Other Poems*, Cambridge: Cambridge University Press, 1916, rev. 1919, 1922;
Jean Moorcroft Wilson (ed.), *The Collected Poems of Charles Hamilton Sorley*, London: Cecil Woolf, 1985

'All the hills and vales along'

All the hills and vales along
Earth is bursting into song,
And the singers are the chaps
Who are going to die perhaps.
   O sing, marching men,
   Till the valleys ring again.
   Give your gladness to earth's keeping,
   So be glad, when you are sleeping.

Cast away regret and rue,
Think what you are marching to.
Little live, great pass.
Jesus Christ and Barabbas
Were found the same day.
This died, that went his way.
   So sing with joyful breath.
   For why, you are going to death.
   Teeming earth will surely store
   All the gladness that you pour.

Earth that never doubts nor fears,
Earth knows of death, not tears,
Earth that bore with joyful ease
Hemlock for Socrates,
Earth that blossomed and was glad
'Neath the cross that Christ had,
Shall rejoice and blossom too
When the bullet reaches you.

   Wherefore, men marching
   On the road to death, sing!
   Pour your gladness on earth's head,
   So be merry so be dead.

From the hills and valleys earth
Shouts back the sound of mirth,
Tramp of feet and lilt of song
Ringing all the road along
All the music of their going,
Ringing swinging glad song-throwing,
Earth will echo still, when foot
Lies numb and voice mute.
   On marching men, on
   To the gates of death with song.
   Sow your gladness for earth's reaping,
   So you may be glad, though sleeping,
   Strew your gladness on earth's bed,
   So be merry, so be dead.

To Germany

You are blind like us. Your hurt no man designed,
And no man claimed the conquest of your land.
But gropers both through fields of thought confined
We stumble and we do not understand.
You only saw your future bigly planned,
And we, the tapering paths of our own mind,
And in each other's dearest ways we stand,
And hiss and hate. And the blind fight the blind.

When it is peace, then we may view again
With new-won eyes each other's truer form
And wonder. Grown more loving-kind and warm
We'll grasp firm hands and laugh at the old pain,
When it is peace. But until peace, the storm
The darkness and the thunder and the rain.

Whom Therefore We Ignorantly Worship

These things are silent. Though it may be told
Of luminous deeds that lighten land and sea,
Strong sounding actions with broad minstrelsy
Of praise, strange hazards and adventures bold,
We hold to the old things that grow not old:
Blind, patient, hungry, hopeless (without fee
Of all our hunger and unhope are we),
To the first ultimate instinct, to God we hold.

They flicker, glitter, flicker. But we bide,
We, the blind weavers of an intense fate,
Asking but this – that we may be denied:
Desiring only desire insatiate,
Unheard, unnamed, unnoticed, crucified
To our unutterable faith, we wait.

September 1914

Two Sonnets

I

Saints have adored the lofty soul of you.
Poets have whitened at your high renown.
We stand among the many millions who
Do hourly wait to pass your pathway down.
You, so familiar, once were strange: we tried
To live as of your presence unaware.
But now in every road on every side
We see your straight and steadfast signpost there.

I think it like that signpost in my land,
Hoary and tall, which pointed me to go
Upward, into the hills, on the right hand,
Where the mists swim and the winds shriek and blow,
A homeless land and friendless, but a land
I did not know and that I wished to know.

II

Such, such is Death: no triumph: no defeat:
Only an empty pail, a slate rubbed clean,
A merciful putting away of what has been.

And this we know: Death is not Life effete,
Life crushed, the broken pail. We who have seen
So marvellous things know well the end not yet.

Victor and vanquished are a-one in death:
Coward and brave: friend, foe. Ghosts do not say
'Come, what was your record when you drew breath?'
But a big blot has hid each yesterday
So poor, so manifestly incomplete.
And your bright Promise, withered long and sped,
Is touched, stirs, rises, opens and grows sweet
And blossoms and is you, when you are dead.

12 June 1915

'When you see millions of the mouthless dead'

When you see millions of the mouthless dead
Across your dreams in pale battalions go,
Say not soft things as other men have said,
That you'll remember. For you need not so.
Give them not praise. For, deaf, how should they know
It is not curses heaped on each gashed head?
Nor tears. Their blind eyes see not your tears flow.
Nor honour. It is easy to be dead.
Say only this, 'They are dead.' Then add thereto,
'Yet many a better one has died before.'
Then, scanning all the o'ercrowded mass, should you
Perceive one face that you loved heretofore,
It is a spook. None wears the face you knew.
Great death has made all his for evermore.

In Memoriam S.C.W., VC

There is not fitter end than this.
    No need is now to yearn nor sigh.
We know the glory that is his,
    A glory that can never die.

Surely we knew it long before,
    Knew all along that he was made
For a swift radiant morning, for
    A sacrificing swift night-shade.

8 September 1915

Mary Symon
1863–1938

Mary Symon was born in Dufftown, Banffshire, the daughter of a small landowner and educated at boarding school in Edinburgh and at the University of St Andrews. Much of her early writing was sentimental verse which was published in the *Scots Magazine*, but she was also a contributor to Hugh MacDiarmid's *Northern Numbers*. Like Violet Jacob (see p 46) another noteworthy poet of the north-east of Scotland, Mary Symon took a good deal of interest in the language, customs and lore of her native countryside. Her poetry shows a genuine concern for the pain and misery caused by war, especially in the small rural communities. She died at her father's estate of Pittyvaich in 1938.

Source: Leslie W. Wheeler, ed. *Ten North-East Poets*, Aberdeen: University Press, Aberdeen, 1985

The Glen's Muster-Roll
The Dominie Loquitur

Hing't up aside the chumley-cheek, the aul' glen's Muster-Roll
A' names we ken fae hut an' ha', fae Penang to the Pole,
An' speir na gin I'm prood o't – losh! coont them line by line,
Near han' a hunner fechtin' men, an' they a' were Loons o' Mine.

A' mine. It's jist like yesterday they sat there raw on raw,
Some tyaavin' wi' the 'Rule o' Three', some widin' throu 'Mensa';
The map o' Asia's shoogly yet faur Dysie's sheemach head
Gaed cleeter-clatter a' the time the carritches was said.
'A limb,' his greetin' granny swore, 'the aul' deil's very limb' –
But Dysie's deid and drooned lang syne; the 'Cressy' coffined
    him.
'Man guns upon the fore barbette!' . . . What's that to me an'
    you?
Here's moss an' burn, the skailin' kirk, aul' Kissack beddin's soo.
It's Peace, it's Hame – but owre the Ben the coastal searchlights
    shine,
And we ken that Britain's bastions mean – that sailor Loon o'
    Mine.

The muirlan's lang, the muirlan's wide, an' fa says 'ships' or 'sea'?
But the tang o' saut that's in wir bleed has puzzled mair than me.
There's Sandy wi' the bristled shins, faur think ye's he the day?
Oot where the hawser's tuggin' taut in the surf o' Suvla Bay;
An' owre the spurs o' Chanak Bahr gaed twa lang stilpert chiels,
I think o' flappin' butteries yet or weyvin' powets' creels –
Exiles on far Australian plains – but the Lord's ain boomerang
'S the Highland heart that's aye for hame hooever far it gang.
An' the winds that wail owre Anzac an' requiem Lone Pine
Are nae jist a' for stranger kin, for some were Loons o' Mine.

They're comin' hame in twas an' threes; there's Tam fae Singapore –
Yon's his, the string o' buckie-beads abeen the aumry door –
An' Dick MacLeod, his sanshach sel' (Guidsake, a bombardier!)
I see them yet ae summer day come hodgin' but the fleer:
'Please, sir,' (a habber an' a hoast), 'Please, sir' (a gasp, a gulp,

Syne wi' a rush) 'Please-sir-can-we-win-oot-to-droon-a-fulp?'
. . . Hi, Rover, here lad! – aye, that's him, the fulp they didna
   droon,
But Tam – puir Tam lies cauld an' stiff on some grey Belgian dune,
An' the Via Dolorosa's there, faur a wee bit cutty quine
Stan's lookin' doon a teem hill road for a sodger Loon o' Mine.

Fa's neist? the Gaup – A Gordon wi' the 'Bydand' on his broo,
Nae murlacks dreetlin' fae his pooch or owre his grauvit noo,
Nae words o' groff-write trackies on the 'Four best ways to
   fooge' –
He steed his grun' an' something mair, they tell me, oot at Hooge.
But owre the dyke I'm hearin' yet: 'Lads, fa's on for a swap? –
A lang sook o' a pandrop for the sense o' verbum sap.
Fack's death, I tried to min' on't – here's my gairten wi the knot –
But – bizz! a dhubrack loupit as I passed the muckle pot.'
. . . Ay, ye dinna ken the classics, never heard o' a co-sine
But here's my aul' lum aff tae ye, dear gowkit Loon o' Mine.

They're handin oot the haloes an' three's come to the glen –
There's Jeemack ta'en his Sam Browne to his mither's but an' ben.
Ay, they ca' me 'Blawin' Beelie,' but I never crawed sae crouse
As the day they gaed the V.C. to my *filius nullius*.
But he winna sit 'Receptions' nor keep on his aureole,
A' he says is 'Dinna haiver, jist rax owre the Bogie Roll.'
An' the Duke an' 's dother shook his han' an' speirt aboot his kin.
'Old family, yes; here sin' the Flood,' I smartly chippit in.
(Fiech! Noah's Na – we'd ane wirsels, ye ken, in '29)
I'm nae the man tae stan' an' hear them lichtlie Loon o' Mine.

Wir Lairdie. That's his mither in her doo's-neck silk gaun by,
The puddock, so she tells me, 's haudin' up the H.L.I.
An' he's stan'in' owre his middle in the Flanders' clort an' dub,
Him 'at eese't to scent his hanky, an' speak o's mornin' 'tub'.
The Manse loon's dellin' divots on the weary road to Lille,
An' he cann flype his stockin's, cause they hinna tae nor heel.
Sennelager's gotten Davie – a' moo fae lug tae lug –
An' the Kaiser's kyaak, he's writin', 'll neither ryve nor rug,
'But mind ye' (so he post-cairds), 'I'm already owre the Rhine.'
Ay, there's nae a wanworth o' them, though they werna Loons o'
   Mine.

. . . You – Robbie. Memory pictures; Front bench, a curly pow,
A chappit hannie grippin' ticht a Homer men't wi' tow –
The lave a' scrammelin' near him, like bummies roon a bike.
'Fat's this?' 'Fats that?' he'd tell them a' – ay, speir they fat they
      like.
My hill-foot lad! A sowl an' brain fae's bonnet to his beets,
A 'Fullerton' in posse, nae the first fun' fowin' peats.
. . . An' I see a blythe young Bajan gang whistlin' doon the brae,
An' I hear a wistful Paladin his patriot credo say.
An' noo, an' noo. I'm waitin' till a puir thing hirples hame –
Ay, 't's the Valley o' the Shadow, nae the mountain heichts o'
      Fame.
An' where's the nimble nostrum, the dogma fair an' fine.
To still the ruggin' heart I hae for you, oh, Loon o' Mine?

My loons, my loons! Yon winnock gets the settin' sun the same,
Here's sklates and skailies, ilka dask a' futtled wi' a name.
An' as I sit a vision comes: Ye're troopin' in aince mair,
Ye're back fae Aisne an' Marne an' Meuse, Ypres an' Festubert;
Ye're back on weary bleeding feet – you, you that danced an'
      ran –
For every lauchin' loon I kent I see a hell-scarred man.
Not mine but yours to question now! You lift unhappy eyes –
'Ah, Maister; tell's fat a' this means.' And I, ye thocht sae wise,
Maun answer wi' the bairn words ye said tae me langsyne:
'I dinna ken, I dinna ken. Fa does, oh, Loons o' Mine?'

A Recruit For The Gordons

I'm aff! The halflin gets my crib,
　　An' keeps the chaumer key;
The morn aul Mains can dicht his nib,
　　An' scoor the lift for me.

I've listed! Dang the nowt an' neeps!
　　I'm aff to fecht or fa';
I ken, withoot their weary threeps,
　　They're mair than needin's a'.

Wi' Huns upon wir thrashel-stane,
　　An' half the world red wud,
Gweed sax feet ane o' brawn an' bane
　　Is nae for plooman dud.

An' sae I paumered back an' fore,
　　Practeesin' in my kilt,
An' Sownock fae the bothy door
　　Kame-sowfed a marital lilt.

They leuch till howe an' hill-top rang –
　　I steppit saft mysel; –
For aye anaith my bonnet sang
　　But things I couldna tell –

The bonnet wi' the aul' 'Bydand'
　　That sat upon my broo –
An' something stirred, grey Mitherland,
　　In my puir hert for you,

As aye an' aye the plaidie green
　　Swung roon my naked knee,
An' mairchin' there anaith the meen,
　　Lord sake! That wasna me.

The eat-meat sumph that kissed the quines,
　　An' took a skyte at Eel;
I was the heir o' brave langsynes,
　　A sodger, head to heel.

Ay me! 'At never shot a craw,
   Nor killed a cushy-doo –
But bleed's aye bleed, an' aul' granda
   Did things at Waterloo.

I'm aff the morn . . . There's nane'll ken
   O' ae broon curly head,
That ees't to lie aside my ain
   In mains' stoupet bed:

It's laich, laich noo, in Flander's sod,
   An' I'm mairchin' wi' the drum,
'Cause doon the lang La Bassée road
   There's dead lips cryin' 'Come!'

The Soldiers' Cairn

Gie me a hill wi heather on't,
  An' a reid sun drappin', doon,
Or the mists o' the mornin' risin' saft
  Wi' the reek owre a wee grey toon.
Gie me a howe by the lang glen road,
  For it's there 'mang the whin an' fern
(D'ye mind on't, Will? Are ye hearin', Dod?)
  That we're biggin the Soldiers' Cairn.

Far awa' in the Flanders land
  Wi' fremmit France atween,
But mony a howe o' them baith the day
  Has a hap o' the Gordon green;
It's them we kent that's lyin' there,
  An it's nae wi' stane or airn,
But wi' brakin' herts an' mem'ries sair
That we're biggin' the Soldiers' Cairn.

Doon, laich doon the Dullan sings –
  An' I ken o' an aul' sauch tree,
Where a wee loon's wahnie's hingin' yet
  That's dead in Picardy;
An' ilka win' fae the Conval's broo
  Bends aye the buss o' ern
Where aince he futtled a name that noo
  I'll read on the Soldiers' Cairn.

Oh! build it fine an' build it fair,
  Till it leaps to the moorland sky –
More, more than death is symbolled there,
  Than tears or triumphs by.
There's the Dream Devine of a starward way
  Oor laggard feet would learn –
It's a new earth's corner-stone we'd lay
  As we fashion the Soldiers' Cairn.

Lads in your plaidies lyin' still
  In lands we'll never see,
This lonely cairn on a hameland hill
  Is a' that oor love can dee;
An' fine an' braw we'll mak' it a',
  But oh, my Bairn, my Bairn,
It's a cradle's croon that'll aye blaw doon
  To me fae the Soldiers' Cairn.

PROSE

J. J. Bell
1871–1934

John Joy Bell was born in Glasgow and was educated at Kelvinside Academy and in Perthshire at Morrison's Academy. He studied Chemistry at Glasgow University but left without taking a degree. While a student he had started writing poetry and his first book *The New Noah's Ark* was published in 1899. Most of his writing at that time was in journalism and it was from a series of sketches published in the *Glasgow Evening Times* between 1901 and 1902 that he came to publish, at his own expense, *Wee MacGreegor*, a pawky novel about a small boy and his adventures in Glasgow. With its sentimental picture of working–class life *Wee MacGreegor* was an instant success; it sold over a quarter of a million copies and was pirated in America. Bell followed the successful formula in its sequels *Wee MacGreegor Again* and *Wee MacGreegor Enlists*. Although less assured and inventive than the original novel, the story of 'Wee MacGreegor's' service in a Scottish regiment captures some of the early enthusiasm for the war.

Source: J. J. Bell, *Wee MacGreegor Enlists*, London: Hodder & Stoughton, 1915

The Alarm

It came, as Christina would have expressed it in her early days, like a 'blot from the blue.' On a certain fine morning, while battalion drill was in progress, a mounted officer dashed upon the scene and was forthwith engaged in earnest conversation with the colonel. The news was evidently urgent, and it was received with an obvious gravity. A thrill ran through the ranks; you would have fancied you heard breaths of anticipation.

A minute later the companies were making for camp at the double. Arrived there they were instructed to repair to billets and, with all speed, pack up. And presently ammunition was being served out, a hundred rounds to each man; and, later, 'iron' rations.

'We're awa' noo!' gasped Macgregor, recovering forcibly from Willie's greedy clutch a pair of socks knitted by Christina.

'Ay, we're awa'; an' I'll bet ye we're for Flanders,' said Willie, no less excited.

'Dardanelles!' shouted Macgregor, above the din that filled the billet.

'Flanders!' yelled Willie, wildly, and started to dance – unfortunately upon a thin piece of soap.

'Dardanelles!' Macgregor repeated as he gave his friend a hand up.

'Oh –!' groaned Willie, rubbing the back of his head. 'But what'll ye bet?'

'What ha'e ye got?'

'I'll bet ye thruppence – the thruppence ye lent me the day afore yesterday.'

'Done! If ye win, we'll be quits; if ye loss –'

'Na, na! If I win, ye'll ha'e to pay me –'

'Ach, I've nae time to listen to ye. I've twa letters to write.'

'Letters! What aboot the bet?'

'Awa' an' chase yersel'! Are ye no gaun to drap a line to yer aunt?'

'No dashed likely! She's never sent the postal order I asked her for. If I had got it, I wud ha'e payed what I'm owin' ye, Macgreegor. By heavens, I wud! I'll tak ma oath I –'

'Aweel, never heed aboot that,' Macgregor said, soothingly. 'Send her a post caird an' let me get peace for three meenutes.'

'Ye canna get peace in this,' said Willie, with a glance round the tumultuous billet.

'I can – if ye haud yer silly tongue.' Macgregor thereupon got his pad and envelopes (a gift from Miss Tod), squatted on his bed, and proceeded to gnaw his pencil. The voice of the sergeant was heard ordering the men to hurry up.

'I'll tell ye what I'll dae,' said Willie, sitting down at his friend's elbow. 'I'll bet ye a' I owe ye to a bob it's Flanders. Ye see, I'll maybe get shot, an' I dinna want to dee in debt. An' I'll send the auld cat a caird wi' something nice on it, to please ye . . . . Eh?'

'Aw, onything ye like, but for ony sake clay up! Shift!' cried the distracted Macgregor.

'Weel gi'e's a fag . . . an' a match,' said Willie.

He received them in his face, but merely grinned as he languidly removed himself.

The two scrawls so hastily and under such difficulties produced by Macgregor are sacred. He would never write anything more boyish and loving, nor yet more manly and brave, than those 'few lines' to his mother and sweetheart. There was no time left for posting them when the order came to fall in, but he anticipated an opportunity at one of the stations on the journey south.

Out in the sunshine stood the hundreds of lads whose training had been so brief that some carried ammunition for the first time. There were few grave faces, though possibly some of the many grins were more reflected than original. Yet there was a fine general air of eagerness, and at the word 'attention' the varied expressions gave place to one of determination.

Boom! boom! boom! . . . Boom! boom! boom! Dirl and skirl; skirl and dirl! So to the heart–lifting, hell–raising music of pipes and drums they marched down to the railway.

At the station it seemed as though they had been expected to break all records in military entraining. There was terrific haste and occasional confusion, the latter at the loading of the vans. The enthusiasm was equalled only by the perspiration. But at last everything and nearly everybody was aboard, and the rumour went along that they had actually broken such and such a battalion's record.

Private William Thomson, however, had already started his inevitable grumbling. There were eight in the compartment, and he had stupidly omitted to secure a corner seat.

'I'll bet ye I'm a corp afore we get to Dover,' he bleated.

'That's as near as ever ye'll be to bein' a corporal,' remarked the cheerful Jake. 'But hoo d'ye ken it'll be Dover?'

'I'll bet ye – Na! I'll no tak' on ony mair wagers. I've a tremenjous bet on wi' this yin' – indicating Macgregor – 'every dashed penny I possess – that we're boun' for Flanders. He says the Dardanelles.'

All excepting Macgregor fell to debating the question. He had just remembered something he had forgotten to say to Christina; also, he was going away without the ring she was to have given him. He was not sorry he was going, but he felt sad . . . .

The debate waxed furious.

'I tell ye,' bawled Willie, 'we're for Flanders! The Ninth's been there since the –'

A sudden silence! What the – was that? Surely not – ay, it was! – an order to detrain!

And soon the whisper went round that they were not bound for anywhere – unless the – old camp. The morning's alarm and all that followed had been merely by way of practice.

At such a time different men have different feelings, or, at least, different ways of expressing them. Jake laughed philosophically and appeared to dismiss the whole affair. Willie swore with a curious and seemingly unnecessary bitterness, at frequent intervals, for the next hour or so. Macgregor remained in a semi-stunned condition of mind until the opportunity came for making a little private bonfire of the two letters; after which melancholy operation he straightway recovered his usual good spirits.

'Never heed, Wullie,' he said, later; 'we'll get oor chance yet.'

Willie exploded. 'What for did ye get me to mak' sic a – cod o' masel'?'

'Cod o' yersel'? Me?'

'Ay, you! – gettin' me to send a caird to ma – aunt! What for did ye dae it?'

Macgregor stared. 'But ye didna post it,' he began.

'Ay, but I did. I gi'ed it to a man at the station.'

'Oh! . . . Weel, ye'll just ha'e to send her anither.'

'That'll no mak' me less o' a cod.'

'What way? What did ye write on the caird?'

Willie hesitated, muttered a few curses, and said slowly yet savagely:–

'Off to Flanders, wi' – wi' kind love' '*oh, dammit!*'

(*from* Wee MacGreegor Enlists)

James Bridie
1888–1951

The pen-name of Osborne Henry Mavor who was born in Glasgow, the son of an engineer. Trained as a doctor at Glasgow University where he was a member of the Officers' Training Corps, Mavor joined the Royal Army Medical Corps (RAMC) at the outbreak of war. With the 42nd Field Ambulance he served in France in 1915 and 1916, mainly in the Ypres sector. (See also David Rorie, p 256.) He was invalided home in 1917 and the rest of his war was spent in Mesopotamia, Persia and Trans-caucasia. This front had come into being as a result of allied attempts to stymie the construction of the German railway to Baghdad but by late 1917 events there had become confused by the Bolshevik Revolution in Russia. Mavor was in Georgia and Azerbaijan in Maj-Gen Dunsterville's force during the fighting and did not return home until 1919. Although Mavor did not write a full account of his war service he did publish a lively and amusing description of the confusion that reigned in Trans-caucasia at the tail-end of the war. The first extract is a typically Bridie-ish account of being under fire on the Western Front.

Sources: James Bridie, *One Way of Living*, London: Constable, 1939; James Bridie, *Some Talk of Alexander*, London: Methuen, 1926

Under Fire On The
Western Front

The fighting at Ypres in the early winter of 1914 was the last attempt made by the British Expeditionary Force to turn the German flank during the 'Race to the Sea'. In the course of the fighting the British lost 50,000 casualties and Ypres became an important symbol of British resistance. A second battle for the Ypres salient was fought in April and May 1915. The Somme offensive of July 1916 turned into a war of attrition which, despite the high British casualties, inflicted permanent damage on the German Army. The Battle of Arras, which Bridie missed, was the main allied offensive of spring 1917.

I was sleeping in the school house at Vlaterminghe. I had ridden in to it on a large horse called Ikey, from a fancied resemblance to a great financier. It had been a bright, sunny day and all that could be seen of war was an aeroplane flying high and surrounded by dabs of cotton wool. The houses were a little battered and the *pavé* was disturbed in places. We cleaned out the school house and established a dressing station and went to sleep. I was awakened by an unpleasant tearing sound. It was partly screech and partly whistle, and the main impression it made on my half-awakened mind was that whatever caused the sound was angry at me and wanted to get me. It was followed by a loud bang that shook the floor and rattled the little windows. These sounds and their climaxes followed each other with great rapidity and I sat up in my sleeping-bag in some consternation. The door opened and Sergeant Gatehouse, a schoolmaster in civil life, put his intelligent face round the door. He said in the army voice he had been at some pains to cultivate during the eight months' training at Tweseldown,

'I have to report, sir, that this dressing station is being consistently shelled.'

'In that case,' I said, 'I'd better get up.'

I found my little advance party in greatcoats and balaclava helmets standing in the roadway in the raw misty May dawn. They were looking at the church a few hundred yards down the road. Against the church steeple and in the graveyard round it light shells were bursting in salvos of four. We stood and coughed and smoked cigarettes and inhaled the throat-catching rime for about twenty minutes, and then they stopped.

In *Journey's End*, you will remember, Osborne's favourite reading was *Alice in Wonderland*. This is a true touch. I discovered on that morning a curious thing about *Alice in Wonderland*. A year or two ago a refugee doctor was going round my wards with me. He said that he had been reading *Alice in Wonderland* and that clearly Lewis Carroll was a schizophrenic dement. I said I didn't think so. I thought he was a prophet.

It seemed to me on that May morning that he had prophesied the Great War.

'Tell us a story!' said the March Hare.

'Yes, please do!' pleaded Alice.

'And be quick about it,' added the Hatter, 'or you'll be asleep again before it's done.'

'Once upon a time there were three little sisters', the Dormouse began in a great hurry; 'and their names were Elsie, Lacie and Tillie; and they lived at the bottom of a well – '.

'What did they live on?' asked Alice, who always took a great interest in questions of eating and drinking.

'They lived on treacle,' said the Dormouse, after thinking a minute or two.

'They couldn't have done that, you know,' Alice gently remarked; 'they'd have been ill.'

'So they were,' said the Dormouse; '*very ill.*'

Alice tried a little to fancy to herself what such an extraordinary way of living would be like, but it puzzled her too much, so she went on: 'But why did they live at the bottom of a well?'

'Take some more tea,' the March Hare said to Alice, very earnestly.

As I stood there chewing my cigarette on that May dawn I thought to myself 'I don't know. I'm not sure. But it looks to me as if this business might quite easily become intolerable.'

It did. I encountered frog footmen, white rabbits, Mad Hatters, Dormice, caterpillars, Dodos, and Cheshire cats, to say nothing of Gryphons and Mock-turtles. Above us gimbled the slithy toves, through their anti-aircraft wabe; borogroves bobbed mimsily along the horizon; frumious bandersnatches brought our hearts to our mouths; the jubjub bird passed overhead like a brewer's dray driving along the roofs of Long Acre and left a hole twenty feet deep where it landed; the jabberwock whiffled continually through woods that became more and more tulgey as the weeks went on. The meaning of it all was as elusive as the egg on the shelf of the sheep-shop. We drifted from Ypres to Arras, from Arras to the Somme and back to Arras again. Before the battle of Arras I turned bright orange and was sent home. A rat-like person with a blue band round his hat sent me to Manchester to spite me. I arrived at Manchester in the dark and a girl threw two red roses into my ambulance.

I got well very quickly. Manchester was very cold and foggy and full of people in soft hats whistling 'The Passing of Salome'. I had one very pleasant dinner with Wallace, Fletcher and Herbert Sidebotham and was returned to my native place with a pulse rate of a hundred and fifty or so but otherwise well. My father was dead, my younger brother Eric had had his thigh shot in two at Gallipoli and my brother Jack, the only soldier of the three of us, was tied by an extraordinary series of accidents to a Royal Engineers training camp. My mother and I stayed with my uncle at Mauchline and then I returned to Sick Light Duty.

Sick Light Duty meant living in the United Services Club and daily taking a taxi up the hill to Edinburgh Castle. In Edinburgh Castle a number of young men yawned, slept, played bridge, read novels or sat on inexacting medical boards. Work for the day finished about five and I returned to the club to dine with Robin Brown, whose ships were anchored at Queensferry. At intervals I was orderly MO and remained in the Castle for the night. There was a night ward visit to do, but no kitchen supper. The whole affair was much more dignified than real life. I lay on my bed and heard the east wind howl round the ramparts.

This pleasant routine was broken by a transfer to Fort George, a sullen dismal place on the Moray Firth. I was attached to the Seaforth's depot and messed with two most charming and characteristic old colonels and a discontented adjutant. Drafts of the HLI were also housed in the Fort, but the Greeks had no dealings with these Samaritans. Among the Samaritans was Esme Percy in a very natty pair of tartan trousers. I had the pleasure of seeing him imitate Fred Emney and speak the Harfleur speech at a smoking concert.

Most of the time I was bored. I sank into a lethargy from which I was roused by the two day visit of a travelling medical board, presided over by an ignorant bully. I wrote a frenzied letter to the DADMS of my division, asking him to arrange for my return to my old field ambulance. The field ambulance was not a highly regarded unit in the British Army, but I was satisfied with mine. I had known the men since they were recruits and seen them level up and level down. They were courageous, honourable, devoted fellows, and I had never seen them tired, or unwilling or unskilful or afraid. Shepherd wrote back that the ADMS would wire for me the moment I landed at Boulogne and that there was a reasonable chance of me being made a temporary lieutenant-colonel. As this was one of the cushiest jobs in the war and carried with it an almost automatic DSO I was very pleased. My delight was short-lived. A note from another official friend told me that I was booked to sail for Mesopotamia on the following week. And to Mesopotamia I went.

(*from* One Way of Living)

The Bloody Affair at Deli Abbas

U nder the patient brown hands of certain members of the Jail Corps, our new mess had arisen like a fairy palace. A frieze representing the camel, or ship of the desert, progressing along the desert in convoy, entirely surrounded the mess-room. A cheerful fire of palm logs twinkled below the gun-rack. Portraits of the ancestors of members of the mess in real frames decorated the walls. Bottles of gin and vermouth and sherry and angostura caught the outermost beams of the fire. Outside, the cloudless sky stretched blue and fair, and some of its blue, dancing on the turbid Tigris, made it seem, for the moment, a tolerable river. And still the barbed wire stood and the bulldog defence of the Sindiyeh-Windiyeh line went on.

By the fireside I found the Colonel and his new DSO ribbon striking a warm and welcome note of colour in that already cheerful scene.

'Good morning, sir,' I said.

'Good morning,' said the Colonel. 'Look here,' he said, 'I am fed up with this d——d hole, and I hear there is a battle on this morning. It is a long time since I saw a battle. Let's turn out the Ford tourer and go and see this combat.'

I pointed out that this battle was none of our affair. It had been my practice in the dear, dead days on the Western Front to avoid all battles to which I had not been specifically detailed. I then reflected that no more had it been my custom to drink sherry and bitters at 11a.m., and that in any event we were east of Suez, and besides that it was a grand morning for an expedition of whatever character. I capitulated, and we set off for the battle-field.

The car contained a driver, the Colonel and myself wrapped in sheepskin, two guns, a luncheon basket with cold starling pie, beef sandwiches, and a quantity of Asahi beer. A lark was singing its 'little guts out'. Mesopotamia was all green and gold – more gold than green, but still the green was there. Blue jays and hoopoes, rabbits, partridges and pi-dogs shared the illimitable with us. The sun shone gaily. The Colonel and I sang 'Drake is going West, lads,' and the prologue to 'Pagliacci,' and felt very content as we bumped along for twenty or thirty miles.

'We should be near Divisional Headquarters by now,' said the Colonel at length, and began to tell me what the General intended to do in this battle, and what far-reaching effects would follow the defeat of the Turkish Army. While he was telling me this we sighted two officers of the Divisional Staff engaged in shooting sand-grouse, so we stopped the Ford and asked them for news of the battle. We also offered them beer, which they accepted at our hands. It appeared that the English had won a great victory, and that the Turks were in full flight before the pursuing cavalry of the Indians.

'You will have to hurry up if you are to see any of the battle at all,' said one of the officers. So we pushed on. At Divisional Headquarters we were told that the General was following up the battle, which must now be upwards of twenty miles north of where it started. The Colonel made a rapid calculation and decided that following up the battle and being home in time for dinner were mutually exclusive. We adjourned to the Field Ambulance to hear the tales of the survivors.

Several rows of Turkish prisoners, under the benevolent eyes of a sentry and a sergeant of the RAMC, were seated on the ground eating and eating and eating.

'They've been at it for the lawst two hours, sir,' said the serjeant. 'Gawd knows when the poor devils lawst looked a tin of bully in the fice. Makes your heart bleed, it does.'

We found the quartermaster in the mess tent, discussing a solitary whisky and soda. He told us that as there were no wounded the Medical Officers had gone pig-sticking.

'The blutlust will out,' said the Colonel, rather wittily, I thought, and we got into the car and drove home to dinner, which, I am happy to say, was well chosen, well cooked, well served, and, in quantity, ample.

And that, as I shall tell my grandchildren, was the only occasion on which I came near to seeing a shot fired in anger in Meso-potamia. . . . If you except the four rounds that two dear friends of mine (the proprietors of a pet tortoise and a little mess threatened by crumbling bank), squeezed out of their tiny pompom before it jammed and refused to fire again at that enterprising German aviator who tried to bomb our bridge head one sultry autumn day.

(*from* Some Talk of Alexander)

John Buchan
1875–1940

During the summer of 1914 Buchan wrote *The Power House*, the first of his 'shockers' (his word) in the style of E. Phillips Oppenheim. This was followed by *The Thirty-Nine Steps* (1915) and *Greenmantle* (1916) which were written as an antidote to his work as a government propagandist. *Mr Standfast*, his war novel, was written between July 1917 and July 1918 and it was highly praised for its realistic backgrounds, especially for Buchan's description of the Western Front. As a war correspondent Buchan had visited Flanders in 1915, he had experienced air-raids in London and he knew intimately the Glasgow which Hannay visits at the beginning of the novel. He had also based Hannay on the person of Field Marshal Lord Edmund Ironside who in real life served on the British front during the German offensive of March 1918. The novel also contains a sympathetic portrait of a conscientious objector, Launcelot Wake. See also p 28.

Source: John Buchan, *Mr Standfast*, London: Hodder and Stoughton, 1919; London: Penguin Books, 1983

A Pacifists' Meeting In Glasgow

Richard Hannay is in Glasgow under the disguise of a South African pacifist called Brand. He is in pursuit of Abel Gresson, an American who is part of a German spy-ring run by Moxom Ivery. The anti-war meeting has been called to found a British Council of Workers and Soldiers.

I followed with extreme nervousness, and to my surprise got a fair hearing. I felt as mean as a mangy dog on a cold morning, for I hated to talk rot before soldiers – especially before a couple of Royal Scots Fusiliers, who, for all I knew, might have been in my own brigade. My line was the plain, practical, patriotic man, just come from the colonies, who looked at things with fresh eyes, and called for a new deal. I was very moderate, but to justify my appearance there I had to put in a wild patch or two, and I got these by impassioned attacks on the Ministry of Munitions. I mixed up a little mild praise of the Germans, whom I said I had known all over the world for decent fellows. I received little applause, but no marked dissent, and sat down with deep thankfulness.

The next speaker put the lid on it. I believe he was a noted agitator, who had already been deported. Towards him there was no lukewarmness, for one half of the audience cheered wildly when he rose, and the other half hissed and groaned. He began with whirlwind abuse of the idle rich, then of the middle-classes (he called them the 'rich man's flunkeys'), and finally of the Government. All that was fairly well received, for it is the fashion of the Briton to run down every Government and yet to be very averse to parting from it. Then he started on the soldiers and slanged the officers ('gentry pups' was his name for them), and the generals, whom he accused of idleness, of cowardice, and of habitual intoxication. He told us that our own kith and kin were sacrificed in every battle by leaders who had not the guts to share their risks. The Scots Fusiliers looked perturbed, as if they were in doubt of his meaning. Then he put it more plainly. 'Will any soldier deny that the men are the barrage to keep the officers' skins whole?'

'That's a bloody lee,' said one of the Fusilier Jocks.

The man took no notice of the interruption, being carried away by the torrent of his own rhetoric, but he had not allowed for the persistence of the interrupter. The Jock got slowly to his feet, and announced that he wanted satisfaction. 'If ye open your dirty gab to blagyird honest men, I'll come up on that platform and wring your neck.'

At that there was a fine old row, some crying out 'Order', some 'Fair play', and some applauding. A Canadian at the back of the hall started a song, and there was an ugly press forward. The hall seemed to be moving up from the back, and already men were standing in all the passages and right to the edge of the platform. I did not like the look in the eyes of these new-comers, and among the crowd I saw several who were obviously plain-clothes policemen.

The chairman whispered a word to the speaker, who continued when the noise had temporarily died down. He kept off the army and returned to the Government, and for a little sluiced out pure anarchism. But he got his foot in it again, for he pointed to the Sinn Feiners as examples of manly independence. At that, pandemonium broke loose, and he never had another look-in. There were several fights going on in the hall between the public and courageous supporters of the orator.

Then Gresson advanced to the edge of the platform in a vain endeavour to retrieve the day. I must say he did it uncommonly well. He was clearly a practised speaker, and for a moment his appeal 'Now, boys, let's cool down a bit and talk sense,' had an effect. But the mischief had been done, and the crowd was surging round the lonely redoubt where we sat. Besides, I could see that for all his clever talk the meeting did not like the look of him. He was as mild as a turtle dove, but they wouldn't stand for it. A missile hurtled past my nose, and I saw a rotten cabbage envelop the baldish head of the ex-deportee. Someone reached out a long arm and grabbed a chair, and with it took the legs from Gresson. Then the lights suddenly went out, and we retreated in good order by the platform door with a yelling crowd at our heels.

It was here that the plain-clothes men came in handy. They held the door while the ex-deportee was smuggled out by some side entrance. That class of lad would soon cease to exist but for the protection of the law which he would abolish. The rest of us, having less to fear, were suffered to leak into Newmilns Street. I found myself next to Gresson, and took his arm. There was something hard in his coat pocket.

Unfortunately there was a big lamp at the point where we emerged, and there for our confusion were the Fusilier Jocks.

Both were strung to fighting pitch, and were determined to have someone's blood. Of me they took no notice, but Gresson had spoken after their ire had been roused, and was marked out as a victim. With a howl of joy they rushed for him.

I felt his hand steal to his side-pocket. 'Let that alone, you fool,' I growled in his ear.

'Sure, mister,' he said, and the next second we were in the thick of it.

It was like so many street fights I have seen – an immense crowd which surged up around us, and yet left a clear ring. Gresson and I got against the wall on the sidewalk, and faced the furious soldiery. My intention was to do as little as possible, but the first minute convinced me that my companion had no idea how to use his fists, and I was mortally afraid that he would get busy with the gun in his pocket. It was that fear that brought me into the scrap. The Jocks were sportsmen every bit of them, and only one advanced to the combat. He hit Gresson a clip on the jaw with his left, and but for the wall would have laid him out. I saw in the lamplight the vicious gleam in the American's eye and the twitch of his hand to his pocket. That decided me to interfere and I got in front of him.

This brought the second Jock into the fray. He was a broad, thickset fellow, of the adorable bandy-legged stocky type that I had seen go through the Railway Triangle at Arras as though it were blotting-paper. He had some notion of fighting, too, and gave me a rough time, for I had to keep edging the other fellow off Gresson.

'Go home, you fool,' I shouted. 'Let this gentleman alone. I don't want to hurt you.'

The only answer was a hook-hit which I just managed to guard, followed by a mighty drive with his right which I dodged so that he barked his knuckles on the wall. I heard a yell of rage, and observed that Gresson seemed to have kicked his assailant on the shin. I began to long for the police.

Then there was that swaying of the crowd which betokens the approach of the forces of law and order. But they were too late to prevent trouble. In self-defence I had to take my Jock seriously, and got in my blow when he had over-reached himself and lost his balance. I never hit anyone so unwillingly in my life. He went over like a poled ox, and measured his length on the causeway.

I found myself explaining things politely to the constables. 'These men objected to this gentleman's speech at the meeting, and I had to interfere to protect him. No, no! I don't want to charge anybody. It was all a misunderstanding.' I helped the stricken Jock to rise and offered him ten bob for consolation.

He looked at me sullenly and spat on the ground. 'Keep your dirty money,' he said. 'I'll be even with ye yet, my man – you and that red-headed scab. I'll mind the looks of ye the next time I see ye.'

Gresson was wiping the blood from his cheek with a silk handkerchief. 'I guess I'm in your debt, Mr Brand,' he said. 'You may bet I won't forget it.'

Back in London after his adventures in Scotland, Richard Hannay is caught up in an air-raid. This time he is in the disguise of a British private soldier.

The Advantages of an Air Raid

The train was abominably late. It was due at eight-twenty-seven, but it was nearly ten when we reached St Pancras. I had resolved to go straight to my rooms in Westminster, buying on the way a cap and waterproof to conceal my uniform should anyone be near my door on my arrival. Then I would ring up Blenkiron and tell him all my adventures. I breakfasted at a coffee-stall, left my pack and rifle in the cloak-room, and walked out into the clear sunny morning.

I was feeling very pleased with myself. Looking back on my madcap journey, I seemed to have had an amazing run of luck and to be entitled to a little credit too. I told myself that persistence always pays and that nobody is beaten till he is dead. All Blenkiron's instructions had been faithfully carried out. I had found Ivery's post office. I had laid the lines of our own special communications with the enemy, and so far as I could see I had left no clue behind me. Ivery and Gresson took me for a well-meaning nincompoop. It was true that I had aroused profound suspicion in the breasts of the Scottish police. But that mattered nothing, for Cornelius Brand, the suspect, would presently disappear, and there was nothing against that rising soldier, Brigadier-General Richard Hannay, who would soon be on his way to France. After all, this piece of service had not been so very unpleasant. I laughed when I remembered my grim forebodings in Gloucestershire. Bullivant had said it would be damnably risky in the long run, but here was the end and I had never been in danger of anything worse than making a fool of myself.

I remember that, as I made my way through Bloomsbury, I was not thinking so much of my triumphant report to Blenkiron as of my speedy return to the Front. Soon I would be with my beloved brigade again. I had missed Messines and the first part of Third Ypres, but the battle was still going on, and I had yet a chance. I might get a division, for there had been talk of that before I left. I knew the Army Commander thought a lot of me. But on the whole I hoped I would be left with the brigade. After all I was an amateur soldier, and I wasn't certain of my powers with a bigger command.

In Charing Cross Road I thought of Mary, and the brigade seemed suddenly less attractive. I hoped the war wouldn't last much longer, though with Russia heading straight for the devil I didn't know how it was going to stop very soon. I was determined to see Mary before I left, and I had a good excuse, for I had taken my orders from her. The prospect entranced me, and I was mooning along in a happy dream, when I collided violently with an agitated citizen.

Then I realized that something very odd was happening.

There was a dull sound like the popping of the corks of flat soda-water bottles. There was a humming, too, from very far up in the skies. People in the street were either staring at the heavens or running wildly for shelter. A motor-bus in front of me emptied its contents in a twinkling; a taxi pulled up with a jar and the driver and fare dived into a second-hand bookshop. It took me a moment or two to realize the meaning of it all, and I had scarcely done this when I got a very practical proof. A hundred yards away a bomb fell on a street island, shivering every window-pane in a wide radius, and sending splinters of stone flying about my head. I did what I had done a hundred times before at the Front, and dropped flat on my face.

The man who says he doesn't mind being bombed or shelled is either a liar or a maniac. This London air-raid seemed to me a singularly unpleasant business. I think it was the sight of the decent civilized life around one and the orderly streets, for what was perfectly natural in a rubble-heap like Ypres or Arras seemed an outrage here. I remember once being in billets in a Flanders village where I had the Maire's house and sat in a room upholstered in cut velvet, with wax flowers on the mantelpiece and oil paintings of three generations on the walls. The Boche took it into his head to shell the place with a long-range naval gun, and I simply loathed it. It was horrible to have dust and splinters blown into the snug, homely room, whereas if I had been in a ruined barn I wouldn't have given the thing two thoughts. In the same way bombs dropping in central London seemed a grotesque indecency. I hated to see plump citizens with wild eyes, and nursemaids with scared children, and miserable women scuttling like rabbits in a warren.

The drone grew louder, and, looking up, I could see the enemy planes flying in a beautiful formation, very leisurely as it seemed, with all London at their mercy. Another bomb fell to the right, and presently bits of our own shrapnel were clattering viciously around me. I thought it about time to take cover, and ran shamelessly for the best place I could see, which was a Tube station. Five minutes before the street had been crowded; now I left behind me a desert dotted with one bus and three empty taxicabs.

I found the Tube entrance filled with excited humanity. One stout lady had fainted, and a nurse had become hysterical, but on the whole people were behaving well. Oddly enough they did not seem inclined to go down the stairs to the complete security of underground; but preferred rather to collect where they could still get a glimpse of the upper world, as if they were torn between fear of their lives and interest in the spectacle. That crowd gave me a good deal of respect for my countrymen.

Like his model Field Marshal Lord Ironside, Hannay is a British field commander during the German offensive of March 1918 which broke the allied lines between Arras and St Quentin. Although Ludendorff's divisions forced a gap, the attack petered out in April due to the superior strength and professionalism of the British Third Army.

The German Offensive of March 1918

This is not the place to write the story of the week that followed. I could not write it even if I wanted to, for I don't know it. There was a plan somewhere, which you will find in the history books, but with me it was blank chaos. Orders came, but long before they arrived the situation had changed, and I could no more obey them than fly to the moon. Often I had lost touch with the divisions on both flanks. Intelligence arrived erratically out of the void, and for the most part we worried along without it. I heard we were under the French – first it was said to be Foch, and then Fayolle, whom I had met in Paris. But the higher command seemed a million miles away, and we were left to use our mother wits. My problem was to give ground as slowly as possible and at the same time not to delay too long, for retreat we must, with the Boche sending in brand-new divisions each morning. It was a kind of war worlds distant from the old trench battles, and since I had been taught no other I had to invent rules as I went along. Looking back, it seems a miracle that any of us came out of it. Only the grace of God and the uncommon toughness of the British soldier bluffed the Hun and prevented him pouring through the breach to Abbeville and the sea. We were no better than a mosquito curtain stuck in a doorway to stop the advance of an angry bull.

The Army Commander was right; we were hanging on with our eyelashes.

We must have been easily the weakest part of the whole front, for we were holding a line which was never less than two miles and was often, as I judged, nearer five, and there was nothing in reserve to us except some oddments of cavalry who chased about the whole battlefield under vague orders. Mercifully for us the Boche blundered. Perhaps he did not know our condition, for our airmen were magnificent and you never saw a Boche plane over our line by day, though they bombed us merrily by night. If he had called our bluff we should have been done, but he put his main strength to the north and the south of us. North he pressed hard on the Third Army, but he got well hammered by the Guards north of Bapaume and he could make no headway at Arras. South he drove at the Paris railway and down the Oise valley, but there Pétain's reserves had arrived, and the French made a noble stand.

Not that he didn't fight hard in the centre where we were, but he hadn't his best troops, and after we got west of the bend of the Somme he was outrunning his heavy guns. Still, it was a desperate enough business, for our flanks were all the time falling back, and we had to conform to movements we could only guess at. After all, we were on the direct route to Amiens, and it was up to us to yield slowly so as to give Haig and Pétain time to get up supports. I was a miser about every yard of ground, for every yard and every minute were precious. We alone stood between the enemy and the city, and in the city was Mary.

If you ask me about our plans I can't tell you. I had a new one every hour. I got instructions from the Corps, but, as I have said, they were usually out of date before they arrived, and most of my

tactics I had to invent myself. I had a plain task, and to fulfil it I had
to use what methods the Almighty allowed me. I hardly slept, I ate
little, I was on the move day and night, but I never felt so strong
in my life. It seemed as if I couldn't tire, and, oddly enough, I
was happy. If a man's whole being is focused on one aim, he has
no time to worry. . . . I remember we were all very gentle and
soft-spoken those days. Lefroy, whose tongue was famous for its
edge, now cooed like a dove. The troops were on their uppers,
but as steady as rocks. We were against the end of the world, and
that stiffens a man. . . .

Day after day saw the same performance. I held my wavering
front with an outpost line which delayed each new attack till I
could take its bearings. I had special companies for counter-attack
at selected points, when I wanted time to retire the rest of the
division. I think we must have fought more than a dozen of such
little battles. We lost men all the time, but the enemy made no
big scoop, though he was always on the edge of one. Looking
back, it seems like a succession of miracles. Often I was in one
end of a village when the Boche was in the other. Our batteries
were always on the move, and the work of the gunners was past
praising. Sometimes we faced east, sometimes north, and once at
a most critical moment due south, for our front waved and blew
like a flag at masthead. . . . Thank God, the enemy was getting
away from his big engine, and his ordinary troops were fagged
and poor in quality. It was when his fresh shock battalions came
on that I held my breath. . . . He had a heathenish amount of
machine-guns and he used them beautifully. Oh, I take my hat
off to the Boche performance. He was doing what we had tried
to do at the Somme and the Aisne and Arras and Ypres, and he
was more or less succeeding. And the reason was that he was going
bald-headed for victory.

The men, as I have said, were wonderfully steady and patient
under the fiercest trial that soldiers can endure. I had all kinds in
the division – old army, new army, Territorials – and you couldn't
pick and choose between them. They fought like Trojans, and,
dirty, weary, and hungry, found still some salt of humour in
their sufferings. It was a proof of the rock-bottom sanity of human
nature.

(*from* Mr Standfast)

R. W. Campbell
b.1876

Robert Walter Campbell served with the Royal Scots Fusiliers during the Boer War and then retired to the Special Reserve. In 1914 he rejoined his regiment and served with the 5th battalion, a Territorial Army formation recruited from Ayrshire. With them he served in Gallipoli, an experience which gave him the background for his first war novel *The Kangaroo Marines* (1915). In 1916 he was transferred once more to the reserve and served for the rest of the war in an administrative capacity. His next novel *Private Spud Tamson* was published in 1916 and quickly went through several editions. Campbell repeated the formula, less successfully, in *Sergeant Spud Tamson VC* and his hero reappeared in 1926 to save a mining village in *Spud Tamson's Pit*. After the war Campbell lived in Lochmaben and Edinburgh but he vanished from the literary scene in the late 1920s and little is known about his subsequent life and career. He was also well known for his jaunty war poems which were published in *The Making of Micky McGhee* (1916). Campbell described the men of the 'Glesca Mileeshy' who took part in the trench fighting as 'a noble force, recruited from the Weary Willies and Never-works of the famous town of Glasgow.'

Source: R. W. Campbell, *Private Spud Tamson*, Edinburgh and London: William Blackwood, 1916

Trench Fighting on the Western Front

The disadvantage of trench-fighting is that it robs even the best soldiers of their dash and initiative. Men who have been stuck in trenches for months get out of condition, and, at times, fail to seize opportunities to strengthen and consolidate their lines. Perhaps that was the reason for the deliberate progression of the Allied Army.

Each week a certain forward movement had to be done, even if this only amounted to a few yards. Saps were made underneath the enemy's barbed wire, explosions levelled these obstructions low, then with a rush our men would have a go to capture another of the German trenches. This work provided scope for all. Variety was frequently afforded in village fighting – the toughest job in war. The most interesting was a fight for a little house which commanded a short bridge and road over a Belgian canal. It was important to gain this point. Half a battalion of the Glesca Mileeshy, under Major Tartan, was ordered out to the job. The house itself was loopholed and sandbagged. There were two machine guns inside as well as fifty snipers. Outside there was a circular redoubt, manned by three hundred more. The whole place was thoroughly protected by barbed wire and other tricky lures.

'It will cost us a lot of men, Major,' said Colonel Corkleg; 'but the Brigadier says it must be done.'

'Yes, and we'll do it, sir,' replied Tartan, with a decision in his words which was inspiring.

'Very well, Tartan, I leave it to you – you know your job.'

Tartan's attack was preceded by a terrific bombardment by our artillery. But these shells did not dislodge the enemy. They stuck gamely to their job, and opened a fierce fusilade on the three skirmishing lines, which moved forward after the bombardment.

Captain Hardup had the first line. He took his men forward inch by inch. Trees, walls, holes, fence-posts, all sorts of cover were used by the men. Now and again a groan and curse was heard as men fell back wounded or dead.

'Come on, lads!' roared Lieutenant Longlegs, who was Hardup's subaltern. They gallantly replied and pushed forward to within one hundred yards of the barbed wire entanglements. Matters were serious here, and casualties heavy. Ten men were knocked out in twenty minutes.

'Sergeant Brown, have a go with your cutters.'

'Right, sir,' said the sturdy little fellow, crawling forward. He wriggled like a snake right up to the wires. Click! went his cutters through one strand, click! through and Longlegs now called them on. With a mighty rush they scaled the great redoubt and leapt down into the ranks of the Germans. Some of the Teutons fought gamely; others cowered back, listless and powerless, an awful fear and awe in their eyes. The sight chilled the men, but a bloodthirsty old sergeant shouted, 'Remember the Belgian atrocities, boys.' That was enough. They bayoneted every man on the spot. During this bloody combat the machine guns and snipers in the house were pumping out volleys of death.

'Take the house now, men,' roared Hardup.

'By God, we'll soon do that,' answered Muldoon, the worst character in the regiment. Running forward to the walls this powerful man got near the mouth of a Maxim gun projecting through the wall. With a terrible swipe he smashed the end of the tube, breaking his butt at the job. Another man did the same for the other gun, while the remainder of the men made for the doors. A check happened here. The doors were barred and the enemy firing furiously from within.

'Smash it in,' ordered Hardup, standing near. Three men sprang forward. First they smashed the protruding rifle barrels and then they tackled the doors. In ten minutes great holes were made. Captain Hardup was the first man through. Longlegs followed at his heels. The captain pinned a great big German with his bayonet, but another of the enemy stuck the gallant officer right through the chest. Longlegs had just got in when he saw his captain fall. Jumping forward he clubbed the man's brains out. The remaining Germans cleared up a stair to the next floor. This gave a breathing space and time to get more men through. When enough had been collected Longlegs led the way. Another barred door was found. Willing hands quickly ended this, and into a room Longlegs and his men dashed. The enemy stood at the end of the room with bayonets fixed.

'Come on, lads – wipe them out.' Forward they went. There was a terrific tussle for five minutes. Longlegs had the muscle of his arm torn away with a bayonet, while three of his men were killed on the spot; but every German was bayoneted to death. Longlegs had his arm hastily bandaged. 'Come on,' he shouted again, and up to the top flat they rushed to end their job. There they found a German officer and a host of men inside a loft. The door of the place was also barred. But this was easily smashed, and into the den the gallants rushed. As they went an old sergeant pushed Longlegs back out of danger.

'What's wrong?' he inquired angrily.

'I'm in charge o' this lot, sir. You're owre braw a fechter tae get kill't.'

'Nonsense, Sergeant.'

'Nae nonsense aboot it, sir. Staund there,' kindly insisted the old non-com., who saw that Longlegs would soon faint from loss of blood. Meantime the din inside the room was deafening. Squeals, groans, and curses rent the air. It was a battle to the death. The officer fought like a Trojan for his life, but, in the end, he was bayoneted to death. Half of the enemy were killed, the other half surrendered or jumped through the windows, smashing their legs on the hard stones below.

'We've won, sir,' reported the sergeant, rushing out of the shambles to where the pale-faced officer was standing at the top of the stair.

'Good!' said the subaltern, tumbling in a heap from loss of blood. At that moment a thundering cheer was heard outside the house. It was the colonel and the other half of the battalion, who had been sent up in support. The job, however, had been well done. Old Corkleg was met at the door by the faithful sergeant.

'We've done it, sir,' said he, saluting.

'Yes,' said the colonel gravely, as he looked at his dead and wounded men. Then looking up, he remarked, 'Where is Major Tartan?'

'Killed, sir.'

'And Captain Hardup?'

'Inside, sir, badly wounded.'

'What about Mr Longlegs?'

'He's lying upstairs wounded too.'

'Any other casualties?'

'Two other officers wounded, sir, and I think we've lost over a hundred men.'

'Sad – very sad, and some of the best,' said the old colonel, turning away to hide the moisture in his eyes.

'Well done, Corkleg,' said the Brigadier, walking up to the scene.

'Yes. Our men have done well, but our casualties have been awful.'

'Still, Corkleg, your men have captured the key to the whole German lines here. They will have to retire for almost a mile now. Good business! Good business! Terrible scamps, these men of yours, but heroes every time. Let me have any recommendations.'

Hardup and Longlegs got the DSO, the old sergeant and wire-cutting corporal received the Distinguished Conduct Medals, while every paper in Britain wrote columns about the gallantry of the Glesca Mileeshy.

'Useful men! Useful men!' said Corkleg, on reading the appreciation in *The Times* a few days later.

'Yes sir,' replied the adjutant.

(*from* Private Spud Tamson)

Lewis Grassic Gibbon
1901–1935

Lewis Grassic Gibbon was the pen-name which James Leslie Mitchell used for his fiction trilogy *A Scots Quair*. The background to the first novel *Sunset Song* is the First World War and the break-up of the already declining small farming communities in the Howe of the Mearns. The unifying figure in each novel is Chris Guthrie, a farmer's daughter, who is torn by the inherent conflicts of her character which pull her between love and hate of the land and lead her to an ambivalent attitude towards English and Scottish culture. In *Sunset Song* she marries the farmer Ewan Tavendale, thereby pledging herself to the land. After he enlists in the army he returns to Chris a changed man and the memory of his brutal behaviour towards her whilst on leave leads him to desert. Like most such offenders during the First World War he was sentenced to death by firing squad, but in the last conversation with his friend Chae Strachan his action is seen as a final heroic attempt to return to the old values of the land.

Source: Lewis Grassic Gibbon, *Sunset Song*, London: Jarrolds, 1932; Edinburgh: Canongate (Canongate Classics), 1988

Shot at Dawn

After joining the army Ewan Tavendale returns to Blawearie a changed man. During his leave he abuses his wife Chris and goes off to fight in France without solving the quarrel between them.

It had burned up as a fire in a whin–bush, that thing in her life, and it burned out again and was finished. She went about the Blawearie biggings next day singing under breath to herself, quiet and unvexed, tending to hens and kye, seeing to young Ewan's sleep in the day and the setting of old Brigson's supper ere he came at night. She felt shamed not at all, all the vexing fears had gone from her, she made no try to turn from the eyes in the glass that looked out at her, wakened and living again. She was glad she'd gone out with Long Rob, glad and content, they were one and the same now, Ewan and her.

So the telegram boy that came riding to Blawearie found her singing there in the close, mending young Ewan's clothes. She heard the click of the gate and he took the telegram out of his wallet and gave it to her and she stared at him and then at her hands. They were quivering like the leaves of the beech in the forecoming of rain, they quivered in a little mist below her eyes. Then she opened the envelope to read the words and she said there was no reply, the boy swung on his bicycle again and rode out, riding and leaning he clicked the gate behind him; and laughed back at her for the cleverness of that.

She stood up then, she put down her work on the hackstock and read again in the telegram, and began to speak to herself till that frightened her and she stopped. But she forgot to be frightened, in a minute she was speaking again, the chirawking hens in the close stopped and came near and turned up bright eyes to her loud and toneless whispering, *What do I do – oh, what do I do?*

She was vexed and startled by that – what was it she did! Did she go out to France and up to the front line, maybe, into a room where they'd show her Ewan lying dead, quiet and dead, white and bloodless, sweat on his hair, killed in action? She went out to the front door and waved to the harvesters, Brigson, young Ewan, and a tink they'd hired, they saw her and stared till she waved again and then John Brigson abandoned the half-loaded cart and came waddling up the park, so slow he was, *Did you cry me, Chris?*

Sweat on his hair as sweat on Ewan's. She stared at that and held out the telegram, he wiped slow hands and took it and read it, while she clung to the door-post and whispered and whispered *What is it I do now, John? Have I to go out to France?* And at last he looked up, his face was grizzled and hot and old, he wiped the sweat from it slow. *God, mistress, this is sore news, but he's died like a man out there, your Ewan's died fine.*

But she wouldn't listen to that, wanting to know the thing she must do; and not till he told her that she did nothing, they could never take all the widows to France and Ewan must already be buried, did she stop from that twisting of her hands and ceaseless whisper. Then anger came, *Why didn't you tell me before? Oh, damn you, you liked tormenting me!* and she turned from him into the house and ran up the stairs to the bed, the bed that was hers and Ewan's, and lay on it, and put her hands over her ears trying not to hear a cry of agony in a lost French field, not to think that the body that had lain by hers, frank and free and kind and young, was torn and dead and unmoving flesh, blood twisted upon it, not Ewan at all, riven and terrible, still and dead when the harvest stood out in Blawearie's land and the snipe were calling up on the loch and the beech trees whispered and rustled. And *SHE KNEW THAT IT WAS A LIE!*

He wasn't dead, he could never have died or been killed for nothing at all, far away from her over the sea, what matter to him their War and their fighting, their King and their country? Kinraddie was his land, Blawearie his, he was never dead for those things of no concern, he'd the crops to put in and the loch to drain and her to come back to. It had nothing to do with Ewan this telegram. They were only tormenting her, cowards and liars and bloody men, the English generals and their like down there in London. But she wouldn't bear it, she'd have the law on them, cowards and liars as she knew them to be!

It was only then that she knew she was moaning, dreadful to hear; and they heard it outside, John Brigson heard it and nearly went daft, he caught up young Ewan and ran with him into the kitchen and then to the foot of the stairs; and told him to go up to his mother, she wanted him. And young Ewan came, it was his hand tugging at her skirts that brought her out of that moaning coma, and he wasn't crying, fearsome the sounds though she made, his face was white and resolute, *Mother, mother!* She picked him up then and held him close, rocking in an agony of despair because of that look on his face, that lost look and the smouldering eyes he had. *Oh Ewan, your father's dead!* she told him the lie that the world believed. And she wept at last, blindly, freeingly, for a little, old Brigson was to say it was the boy that had saved her from going mad.

But throughout Kinraddie the news went underbreath that mad she'd gone, the death of her man had fair unhinged her. For still she swore it was a lie, that Ewan wasn't dead, he could never have died for nothing. Kirsty Strachan and Mistress Munro came up to see her, they shook their heads and said he'd died fine, for his country and his King he'd died, young Ewan would grow up to be proud of his father. They said that sitting at tea, with long faces on them, and then Chris laughed, they quivered away from her at that laugh.

Country and King? You're havering, havering! What have they to do with my Ewan, what was the King to him, what their damned country? Blawearie's his land, it's not his wight that others fight wars!

She went fair daft with rage then, seeing the pity in their faces. And also it was then, and then only, staring through an angry haze at them, that she knew at last she was living a dream in a world gone mad. Ewan was dead, they knew it and she knew it herself; and he'd died for nothing, for nothing, hurt and murdered and crying for her, maybe, killed for nothing: and those bitches sat and spoke of their King and country. . . .

They ran out of the house and down the brae, and, panting, she stood and screamed after them. It was fair the speak of Kinraddie next day the way she'd behaved, and nobody else came up to see her. But she'd finished with screaming, she went quiet and cold. Mornings came up, and she saw them come, she minded that morning she'd sent him away, and she might not cry him back. Noons with their sun and rain came over the Howe and she saw the cruelty and pain of life as crimson rainbows that spanned the horizons of the wheeling hours. Nights came soft and grey and quiet across Kinraddie's fields, they brought neither terror nor hope to her now. Behind the walls of a sanity cold and high, locked in from the lie of life, she would live, from the world that had murdered her man for nothing, for a madman's gibberish heard in the night behind the hills.

And then Chae Strachan came home at last on leave, he came home and came swift to Blawearie. She met him out by the kitchen door, a sergeant by then, grown thinner and taller, and he stopped and looked in her frozen face. Then, as her hand dropped down from his, he went past her with swinging kilts, into the kitchen, and sat him down and took off his bonnet. *Chris, I've come to tell you of Ewan.*

She stared at him, waking, a hope like a fluttering bird in her breast. *Ewan? Chae – Chae's, he's not living?* And then, as he shook his head, the frozen wall came down on her heart again. *Ewan's dead, don't vex yourself hoping else. They can't hurt him more, even this can't hurt him, though I swore I'd tell you nothing about it. But I know right well you should know it, Chris. Ewan was shot as a coward and deserter out there in France.*

. . . . .

Chae had lain in a camp near by and had heard of the thing by chance, he'd read Ewan's name in some list of papers that was posted up. And he'd gone the night before Ewan was shot, and they'd let him see Ewan, and he'd heard it all, the story he was telling her now – *better always to know what truth's in a thing, for lies come creeping home to roost on unco rees, Chris quean. You're young yet, you've hardly begun to live, and I swore to myself that I'd tell you it all, that you'd never be vexed with some twisted bit in the years to come. Ewan was shot as a deserter, it was fair enough, he'd deserted from the front line trenches.*

He had deserted in a blink of fine weather between the rains that splashed the glutted rat-runs of the front. He had done it quickly and easily, he told to Chae, he had just turned and walked back. And other soldiers that met him had thought him a messenger, or wounded, or maybe on leave, none had questioned him, he'd set out at ten o'clock in the morning and by afternoon, taking to the fields, was ten miles or more from the front. Then the military policemen came on him and took him, he was marched back and court-martialled and found to be guilty.

And Chae said to him, they sat together in the hut where he waited the coming of the morning, *But why did you do it, Ewan? You might well have known you'd never get free.* And Ewan looked at him and shook his head, *It was that wind that came with the sun, I minded Blawearie, I seemed to waken up smelling that smell. And I couldn't believe it was me that stood in the trench, it was just daft to be there. So I turned and got out of it.*

In a flash it had come on him, he had wakened up, he was daft and a fool to be there; and, like somebody minding things done in a coarse wild dream there had flashed on him memory of Chris at Blawearie and his last days there, mad and mad he had been, he had treated her as a devil might, he had tried to hurt her and maul her, trying in the nightmare to waken, to make her waken him up; and now in the blink of sun he saw her face as last he'd seen it while she quivered away from his taunts. He knew he had lost her, she'd never be his again, he'd known it in that moment he clambered back from the trenches; but he knew that he'd be a coward if he didn't try though all hope was past.

So out he had gone for that, remembering Chris, wanting to reach her, knowing as he tramped mile on mile that he never would. But he'd made her that promise that he'd never fail her, long syne he had made it that night when he'd held her so bonny and sweet and a quean in his arms, young and desirous and kind. So mile on mile on the laired French roads; she was lost to him, but that didn't help, he'd try to win to her side again, to see her again, to tell her nothing he'd said was his saying, it was the foulness dripping from the dream that devoured him. And young Ewan came into his thoughts, he'd so much to tell her of him, so much he'd to say and do if only he might win to Blawearie. . . .

Then the military policemen had taken him and he'd listened to them and others in the days that followed, listening and not listening at all, wearied and quiet. *Oh, wearied and wakened at last, Chae, and I haven't cared, they can take me out fine and shoot me to-morrow, I'll be glad for the rest of it, Chris lost to me through my own coarse daftness. She didn't even come to give me a kiss at goodbye, Chae, we never said goodbye; but I mind the bonny head of her down-bent there in the close. She'll never know, my dear quean, and that's best—they tell lies about folk they shoot and she'll think I just died like the rest; you're not to tell her.*

Then he'd been silent long, and Chae'd had nothing to say, he knew it was useless to make try for reprieve, he was only a sergeant and had no business even in the hut with the prisoner. And then Ewan said, sudden-like, it clean took Chae by surprise, *Mind the smell of dung in the parks on an April morning, Chae? And the peewits over the rigs? Bonny they're flying this night in Kinraddie, and Chris sleeping there, and all the Howe happed in mist.* Chae said that he mustn't mind about that, he was feared that the dawn was close, and Ewan should be thinking of other things now, had he seen a minister? And Ewan said that an old bit billy had come and blethered, an officer creature, but he'd paid no heed, it had nothing to do with him. Even as he spoke there rose a great clamour of guns far up in the front, it was four miles off, not more; and Chae thought of the hurried watches climbing to their posts and the blash and flare of the Verey lights, the machine-gun crackle from pits in the mud, things he himself mightn't hear for long: Ewan'd never hear it at all beyond this night.

And not feared at all he looked, Chae saw, he sat there in his kilt and shirt-sleeves, and he looked no more than a young lad still, his head between his hands, he didn't seem to be thinking at all of the morning so close. For he started to speak of Blawearie then and the parks that he would have drained, though he thought the land would go fair to hell without the woods to shelter it. And Chae said that he thought the same, there were sore changes waiting them when they went back; and then he minded that Ewan would never go back, and could near have bitten his tongue in half, but Ewan hadn't noticed, he'd been speaking of the horses he'd had, Clyde and old Bess, fine beasts, fine beasts – did Chae mind that night of lightning when they found Chris wandering in the fields with those two horses? That was the night he had known she liked him well – *nothing more than that, so quick and fierce she was, Chae man, she guarded herself like a queen in a palace, there was nothing between her and me till the night we married. Mind that – and the singing there was, Chae? What was it that Chris sang then?*

And neither could remember that, it had vexed Ewan a while, and then he forgot it, sitting quiet in that hut on the edge of morning. Then at last he'd stood up and gone to the window and said *There's bare a quarter of an hour now, Chae, you'll need to be getting back.*

And they'd shaken hands, the sentry opened the door for Chae, and he tried to say all he could for comfort, the foreshadowing of the morning in Ewan's young eyes was strange and terrible, he couldn't take out his hand from that grip. And all that Ewan said was *Oh man, mind me when next you hear the peewits over Blawearie – look at my lass for me when you see her again, close and close, for that kiss that I'll never give her.* So he'd turned back into the hut, he wasn't feared or crying, he went quiet and calm; and Chae went down through the hut lines grouped about that place, a farm-place it had been, he'd got to the lorry that waited him, he was cursing and weeping then and the driver thought him daft, he hadn't known himself how he'd been. So they'd driven off, the wet morning had come crawling across the laired fields, and Chae had never seen Ewan again, they killed him that morning.

(*from* Sunset Song)

Sir Ian Hamilton
1853–1947

Ian Standish Monteith Hamilton was born in Corfu and was brought up at Hafton in Argyll, the home of his grandparents. He was educated at Wellington College and Sandhurst and in 1872 he was commissioned into the 12th (East Suffolk) Foot. Later he transferred to the 92nd (Gordon Highlanders) Foot in order to serve in India. During the first Boer War he was badly injured at the Battle of Majuba Hill but was one of the few British officers to be specially mentioned in despatches for his conspicuous bravery. It marked the beginning of a rapid rise in his fortunes and by the beginning of the war in South Africa in 1899 he was a lieutenant-general. During the Boer War he served as Chief of Staff to Lord Kitchener and in 1904 he was the head of the British Military Mission to the Russo-Japanese War. The publication of his diaries under the title *A Staff Officer's Scrap Book* (1905–1907) confirmed Hamilton as a trenchant observer of warfare and military life. His supreme moment came in March 1915 when he was appointed to command the allied forces in the Dardanelles; the intention was to open a second front, to take Constantinople and to knock Turkey out of the war. Lack of secrecy, inadequate forces and untried field commanders led to a costly allied failure and Hamilton was replaced in some disgrace. (See also Compton Mackenzie, *Gallipoli Memories*, p 215.) Although charming and highly personable, Hamilton seems to have lacked the dominating personality and iron will demanded of the successful commander-in-chief. After his retirement he published his *Gallipoli Diaries*, a factual record of his experiences and a revealing self-portrait. The extract describes the first phase of the operation, the Anglo–French naval attack on the Turkish forts which guarded the straits; its failure led to the use of land forces in an attempt to capture the Gallipoli Peninsula. Hamilton retained his popularity long after the war and was much admired for the honesty of his attitudes towards his leadership during the conflict. In his 'Contemporary Scottish Studies' column in the *Scottish Educational Journal* of 25 August 1925 Hugh MacDiarmid wrote: 'The war may have been for the British War Office a

war to save civilisation – Sir Ian was one of the very few of
our military leaders who had that civilisation in a degree worth
saving.'

Source: General Sir Ian Hamilton: *Gallipoli Diaries*, vol. I, London: Edward
Arnold, 1920

The Straits

On 18 March 1915 Admiral de Robeck, the allied naval commander, ordered the first phase of the attack on the Dardanelles. No less than 18 battleships, surrounded by an armada of cruisers and destroyers, swept through into the waters of the Straits which led into the Black Sea. Although the force included capital ships like the super-dreadnought HMS Queen Elizabeth, the attack ended in disaster. The French battleship Bouvet was sunk first, followed by the British dreadnoughts Irresistible and Ocean. The Turkish forces suffered 8 guns hit and 40 men killed. Hamilton watched the operation from the cruiser HMS Phaeton.

1 *8th March 1915.* HMS *Phaeton.* Cleared Tenedos Harbour at 4a.m. and reached Lemnos at 6a.m. I never saw so many ships collected together in my life; no, not even at Hong Kong, Bombay or New York. Filled up with oil fuel and at 7 a.m. d'Amade and Major-General Paris, commanding the Royal Naval Division, came on board with one or two Staff officers. After consulting these officers as well as McLagan, the Australian Brigadier, cabled Lord K. to say Alexandria *must* be our base as 'the Naval Division transports have been loaded up as in peace time and they must be completely discharged and every ship reloaded,' in war fashion. At Lemnos, where there are neither wharfs, piers, labour nor water, the thing could not be done. Therefore, 'the closeness of Lemnos to the Dardanelles, as implying the rapid transport of troops, is illusory.'

The moment I got this done, namely, at 8.30 a.m., we worked our way out of the long narrow neck of Mudros Harbour and sailed for the Gulf of Saros. Spent the first half of the sixty mile run to the Dardanelles in scribbling. Wrote my first epistle to K., using for the first time the formal 'Dear Lord Kitchener.' My letters to him will have to be formal, and dull also, as he may hand them around. I begin, 'I have just sent you off a cable giving my first impressions of the situation, and am now steaming in company with Generals d'Amade and Paris to inspect the North-western coast of the Gallipoli Peninsula.' I tell him that the real place 'looks a much tougher nut to crack than it did over the map,' – I say that his 'impression that the ground between Cape Helles and Krithia was clear of the enemy,' was mistaken. 'Not a bit of it.' I say, 'The Admiral tells me that there is a large number of men tucked away in the folds of the ground there, not to speak of several field Batteries.' Therefore, I conclude, 'If it eventually becomes necessary to take the Gallipoli Peninsula by military force, we shall have to proceed bit by bit.' This will vex him no doubt. He likes plans to move as fast as his own wishes and is apt to forget, or to pretend he has forgotten, that swiftness in war comes from slow preparations. It is fairer to tell K. this now, when the question has not yet arisen, than hereafter if it does then arise.

Passing the mouth of the Dardanelles we got a wonderful view of the stage whereon the Great Showman has caused so many of his amusing puppets to strut their tiny hour. For the purpose it stands matchless. No other panorama can touch it. There, Hero trimmed her little lamp; yonder the amorous breath of Leander changed to soft sea form. Far away to the Eastwards, painted in dim and lovely hues, lies Mount Ida. Just so, on the far horizon line she lay fair and still, when Hector fell and smoke from burning Troy blackened the midday sun. Against this enchanted background to deeds done by immortals and mortals as they struggled for ten long years five thousand years ago, stands forth formidably the Peninsula. Glowing with bright, springtime colours it sweeps upwards from the sea like the glacis of a giant's fortress.

So we sailed on northwards, giving a wide berth to the shore. When we got within a mile of the head of the Gulf of Saros, we turned, steering a South-westerly course, parallel to, and one to two miles distant from, the coastline. Then my first fears as to the outworks of the fortress were strengthened. The head of the Gulf is filled in with a horrible marsh. No landing there. Did we land far away to the Westward we must still march round the marsh, or else we must cross it on one single road whose long and easily destructible bridges we could see spanning the bog holes some three miles inland. Opposite the fortified lines we stood in to within easy field gun range, trusting that the Turks would not wish prematurely to disclose their artillery positions. So we managed a peep at close quarters, and were startled to see the ramifications and extent of the spider's web of deep, narrow trenches along the coast and on either front of the lines of Bulair. My Staff agree that they must have taken ten thousand men a month's hard work from dark to dawn. In advance of the trenches, Williams in the crow's nest reported that with his strong glasses he could pick out the glitter of wire over a wide expanse of ground. To the depth of a mile the whole Aegean slope of the neck of the Peninsula was scarred with spade work and it is clear to a tiro that to take these trenches would take from us a bigger toll of ammunition and life than we can afford: especially so seeing that we can only see one half of the theatre; the other half would have to be worked out of sight and support of our own ships and in view of the Turkish Fleet. Only one small dent in the rockbound coast offered a chance of landing but that was also heavily dug in. In a word, if Bulair had been the only way open to me and I had no alternative but to take it or wash my hands of the whole business, I should have to go right about turn and cable my master he had sent me on a fool's errand.

Between Bulair and Suvla Bay the coastline was precipitous; high cliffs and no sort of creeks or beaches – impracticable. Suvla Bay itself seems a fine harbour but too far North were the aim to combine a landing there together with an attack on the Southern end of the Peninsula. Were we, on the other hand, to try to work the whole force ashore from Suvla Bay, the country is too big; it is the broadest part of the Peninsula; also, we should be too far from its waist and from the Narrows we wish to dominate. Merely to hold our line of Communications we should need a couple of Divisions. All the coast between Suvla Bay and for a little way South of Gaba Tepe seems feasible for landing. I mean we could get ashore on a calm day if there was no enemy. Gaba Tepe itself would be ideal, but, alas, the Turks are not blind; it is a mass of trenches and wire. Further, it must be well under fire of guns from Kilid Bahr plateau, and is entirely commanded by the high ridge to the North of it. To land there would be to enter a defile without first crowning the heights.

Between Gaba Tepe and Cape Helles, the point of the Peninsula, the coastline consists of cliffs from 100 to 300 feet high. But there are, in many places, sandy strips at their base. Opinions differ but I believe myself the cliffs are not unclimbable. I thoroughly believe also in going for at least one spot that *seems* impracticable.

Sailing Southwards we are becoming more and more

conscious of the tremendous bombardment going on in the Straits. Now and then, too, we can see a hugh shell hit the top of Achi Baba and turn it into the semblance of a volcano. Everyone excited and trying to look calm.

At 4p.m., precisely, we rounded Cape Helles. I had promised de Robeck not to take his fastest cruiser, fragile as an egg, into the actual Straits, but the Captain and the Commander (Cameron and Rosomore), were frightfully keen to see the fight, and I thought it fair to allow one mile as being the *mouth* of the Straits and not *the* Straits. Before we had covered that mile we found ourselves on the outskirts of – dream of my life – a naval battle! Nor did the reality pan out short of my hopes. Here it was; we had only to keep on at thirty knots; in one minute we should be in the thick of it; and who would be brave enough to cry halt!

The world has gone mad; common sense was only moonshine after all; the elephant and the whale of Bismarckian parable were at it tooth and nail! Shells of all sizes flew hissing through the skies. Before my very eyes, the graves of those old Gods whom Christ had risen from the dead to destroy were shaking to the shock of Messrs. Armstrong's patent thunder bolts!

Ever since the faraway days of Afghanistan and Majuba Hill friends have been fond of asking me what soldiers feel when death draws close up beside them. Before he charged in at Edgehill, Astley (if my memory serves me) exclaimed, 'O, God, I've been too busy fixing up this battle to think much about you, but, for Heaven's sake, don't you go and forget about me,' or words to that effect.

The Yankee's prayer for fair play just as he joined issue with the grizzly bear gives another glimpse of these secrets between man and his Maker. As for myself, there are two moments; one when I think I would not miss the show for millions; another when I think 'what an ass I am to be here': and between these two moments there *is* a border land when the mind runs all about Life's workshop and tries to do one last bit of stock-taking.

But the process can no more be fixed in the memory than the sequence of a dream when the dew is off the grass. All I remember is a sort of wonder: – why these incredible pains to seek out an amphibious battleground whereon two sets of people who have no cause of quarrel can blow one another to atoms? Why are these Straits the cockpit of the world? What is it all about? What on earth has happened to sanity when the whale and the elephant are locked in mortal combat making between them a picture which might be painted by one of HM's Commissioners in Lunacy to decorate an asylum for homicides.

Whizz – flop – bang – what an ass I am to be here. If we keep on another thirty seconds we are in for a visit to Davy Jones's Locker.

Now above the *Queen Elizabeth*, making slowly backwards and forwards up in the neck of the Narrows, were other men-o'-war spitting tons of hot metal at the Turks. The Forts made no reply – or none that we could make out, either with our ears or with glasses. Perhaps there was an attempt; if so, it must have been very half-hearted. The enemy's fixed defences were silenced but the concealed mobile guns from the Peninsula and from Asia were far too busy and were having it all their own way.

Close to us were steam trawlers and mine-sweepers steaming along with columns of spray spouting up close by them from falling field gun shells, with here and there a biggish fellow amongst them, probably a five or six inch field howitzer. One of them was in the act of catching a great mine as we drew up level with her. Some 250 yards from us was the *Inflexible* slowly coming out of the Straits, her wireless cut away and a number of shrapnel holes through her tops and crow's nest. Suddenly, so quickly did we turn that, going at speed, the decks were at an angle of 45 degrees and several of us (d'Amade for one) narrowly escaped slipping down the railless decks into the sea. The *Inflexible* had signalled us she had struck a mine, and that we must stand by and see her home to Tenedos. We spun round like a top (escaping thereby a salvo of four from a field battery) and followed as close as we dared.

My blood ran cold – for sheer deliberate awfulness this beat everything. We gazed spellbound: no one knew what moment the great ship might dive into the depths. The pumps were going hard. We fixed our eyes on marks about the water-line to see if the sea was gaining upon them or not. She was very much down by the bows, that was a sure thing. Crew and stokers were in a mass standing strictly at attention on the main deck. A whole bevy of destroyers crowded round the wounded warrior. In the sight of all those men standing still,

silent, orderly in their ranks, facing the imminence of death, I
got my answer to the hasty moralizings about war, drawn from
me (really) by a regret that I would very soon be drowned. On
the deck of that battleship staggering along at a stone's throw
was a vindication of war itself; of war, the state of being, quite
apart from war motives or gains. Ten thousand years of peace
would fail to produce a spectacle of so great virtue. Where, in
peace, passengers have also shown high constancy, it is because
war and martial discipline have lent them its standards. Once in a
generation a mysterious wish for war passes through the people.
Their instinct tells them that *there is no other way* of progress and
of escape from habits that no longer fit them. Whole generations
of statesmen will fumble over reforms for a lifetime which are
put into full-blooded execution within a week of a declaration of
war. There is *no other way*. Only by intense sufferings can the
nations grow, just as the snake once a year must with anguish
slough off the once beautiful coat which has now become a strait
jacket.

How was it going to end? How touching the devotion of all
these small satellites so anxiously forming escort? Onwards, at
snail's pace, moved our cortege which might at any moment
be transformed into a funeral affair, but slow as we went we
yet went fast enough to give the go-by to the French battleship
Gaulois, also creeping out towards Tenedos in a lamentable
manner attended by another crowd of TBs and destroyers eager
to stand to and save.

The *Inflexible* managed to crawl into Tenedos under her own
steam but we stood by until we saw the *Gaulois* ground on some
rocks called Rabbit Island, when I decided to clear right out so
as not to be in the way of the Navy at a time of so much stress.
After we had gone ten miles or so, the *Phaeton* intercepted a
wireless from the *Queen Elizabeth*, ordering the *Ocean* to take
the *Irresistible* in tow, from which it would appear that she (the
Irresistible) has also met with some misfortune.

Thank God we were in time! That is my dominant feeling.
We have seen a spectacle which would be purchased cheap by
five years of life and, more vital yet, I have caught a glimpse
of the forces of the enemy and of their Forts. What with my
hurried scamper down the Aegean coast of the Peninsula and
the battle in the Straits, I begin to form some first-hand notion
of my problem. More by good luck than good guidance I have

got into personal touch with the outer fringes of the thing we are up against and that is so much to the good. But oh, that we had been here earlier! Winston in his hurry to push me out has shown a more soldierly grip than those who said there was no hurry. It is up to me now to revolve today's doings in my mind; to digest them and to turn myself into the eyes and ears of the War Office whose own so far have certainly not proved themselves very acute. How much better would I be able to make them see and hear had I been out a week or two; did I know the outside of the Peninsula by heart; had I made friends with the Fleet! And why should I not have been?

Have added a PS to K.'s letter: –

'Between Tenedos and Lemnos. 6p.m. – This has been a very bad day for us judging by what has come under my own personal observation. After going right up to Bulair and down again to the South-west point looking at the network of trenches the Turks have dug commanding all possible landing places, we turned into the Dardanelles themselves and went up about a mile. The scene was what I believe Naval writers describe as "lively".' (Then follows an account based on my Diary jottings.) I end:

'I have not had time to reflect over these matters, nor can I yet realise on my present slight information the extent of these losses. Certainly it looks at present as if the Fleet would not be able to carry on at this rate, and, if so, the soldiers will have to do the trick.'

'*Later*.

'The *Irresistible*, the *Ocean* and the *Bouvet* are gone! The *Bouvet*, they say, just slithered down like a saucer slithers down in a bath. The *Inflexible* and the *Gaulois* are badly mauled.'

(*from* Gallipoli Diary)

Ian Hay
1876–1952

The pen-name of John Hay Beith who was a schoolmaster at
Fettes College in Edinburgh. After the publication of his first
novel, *Pip*, in 1907 he became a regular contributor to *Blackwood's
Magazine*; five years later he gave up teaching to become a full-time
writer, encouraged by the success of his light romantic novels.
An officer in the Territorial Army since 1908, he enlisted for
regular service at the outbreak of war and served with the Argyll
and Sutherland Highlanders. In January 1915 Neil Munro (see
p 94) reported to Blackwood a sighting of Ian Hay with his
battalion on Loch Lomondside, 'trudging in front of his platoon,
his shoulders covered by an old waterproof sheet which spouted
rain down his kilt and legs. He was carrying the rifle of a dejected
Tommy who limped behind him in the first section of fours.'
By then Hay had started contributing to *Blackwood's Magazine*
the scenes of life in Kitchener's volunteer army which were
published later that year as *The First Hundred Thousand*. For
this and its successor *Carrying On* (1917) he adopted a new
pseudonym 'The Junior Sub'. The extract '. . . And Some Fell
by the Wayside' appeared in the April 1915 issue of *Blackwood's
Magazine*.

Source: Ian Hay, *The First Hundred Thousand*, Edinburgh and London: 1915;
Glasgow: Richard Drew (The Scottish Collection), 1985

. . . And Some Fell By The Wayside

'Firing parrty, revairse arrms!'

Thus the platoon-sergeant – a little anxiously; for we are new to this feat, and only rehearsed it for a few minutes this morning.

It is a sunny afternoon in late February. The winter of our discontent is past. (At least, we hope so.) Comfortless months of training are safely behind us, and lo, we have grown from a fortuitous concourse of atoms to a cohesive unit of fighting men. Spring is coming; spring is coming; our blood runs quicker; active service is within measurable distance; and the future beckons to us with both hands to step down at last into the arena, and try our fortune amid the uncertain but illimitable chances of the greatest game in the world.

To all of us, that is, save one.

The road running up the hill from the little mortuary is lined on either side by members of our company, specklessly turned out and standing to attention. At the foot of the slope a gun-carriage is waiting, drawn by two great dray-horses and controlled by a private of the Army Service Corps, who looks incongruously perky and cockney amid that silent, kilted assemblage. The firing party form a short lane from the gun-carriage to the door of the mortuary. In response to the sergeant's command, each man turns over his rifle, and setting the muzzle carefully upon his right boot – after all, it argues no extra respect to the dead to get your barrel filled with mud – rests his hands upon the buttplate and bows his head, as laid down in the King's Regulations.

The bearers move slowly down the path from the mortuary, and place the coffin upon the gun-carriage. Upon the lid lie a very dingy glengarry, a stained leather belt, and a bayonet. They are humble trophies, but we pay them as much reverence as we would to the baton and cocked hat of a field-marshal, for they are the insignia of a man who has given his life for his country.

On the hill-top above us, where the great military hospital rears its clock-tower four-square to the sky, a line of convalescents, in natty blue uniforms with white facings and red ties, lean over the railings deeply interested. Some of them are bandaged, others are in slings, and all are more or less maimed. They follow the obsequies below with critical approval. They have been present at

enough hurried and promiscuous interments of late – more than
one of them has only just escaped being the central figure at one
of these functions – that they are capable of appreciating a properly
conducted funeral at its true value.

'They're puttin' away a bloomin' Jock,' remarks a gentleman
with an empty sleeve.

'And very nice, too,' responds another on crutches, as the firing
party present arms with creditable precision. 'Not 'arf a bad bit of
eye-wash at all for a bandy-legged lot of coal-shovellers.'

'That lot's out of K(i),' explains a well-informed invalid with his
head in bandages. 'Pretty 'ot stuff they're gettin'. *Très moutarde!*
Now we're off.'

The signal is passed up the road to the band, who are waiting
at the head of the procession, and the pipes break into a lament.
Corporals step forward and lay four wreaths upon the coffin –
one from each company. Not a man in the battalion has failed
to contribute his penny to those wreaths; and pennies are not
too common with us, especially on a Thursday, which comes
just before pay-day. The British private is commonly reputed to
spend all, or most of, his pocket-money upon beer. But I can tell
you this, that if you give him his choice between buying himself
a pint of beer and subscribing to a wreath, he will most decidedly
go thirsty.

The serio-comic charioteer gives his reins a twitch, the horses
wake up, and the gun-carriage begins to move slowly along the
lane of mourners. As the dead private passes on his way the walls
of the lane melt, and his comrades fall into their usual fours behind
the gun-carriage.

So we pass up the hill towards the military cemetery, with the
pipes wailing their hearts out, and the muffled drums marking the
time of our regulation slow step. Each foot seems to hang in the
air before the drums bid us put it down.

In the very rear of the procession you may see the company
commander and three subalterns. They give no orders, and exact
no attention. To employ a colloquialism, this is not their funeral.

Just behind the gun-carriage stalks a solitary figure in civilian
clothes – the unmistakable 'blacks' of an Elder of the Kirk. At
first sight, you have a feeling that someone has strayed into the
procession who has no right there. But no one has a better. The
sturdy old man behind the coffin is named Adam Carmichael, and
he is here, having travelled south from Dumbarton by the night
train, to attend the funeral of his only son.

Peter Carmichael was one of the first to enlist in the regiment. There was another Carmichael in the same company, so Peter at roll-call was usually addressed by the sergeant as 'Twenty-seeven fufty-fower Carmichael,' 2754 being his regimental number. The army does not encourage Christian names. When his attestation paper was filled up, he gave his age as nineteen; his address, vaguely, as Renfrewshire; and his trade, not without an air, as a 'holder-on'. To the mystified Bobby Little he entered upon a lengthy explanation of the term in a language composed almost entirely of vowels, from which that officer gathered, dimly, that holding-on had something to do with shipbuilding.

Upon the barrack-square his platoon-commander's attention was again drawn to Peter, owing to the passionate enthusiasm with which he performed the simplest evolutions, such as forming fours and sloping arms – military exercises which do not intrigue the average private to any great extent. Unfortunately, desire frequently outran performance. Peter was undersized, unmuscular, and extraordinarily clumsy. For a long time Bobby Little thought that Peter, like one or two of his comrades, was left-handed, so made allowances. Ultimately he discovered that his indulgence was misplaced: Peter was equally incompetent with either hand. He took longer in learning to fix bayonets or present arms than any other man in the platoon. To be fair, Nature had done little to help him. He was thirty-three inches round the chest, five feet four in height, and weighed possibly nine stone. His complexion was pasty, and, as Captain Wagstaffe remarked, you could hang your hat on any bone in his body. His eyesight was not all that the Regulations require, and on the musketry-range he was 'put back', to his deep distress, 'for further instruction'. Altogether, if you had not known the doctor who passed him, you would have said it was a mystery how he passed the doctor.

But he possessed the one essential attribute of the soldier. He had a big heart. He was keen. He allowed nothing to come between him and his beloved duties. ('He was aye daft for to go sogerin',' his father explained to Captain Blaikie, 'but his mother would never let him away. He was ower wee, and ower young.') His rifle, buttons, and boots were always without blemish. Further, he was of the opinion that a merry heart goes all the way. He never sulked when the platoon were kept on parade five minutes after the breakfast bugle had sounded. He made no bones about obeying orders and saluting officers – acts of abasement which grated sorely at times upon his colleagues, who reverenced no one except themselves and their Union. He appeared to revel in muddy route-marches, and invariably provoked and led the choruses. The men called him 'Wee Pe'er', and ultimately adopted him as a sort of company mascot. Whereat Pe'er's heart glowed; for when your associates attach a diminutive to your Christian name, you possess something which millionaires would gladly give half their fortune to purchase.

And certainly he required all the social success he could win, for professionally Peter found life a rigorous affair. Sometimes, as he staggered into barracks after a long day, carrying a rifle made of lead and wearing a pair of boots weighing a hundredweight apiece, he dropped dead asleep on his bedding before he could eat his dinner. But he always hotly denied the imputation that he was 'sick'.

Time passed. The regiment was shaking down. Seven of Peter's particular cronies were raised to the rank of lance-corporal – but not Peter. He was 'off the square' now – that is to say, he was done with recruit drill for ever. He possessed a sound knowledge of advance-guard and outpost work; his conduct-sheet was a blank page. But he was not promoted. He was 'ower wee for a stripe,' he told himself. For the present he must expect to be passed over. His chance would come later, when he had filled out a little and got rid of his cough.

The winter dragged on: the weather was appalling: the grousers gave tongue with no uncertain voice, each streaming field-day. But Wee Pe'er enjoyed it all. He did not care if it snowed ink. He was a 'sojer'.

One day, to his great delight, he was 'warned for guard' – a particularly unpopular branch of a soldier's duties, for it means sitting in the guardroom for twenty-four hours at a stretch, fully dressed and accoutred, with intervals of sentry-go, usually in heavy rain, by way of exercise. When Peter's turn for sentry-go came on he splashed up and down his muddy beat – the battalion was in billets now, and the usual sentry's veranda was lacking – as proud as a peacock, saluting officers according to their rank, challenging stray civilians with great severity, and turning out the guard on the slightest provocation. He was at his post, soaked right through his greatcoat, when the orderly officer made his night round.

Peter summoned his colleagues; the usual inspection of the guard took place; and the sleepy men were then dismissed to their fireside. Peter remained; the officer hesitated. He was supposed to examine the sentry in his knowledge of his duties. It was a profitless task as a rule. The tongue-tied youth merely gaped like a stranded fish, until the sergeant mercifully intervened, in some such words as these, 'This man, sirr, is liable to get over-excited when addressed by an officer.'

Then soothingly, 'Now, Jimmy, tell the officer what would ye dae in case of fire?'

'Present airrms!' announces the desperate James. Or else, almost tearfully, 'I canna mind. I had it all fine just noo, but it's awa' oot o' ma heid!'

Therefore it was with no great sense of anticipation that the orderly officer said to Private Carmichael, 'Now, sentry, can you repeat any of your duties?'

Peter saluted, took a full breath, closed both eyes, and replied rapidly, 'For tae tak' chairge of all Government property within sicht of this guairdhoose tae turrn oot the guaird for all arrmed pairties approaching also the commanding officer once a day tae salute all officers tae challenge all pairsons approaching this post tae . . .'

His recital was interrupted by a fit of coughing.

'Thank you,' said the officer hastily, 'that will do. Good night!'

Peter, not sure whether it would be correct to say 'good night' too, saluted again, and returned to his cough.

'I say,' said the officer, turning back, 'you have a shocking cold.'

'Och, never heed it, sirr,' gasped Peter politely.

'Call the sergeant,' said the officer.

The fat sergeant came out of the guardhouse again buttoning his tunic.

'Sirr?'

'Take this man off sentry-duty and roast him at the guardroom fire.'

'I will, sirr,' replied the sergeant; and added, paternally, 'This man has no right for to be here at all. He should have reported sick when warned for guard; but he would not. He is very attentive to his duties, sirr.'

'Good boy!' said the officer to Peter. 'I wish we had more like you.'

Wee Pe'er blushed, his teeth momentarily ceased chattering, his heart swelled. Appearances to the contrary, he felt warm all through. The sergeant laid a fatherly hand upon his shoulder.

'Go you your ways intil the guardroom, boy,' he commanded, 'and send oot Dunshie. He'll no hurt. Get close in ahint the stove, or you'll be for Cambridge!'

(The last phrase carries no academic significance. It simply means that you are likely to become an inmate of the great Cambridge Hospital at Aldershot.)

Peter, feeling thoroughly disgraced, cast an appealing look at the officer.

'In you go!' said that martinet.

Peter silently obeyed. It was the only time in his life that he ever felt mutinous.

A month later Brigade Training set in with customary severity. The life of company officers became a burden. They spent hours in thick woods with their followers, taking cover, ostensibly from the enemy, in reality from brigade-majors and staff officers. A subaltern never tied his platoon in a knot but a general came trotting round the corner. The wet weather had ceased, and a biting east wind reigned in its stead.

On one occasion an elaborate night operation was arranged. Four battalions were to assemble at a given point five miles from camp, and then advance in column across country by the light of the stars to a position indicated on the map, where they were to deploy and dig themselves in. It sounded simple enough in operation orders; but when you try to move four thousand troops – even well-trained troops – across three miles of broken country on a pitch-dark night, there is always a possibility that someone will get mislaid. On this particular occasion a whole battalion lost itself without any delay or difficulty whatsoever. The other three were compelled to wait for two hours and a half, stamping their feet and blowing on their fingers, while overheated staff officers scoured the country for the truants. They were discovered at last waiting virtuously at the wrong rendezvous, three-quarters of a mile away. The brazen-hatted strategist who drew up the operation orders had given the point of assembly for the brigade as:
. . . the field SW of WELLINGTON WOOD and due E of HANGMAN'S COPSE, immediately below the first O in GHOSTLY BOTTOM, but omitted to underline the O

indicated. The result was that three battalion commanders assembled at the O in 'ghostly' while the fourth, ignoring the adjective in favour of the noun, took up his station at the first O in 'bottom'.

The operations had been somewhat optimistically timed to end at 11p.m., but by the time that the four battalions had effected a most unloverly tryst, it was close on ten, and beginning to rain. The consequence was that the men got home to bed, soaked to the skin, and asking the Powers Above rhetorical questions, at three o'clock in the morning.

Next day Brigade Orders announced that the movement would be continued at nightfall, by the occupation of the hastily-dug trenches, followed by a night attack upon the hill in front. The captured position would then be re-trenched.

When the tidings went round, fourteen of the more quick-witted spirits of 'A' Company hurriedly paraded before the Medical Officer and announced that they were 'sick in the stomach'. Seven more discovered abrasions upon their feet, and proffered their sores for inspection, after the manner of oriental mendicants. One skrim-shanker, despairing of producing any bodily ailment, rather ingeniously assaulted a comrade-in-arms, and was led away, deeply grateful, to the guardroom. Wee Peter, who in the course of last night's operations had stumbled into an old trench half-filled with ice-cold water, and whose temperature today, had he known it, was a hundred and two, paraded with his company at the appointed time. The company, he reflected, would get a bad name if too many men reported sick at once.

Next day he was absent from parade. He was 'for Cambridge' at last.

Before he died, he sent for the officer who had befriended him, and supplemented, or rather corrected, some of the information contained in his attestation paper.

He lived in Dumbarton, not Renfrewshire. He was just sixteen. He was not – this confession cost him a great effort – a full-blown 'holder-on' at all; only an apprentice. His father was 'weel kent' in the town of Dumbarton, being a chief engineer, employed by a great firm of ship-builders to extend new machinery on trial trips.

Needless to say, he made a great fight. But though his heart was big enough, his body was too frail. As they say on the sea, he was over-engined for his beam.

And so, three days later, the simple soul of Twenty-seven fifty-four Carmichael, 'A' Company, was transferred, on promotion, to another company – the great Company of Happy Warriors who walk the Elysian Fields.

'Firing parrty, one round blank-load!'

There is a rattle of bolts, and a dozen barrels are pointed heavenwards. The company stands rigid, except the buglers, who are beginning to finger their instruments.

'Fire!'

There is a crackling volley, and the pipes break into a brief, sobbing wail. Wayfarers upon the road below look up curiously. One or two young females with perambulators come hurrying across the grass, exhorting apathetic babies to sit up and admire the pretty funeral.

Twice more the rifles ring out. The pipes cease their wailing, and there is an expectant silence.

The drum-major crooks his little finger, and eight bugles come to the 'ready'. Then 'Last Post', the requiem of every soldier of the King, swells out, sweet and true.

The echoes lose themselves among the dripping pines. The chaplain closes his book, takes off his spectacles, and departs.

Old Carmichael permits himself one brief look into his son's grave, resumes his crape-bound tall hat, and turns heavily away. He finds Captain Blaikie's hand waiting for him. He grips it, and says, 'Weel, the laddie has had a grand sojer's funeral. His mother will be pleased to hear that.'

He passes on, and shakes hands with the platoon sergeant and one or two of Peter's cronies. He declines an invitation to the Sergeants' Mess.

'I hae a trial-trup the morn,' he explains. 'I must be steppin'. God keep ye all, brave lads!'

The old gentleman sets off down the station road. The company falls in, and we march back to barracks, leaving Wee Pe'er – the first name on our Roll of Honour – alone in his glory beneath the Hampshire pines.

(from The First Hundred Thousand)

Harry Lauder
1870–1950

Harold MacLennan Lauder was born in Portobello, Edinburgh and his childhood years were spent in Arbroath and Hamilton. He started singing in public at miners' concerts in Lanarkshire and turned professional in 1894. The success of songs like 'I love a Lassie' and 'Roamin' in the Gloamin' helped to make him one of the most successful vaudeville artists of his day. At the outbreak of the war Lauder had just completed a world tour but he threw himself into a fresh round of concerts to boost recruiting and, in the United States, to promote the British war effort. His only son, John, a Territorial Army officer and Cambridge graduate, was killed on 28 December 1916 while serving with the 8th Argyll and Sutherland Highlanders between Courcellete and Poizieres. The news reached Lauder on New Year's Eve while he was in London starring in a popular revue called *Three Cheers* in which he performed his famous wartime song 'The Laddies Who Fought and Won'. Defying the shock of his personal tragedy Lauder returned to the stage a few days later, and in 1917 he crossed over to France to give a programme of concerts to troops on the Western Front. For his war work, Lauder was knighted in 1919.

Source: Harry Lauder, *A Minstrel in France*, London: Andrew Melrose, 1918

Death of a Son

Harry Lauder was one of the many thousand British parents who lost loved ones during the First World War. The announcement of casualties was made by War Office telegram, usually several days later.

It was on Monday morning, January the first, 1917, that I learned of my boy's death. And he had been killed the Thursday before! He had been dead four days before I knew it! And yet – I had known. Let no one ever again tell me that there is nothing in presentiment. Why else had I been so sad and uneasy in my mind? Why else, all through that Sunday, had it been so impossible for me to take comfort in what was said to cheer me? Some warning had come to me, some sense that all was not well.

Realization came to me slowly. I sat and stared at that slip of paper, that had come to me like the breath of doom. Dead! Dead these four days! I was never to see the light of his eyes again. I was never to hear that laugh of his. I had looked on my boy for the last time. Could it be true? Ah, I knew it was. And it was for this moment that I had been waiting, that we had all been waiting, ever since we had sent John away to fight for his country and do his part. I think we had all felt that it must come. We had all known that it was too much to hope that he should be one of those to be spared.

The black despair that had been hovering over me for hours closed down now and enveloped all my senses. Everything was unreal. For a time I was quite numb. But then, as I began to realize and to visualize what it was to mean in my life that my boy was dead, there came a great pain. The iron of realization slowly seared every word of that curt telegram upon my heart. I said it to myself, over and over again. And I whispered to myself, as my thoughts took form, over and over, the one terrible word: 'Dead!'

I felt that for me everything had come to an end with the reading of that dire message. It seemed to me that for me the board of life was black and blank. For me there was no past and there could be no future. Everything had been swept away, erased, by one sweep of the hand of a cruel fate. Oh, there was a past, though! And it was in that past that I began to delve. It was made up of every memory I had of my boy. I fell at once to remembering him. I clutched at every memory, as if I must grasp them and make sure of them; lest they be taken from me as well as the hope of seeing him again that the telegram had forever snatched away.

I would have been destitute indeed in that event. It was as if I must fix in my mind the way he had been wont to look, and recall to my ears every tone of his voice, every trick of his speech. There was something left of him that I must keep, I realized, even then, at all costs, if I was to be able to bear his loss at all.

There was a vision of him before my eyes. My bonnie Highland laddie, brave and strong, in his kilt and the uniform of his country, going out to his death with a smile on his face. And there was another vision that came up now, unbidden. It was a vision of him lying stark and cold upon the battlefield, the mud on his uniform. And when I saw that vision I was like a man gone mad and possessed of devils who had stolen away his faculties. I cursed war as I saw that vision, and the men who caused war. And when I thought of the Germans who had killed my boy, a terrible and savage hatred swept me, and I longed to go out there and kill with my bare hands, until I had avenged him or they had killed me too.

But then I was a little softened. I thought of his mother back in our wee hoose at Dunoon. And the thought of her, bereft even as I was, sorrowing, even as I was, and lost in her frightful loneliness, was pitiful, so that I had but the one desire and wish – to go to her, and join my tears with hers, that we who were left alone to bear our grief, might bear it together and give one to the other such comfort as there might be in life for us. And so I fell upon my knees and prayed, there in my lonely room in the hotel. I prayed to God that He might give us both, John's mother and myself, strength to bear the blow that had been dealt us, and to endure the sacrifice that He and our country had demanded of us.

My friends came to me. They came rushing to me. Never did man have better friends, and kindlier friends than mine proved themselves to me on that day of sorrow. They did all that good men and women could do. But there was no help for me in the ministration of friends. I was beyond the power of human words to comfort or solace. I was glad of their kindness, and the memory of it now is a precious one, which I would not be without. But at such a time I could not gain from them what they were eager to give me. I could only bow my head and pray for strength.

That night, that New Year's night that I shall never forget, no matter how long God may let me live, I went north. I took a train from London to Glasgow, and the next day I came to our wee hoose – a sad, lonely wee hoosé it had become now! – on the Clyde at Dunoon, and was with John's mother. It was the place for me. It was there that I wanted to be, and it was with her, who must hereafter be all the world to me. And I was eager to be with her, too, who had given John to me. Sore as my grief was, stricken as I was, I could comfort her as no one else could hope to do, and she could do as much for me. We belonged together.

I can scarce remember, even for myself, what happened there at Dunoon. I cannot tell you what I said or what I did, or what words and what thoughts passed between John's mother and myself. But there are some things that I do know and that I will tell you.

Almighty God, to whom we prayed, was kind, and He was pitiful and merciful. For presently He brought us both a sort of sad composure. Presently He assuaged our grief a little, and gave us the strength that we must have to meet the needs of life and the thought of going on in a world that was darkened by the loss of the boy in whom all our thoughts and all our hopes had been centred. I thanked God then, and I thank God now, that I have never denied Him nor taken His name in vain.

For God gave me great thoughts about my boy and about death. Slowly, gradually, He made me to see things in their true light, and He took away the sharp agony of my first grief and sorrow, and gave me a sort of peace.

John died in the most glorious cause, and he died the most glorious death it may be given to a man to die. He died for humanity. He died for liberty, and that this world in which life must go on, no matter how many die, may be a better world to live in. He died in a struggle against the blackest force and the direst threat that has appeared against liberty and humanity within the memory of man. And were he alive now, and were he called again today to go out for the same cause, knowing that he must meet death – as he did meet it – he would go as smilingly and as willingly as he went then. He would go as a British soldier and a British gentleman, to fight and die for his King and his country. And I would bid him go.

After visiting the Western Front in 1917 Harry Lauder reflected on the indomitable spirit of the Scottish soldier.

The Scottish Soldier

Let me tell you how Scotland takes this war. Let me show you the home-coming of a Scottish soldier, back from the trenches on leave. Why, he is received with no more ceremony than if he were coming home from his day's work!

Donald – or Jock might be his name, or Andy! – steps from the train at his old hame town. He is fresh from the mud of the Flanders trenches, and all his possessions and his kit are on his back, so that he is more like a beast of burden than the natty creature old tradition taught us to think a soldier must always be. On his boots there are still dried blobs of mud from some hole in France that is like a crater in hell. His uniform will be pretty sure to be dirty, too, and torn; and perhaps, if you looked closely at it, you would see stains upon it that you might not be far wrong in guessing to be blood.

Leave long enough to let him come home to Scotland – a long road it is from France to Scotland these days – has been a rare thing for Jock. He will have been campaigning a long time to earn it; months certainly, and maybe even years. Perhaps he was one of those who went out first. He may have been mentioned in dispatches; there may be a distinguished conduct medal hidden about him somewhere; worth all the iron crosses the Kaiser ever gave! He has seen many a bloody field, be sure of that. He has heard the sounding of the gas alarm, and maybe got a whiff of the dirty poison gas Huns turned loose against our boys. He has looked Death in the face so often that he has grown used to him. But now he is back in Scotland, safe and sound, free from battle and the work of the trenches for a space, home to gain new strength for his next bout with Fritz across the water.

When he gets off the train Jock looks about him, from force of habit. But no one has come to the station to meet him, and he looks as if that gave him neither surprise nor concern. For a minute, perhaps, he will look around him, wondering, I think, that things are so much as they were; fixing in his mind the old familiar scenes that have brought him cheer so often in black, deadly nights in the trenches or in lonely billets out there in France. And then, quietly, and as if he were indeed just home from some short trip, he shifts his pack, so that it lies comfortably across his back, and trudges off. There would be cabs around the station, but it would not come into Jock's mind to hail one of the drivers. He has been used to using Shanks's Mare in France when he wanted to go anywhere, and so now he sets off quietly with his long, swinging soldier's stride.

As he walks along he is among scenes familiar to him since his boyhood. Yon house, yon barn, yon wooded rise against the sky, are landmarks for him. And he is pretty sure to meet old friends. They nod to him, pleasantly, and with a smile, but there is no excitement, no strangeness, in their greeting. For all the emotion they show, these folk to whom he has come back, as from the grave, they might have seen him yesterday, and the day before that, and the war never have been at all. And Jock thinks nothing of it that they are not more excited about him. You and I may be thinking of Jock as a hero, but that is not his idea about himself. He is just a Tommy, home on leave from France, one of a hundred thousand, maybe. And if he thought at all about the way his home folk greeted him it would be just that he could not expect them to be making a fuss about one soldier out of so many. And, since he, Jock, is not much excited, not much worked up, because he is seeing these good folk again, he does not think it strange that they are not more excited about the sight of him. It would be if they did make a fuss over him, and welcome him loudly, that he would think it strange!

And at last he comes to his own old home. He will stop and look around a bit. Maybe he has seen that old house a thousand times out there, tried to remember every line and corner of it. And maybe, as he looks down the quiet village street, he is thinking of how different France is. And, deep down in his heart, Jock is glad that everything is as it was, and that nothing has been changed. He could not tell you why; he could not put his feeling into words. But it is there, deep down, and the truer and the keener because it is so deep. Ah, Jock may take it quietly, and there may be no way for him to show his heart, but he is glad to be home.

And at his gate will come, as a rule, Jock's first real greeting. A dog, grown old since his departure, will come rushing out, barking, wagging his tail, and licking the soldier's hand. And Jock will lean down, and give his old dog a pat. If the dog had not come he would have been surprised and disappointed. And so, glad with every fibre of his being, Jock goes in, and finds father and mother and sisters within. They look up at his coming, and their happiness shines for a moment in their eyes. But they are not the sort of people to show their emotions or make a fuss. Mother and girls will rise and kiss him, and begin to take his gear, and his father will shake him by the hand.

'Well,' the father will ask, 'how are you getting along, lad?'

And – 'All right,' he will answer. That is the British soldier's answer to that question, always and everywhere.

Then he sits down, happy and at rest, and lights his pipe, maybe, and looks about the old room which holds so many memories for him. And supper will be ready, you may be sure. They will not have much to say, these folk of Jock's; but if you look at his face as dish after dish is set before him, you will understand that this is a feast that has been prepared for him. They may have been going without all sorts of good things themselves, but they have contrived, in some fashion, to have them all for Jock. All Scotland has tightened its belt, and done its part, in that fashion, as in every other, toward the winning of the war. But for the soldiers the best is none too good. And Jock's folk would rather make him welcome so, by proof that takes no words, than by demonstrations of delight and of affection.

As he eats, they gather round him at the board, and they tell him all the gossip of the neighbourhood. He does not talk about the war, and, if they are curious – probably they are not! – they do not ask him questions. They think that he wants to forget about the war and the trenches and the mud, and they are right. And so, after he has eaten his fill, he lights his pipe again, and sits about. And maybe, as it grows dark, he takes a bit walk into town. He walks slowly, as if he is glad that for once he need not be in a hurry, and he stops to look into shop windows as if he had never seen their stocks before, though you may be sure that, in a Scottish village, he has seen everything they have to offer, hundreds of times.

He will meet friends, maybe, and they will stop and nod to him. And perhaps one of six will stop longer.

'How are you getting on, Jock?' will be the question.

'All right!' Jock will say. And he will think the question rather fatuous, maybe. If he were not all right, how should he be there? But if Jock had lost both legs, or an arm, or if he had been blinded, that would still be his answer. Those words have become a sort of slogan for the British Army, a phrase that typifies its spirit.

Jock's walk is soon over, and he goes home by an old path that is known to him, every foot of it, and goes to bed in his own old bed. He has not broken into the routine of the household, and he sees no reason why he should. And the next day it is much the same for him. He gets up as early as he ever did, and he is likely to do a few odd bits of work that his father has not had time to come to. He talks with his mother and the girls of all sorts of little, commonplace things, and with his father he discusses the affairs of the community. And in the evening he strolls down town again, and exchanges a few words with friends, and learns, perhaps, of boys who haven't been lucky enough to get home on leave; of boys with whom he grew up, who have gone west.

So it goes on for several days, each day the same. Jock is quietly happy. It is no task to entertain him; he does not want to be entertained. The peace and quiet of home are enough for him; they are change enough from the turmoil of the front and the ceaseless grind of the life in the army in France.

And then Jock's leave nears its end, and it is time for him to go back. He tells them, and he makes his few small preparations. They will have cleaned his kit for him, and mended some of his things that needed mending. And when it is time for him to go they help him on with his pack and he kisses his mother and the girls goodbye, and shakes hands with his father.

'Well, goodbye,' Jock says. He might be going to work in a factory a few miles off. 'I'll be all right. Goodbye, now. Don't you cry, now, mother, and you, Jeannie and Maggie. Don't you fash yourselves about me. I'll be back again. And if I shouldn't come back – why, I'll be all right.'

So he goes, and they stand looking after him, and his old dog wonders why he is going, and where, and makes a move to follow him, maybe. But he marches off down the street, alone, never looking back, and is waiting when the train comes. It will be full of other Jocks and Andrews, and Tams, on their way back to France, like him, and he will nod to some he knows as he settles down in the carriage.

And in just two days Jock will have travelled the length of England, and crossed the Channel, and ridden up to the front. He will have reported himself, and have been ordered, with his company, into the trenches. And on the third night, had you followed him, you might see him peering over the parapet at the lines of the Hun, across No Man's Land, and listening to the whine of bullets and the shriek of shells over his head, with a star shell, maybe, to throw a green light upon him for a moment.

So it is that a warrior comes and that a warrior goes, in a land where war is war; in a land where war has become the business of all, every day, and has settled down into a matter of routine.

(*from* A Minstrel in France)

Eric Linklater
1899–1974

Eric Linklater was born in Penarth, South Wales, the son of a shipmaster, but his family had their roots in Orkney where he spent most of his childhood and much of his later life. He was educated at Aberdeen Grammmar School and Aberdeen University where he set out to study medicine before war interrupted his studies. In 1917 he enlisted in the Fife and Forfar Yeomanry but transferred to the 4th/5th Black Watch in order to serve in France. The battalion was stationed in the Arras sector and played a role in stemming the German offensive in March 1918 (see also John Buchan, *Mr Standfast*, pp 145). During the counter-offensive south of the River Aisne, Linklater was shot in the head and badly wounded on 11 April 1918. The steel helmet which saved his life became a prized possession and in later life the furrow in his skull left by the bullet was one of his distinguishing features. After the war Linklater returned to Aberdeen, this time to study English, but he did not write about his wartime experiences until the publication of his first volume of autobiography *The Man on My Back*. He made some use of his military memories in *Magnus Merriman* whose eponymous hero is endowed with adventures which clearly resemble those of his creator.

Sources: Eric Linklater, *The Man on My Back*, London: Macmillan, 1941; Eric Linklater, *Magnus Merriman*, London: Cape, 1934, Edinburgh: Macdonald, 1982

The Sniper Sniped

A ccording to the official history of the Black Watch, the remnant strength of the battalion, when the retreat was over, was one officer and thirty men. But we had two or three more than that, I fancy, and one of them a piper. The next day, marching peacefully in the morning light of France along a pleasant road, we encountered the tattered fragment of a battalion of Foot Guards, and the piper, puffing breath into his bag and playing so that he filled the air like the massed bands of the Highland Division, saluted the tall Coldstreamers, who had a drum or two and some instruments of brass that made also a gallant music. Stiffly we passed each other, swollen of chest, heads tautly to the right, kilts swinging to answer the swagger of the Guards, and the Red Hackle in our bonnets like the monstrance of a bruised but resilient faith. We were bearded and stained with mud – the Guards, the fifty men that were left of a battalion, were button-bright and cleanly shaven – we were a tatterdemalion crew from the coal-mines of Fife and the back streets of Dundee, but we trod quick-stepping to the brawling tune of *Hielan' Laddie*, and suddenly I was crying with a fool's delight and the sheer gladness of being in such company.

They were brave comrades, but they could not speak French. A day or so later we were in a poor little village, and for some reason more hungry than usual. But the villagers were as hungry as ourselves, and though there was a baker's shop in the muddy street, the baker would give us no bread. His people, he said, were rationed like soldiers – the French were a nation of soldiers – and therefore not a loaf could be spared. Absolutely and definitely, he refused to sell. But he had a daughter, a plump girl with fair hair, with pale fat cheeks and little dark brown eyes that looked quickly from one to another of the kilted troops, and saw in them some recondite cause for often giggling.

'Here, you!' exclaimed a lean and hardy private. I turned obediently. 'If you can parly-voo the old man, you can parly-voo the lassie. Away and ask her for a promenade the night, and gie her a bit cuddle, and see what you can do. You'll maybe get twa-three loaves out of her the morn's morn.'

'But I'm on guard tonight,' I said.

'I'll tak your guard. Away you and clean your buttons, and see if you ken the French for square-pushing.'

So in laborious and schoolboy terms I made love to the baker's daughter, and an hour before dawn I was at the bakehouse door, and she came hurriedly, and without another word put half a dozen crisp long loaves into my arms.

I prided myself on a conquest, but so apparently did she, and spread the news of it. For in the afternoon I was walking down the street, and passing two thin and dirty little boys, I heard one say to the other in solemn tones, '*Voilà l'Écossais qui parle français!*'

It was a very gratifying moment.

We continued marching westward and came to Arques, where we were billeted in what seemed to be a deserted factory. I threw my kit into a corner – the farthest corner from the door – and went out for a stroll; but when I came back my belongings were in the middle of the floor, and in my chosen corner was a black-avised and surly man with a short pipe in his mouth and an air of possession.

'That was my place,' I said.

'Weel, it's mine noo,' he answered grimly.

Everybody, with happy anticipation, was watching us; and sadly I realised that I must challenge him to fight. I was clearing my throat – for the words were curiously slow in coming – when a sergeant shouted through the open door, 'Stand to! Get your kits packed, and on parade. Full marching order.'

'What's the matter now?' they asked him.

'We're going up the bloody line again: that's all!'

It was true, and I was thankful to hear it; for the order came just in time to save me from a thrashing.

For the next two or three weeks the war was in a state of singular confusion. We were in the neighbourhood of Ypres again – at Zillebeke and Voormezeele – and wherever we went we were digging trenches and fighting off an enemy who generally appeared from some entirely unexpected quarter. It was the season for low-lying fog, and on one occasion we refrained, in the nick of time, from opening fire on a battalion of Cameron Highlanders who, in the most mysterious fashion, came charging towards us out of what we thought was the German line. We were now a composite battalion, made from Cambridgeshires, Cheshires, KRRs, Black Watch, certain Welshmen, and other remnants of the 39th Division; and when, about this time, Haig issued the celebrated order in which he said we were fighting with our backs to the wall, there was laughter from one end of the country to the other; for we had no such illusion of support, and were more likely to be fighting with our backs to the enemy, since the Germans often appeared on both sides of us.

Nothing occurred of any military importance – though a good many lives were lost – but to myself there happened something of a startling interest. I nearly became a good soldier. It began with a gumboil and outrageous toothache that swelled my cheek to the likeness of a dumpling, and put me into the vilest temper. When the gumboil subsided, I discovered to my amazement that I had acquired not only confidence, but a new capacity of enjoyment. Rations were plentiful: I ate with good appetite, and swigged my rum with enormous pleasure. I was still afraid, especially of being taken prisoner, and of heavy trench-mortars that shook the earth with the close violence of their explosion; but my fear was under control, and far less tiresome than toothache.

It is true that I never learnt to handle pick and spade very cleverly, and as many of my fellow privates had been miners, my ineptitude was the more apparent by contrast. Once, while we were digging a new line, the Commanding Officer came to inspect our work and stood for a long time behind me. Compared with the deep excavation of my comrades, I had made, I confess, but a shallow hole; and his voice, when at last he spoke, was recognisably unfriendly.

His first question was insulting. 'What are you doing?' he asked.

I turned and stood rigidly at attention: 'Digging a trench, sir.'

'My wife,' he said, 'has a small dog, a Pekinese, that goes out every morning to do its business in the garden. And that little Pekinese dog makes a bigger hole than you do.'

Glumly, amid sycophantic laughter, I waited for the inevitable conclusion. It came. He turned to the NCO beside him and said coldly, 'Take his name, sergeant.'

But I found compensation when, in a rather casual way, I became a sniper. Because of the composite nature of the battalion, organisation was a little sketchy, and appointments were made in a somewhat perfunctory fashion. At stand-to one morning the company sergeant-major enquired for marksmen, and though others kept a prudent silence, I stood proudly forward, exclaiming, 'Here, sir!'

'All right,' he said, 'you're a sniper. There's a hole about twenty yards in front of that sap that'll give you a good field of fire. You'd better get into it before the mist rises.'

And then I earned my pay, and in a taut unresting way enjoyed myself. I had found a rifle that was unusually well balanced, and I got the nose of the sear so filed that little more than blood-pressure on the trigger would fire it. It was a good rifle. Twice we were attacked, and the attacks were beaten off; and there were German working-parties within easy range. I earned my rations, and for a few days lived at the full pitch of strenuous excitement.

But my little while of active service was nearly over. Early one morning we were driven out of the ruined village of Voormezeele and, in a most unwilling counter-attack, recaptured it an hour or so later. Pressing hard, and vastly outnumbering us, the Germans came back. They turned our flank, and my platoon was left in an unfinished trench that thrust like a tongue into their midst. I was at the extreme end of it, because from there ran a sap I had used for sniping. They were very close. One could see the agitation of their features, and the shape of their helmets appeared more sinister than ever. I had used all my ammunition – I had been shooting badly – and in any case my rifle was too hot to hold. But I had a box of bombs, already detonated, and I threw one that fell short. I was swinging for the second when I hear a wild shout behind me, and looking round saw the trench was empty save for one man, who had come back to warn me that we were retreating. He was an old regular soldier, and had also been a nurse in a lunatic asylum. He was a big good-looking man, but his cheeks had strangely fallen in. He must have lost his false teeth, I thought.

I threw my second bomb, more usefully than the first, and turned to run. I ran so very fast that, although I was the last by a long way to leave the trench, within two hundred yards I had passed several of those who preceded me; including an officer who was looking back with an expression of reluctance that, in the circumstances, appeared strangely ill-timed.

I continued to run till in a mingling of righteous indignation and utter dismay I felt on my head a blow of indescribable force. It was a bullet, and probably a machine-gun bullet; for the rifle-fire of the German infantry was poor.

When I recovered consciousness the surrounding landscape appeared entirely empty. But I could not see very well, and perhaps I was mistaken. A few shots, that were evidently hostile, gave me a rough direction, and with clumsy fingers I took from a pocket in the lining of my tunic a little package of field-dressings. I could not undo it, but stuck it whole on the back of my head, where I judged the wound to be, and kept it in position with my steel helmet, that a chin-strap held tightly on.

Scarcely had I made these arrangements when, my sight growing more foggy, I fell into a water-logged trench. It was deep, and full to the brim, and the sides were so well revetted that I had great difficulty in getting out. I was nearly drowned, indeed, and lost my good rifle there. But the cold water revived me, and now my only feeling of discomfort was extreme weariness. So I threw off my equipment and my tunic, and found progress a little easier. Presently, after walking, as I thought, for many miles, someone came to help me, and I saw a cluster of men in kilt and kilt-apron, who looked familiar. I waved my hand to them. It was the very last, the ultimate remnant of the battalion, and already they were forming for the counter-attack. In the afternoon they recaptured Voormezeele.

My wound was dressed and I was given a coat. I lay for some time among dying men, and grew so displeased with such company that I got up and, joining a party of walking wounded, found something to eat. I was ravenously hungry. Then we were put into an ambulance, and the jolting of that was an agony that drove one nearly mad. The ambulance stopped, and we had to get out and walk to a train. Watching us were thirty or forty men of the Chinese Labour Corps. Moon-faced, thickly wadded coolies like those I had been warder among in the long hut at Calais. The same men, perhaps.

They began to laugh at us. We were a ludicrous company, tottering and misshapen, roughly bandaged; but only the dreadful sanity of China could have seen the joke, I think.

Thin of voice, the coolies tittered with laughter; then as their mirth grew, doubled-down and held their sides, or clapped each other on the back. Peal upon peal their laughter rang, and they pointed to the saviours of the western world.

(*from* The Man on My Back)

Magnus Merriman's War

The early life of Magnus Merriman was uneventful except for the usual essays and accidents of boyhood which, though they might be magnified into special significance by anyone with a case to prove, were truly of no great interest. The only remarkable feature of his youthful development was a curious change of temper that occurred when he was twelve or thirteen years old. Till then he had been unduly sensitive, sulky, and unhappy. A disorderly imagination had made him cowardly, while a mixture of laziness and false shame induced a constipated habit that naturally affected his temper. But suddenly, as though he had been waiting for his voice to break before he declared his authority, he became a leader of the neighbouring children, and displaying a talent for noise and vulgarity that none had previously suspected, turned the tables on time by bullying the small brothers of the boys who had previously tortured him. At the same time his brain quickened, and he showed abundant cleverness of that youthful kind which so often is regarded as the prelude to a brilliant maturity. But the abruptness with which the costive timidity of his childhood had been overlaid with the truculent inspiration of adolescence gave little promise of stability.

The son of a country schoolmaster in the parish of St. Magnus, in the Mainland of Orkney, Magnus was born in 1897. Having acquired from his father and a female assistant teacher in his father's school the useful and customary elements of education, he was sent to the city of Inverdoon, the seat of the most northerly university in Britain and of a school some six hundred years old that was well thought of locally, but whose tradition of classical education had been much impaired by modern commercialism and the resulting importance attached to certain statutory examinations. From his teachers at the Inverdoon Academy, solid unimaginative men, Magnus obtained a moderate amount of information, often accompanied by thrashing with a leather strap, but neither incentive to further scholarship nor stimulus to the creative spirit that was dormant in him.

In 1914, shortly after the outbreak of war, he returned to Inverdoon from his summer vacation in Orkney with the intention of proceeding to the University, but instead of that enlisted in a Territorial Battalion of the Gordon Highlanders and spent the next few months in training at Bedford. He found discipline irksome, and was at first extremely clumsy in performing the simple exercises demanded of a private soldier. At the handling of arms and on the range he became tolerably expert in time, but fatigue duties he constantly endeavoured to escape without the ingenuity necessary to their successful evasion, and such matters as maintaining his equipment in military tidiness, and producing in due form and order the requisite number of articles at the weekly kit-inspection, were for ever beyond his power. In consequence of this he endured a multitude of minor punishments and acquired the habit, on pay-nights, of forgetting the unhappiness of his existence in the canteen. At the age of seventeen a few glasses of beer were sufficient to fortify his spirit with remarkable gaiety, and he discovered under their influence an extravagant improper humour that was greatly to the liking of his companions, who encouraged him to drink more and more when they found that he was able to compose, with sufficient stimulation, witty and slanderous verses about the officers and sergeants of their battalion. These canteen lampoons were Merriman's first experiment in literature.

He went to France with the reputation of a troublesome and unprofitable soldier, but when the formality of army life grew thin, as it did in the trenches, and when dirtiness became a uniform condition rather than a crime, he found fewer difficulties to contend with and was increasingly well-thought-of by his superiors. He was strongly built, but slender, and though above the middle size he was not so tall as to find his height a handicap in troglodyte warfare. He was never notable for bravery, but on occasion showed something like recklessness, that was due either to excitement or to inadequate apprehension of the circumstances: for he became interested in the war, or such a minute portion of it as he was acquainted with, and was inclined to form heterodox opinions about its conduct. He was promoted to the rank of corporal and began to think hungrily of decorations. He decided to win a Distinguished Conduct Medal and some French award before applying for a commission, so that his uniform might be well prepared for the additional glories, in time, of a Military Cross and the Distinguished Service Order. And while his thoughts grew more and more romantic his conduct became increasingly efficient, so that Captain Duguid, his company commander, once said somewhat optimistically, 'Merriman is the best NCO in the battalion.'

Unfortunately an incident occurred soon after this that entirely changed Captain Duguid's opinion and completely destroyed Merriman's ambition, at least for some considerable time. It was an incident of a type that he was to become familiar with later in his life, for in his fortune there seemed, ever and again, to be an element of buffoonery that would trip his heels whenever his head was highest, and lay clownish traps for him in the most serious places. He adventured for a medal and had his stripes cut away; whenever he played Romeo he tripped over the chamber pot; and his political hopes were to be spoiled by a ludicrous combination of circumstances. But in 1916 those catastrophes lay far away in the future, unimagined, almost unimaginable, for the horizon was still occluded by war.

One morning Corporal Merriman was informed that he was to accompany Captain Duguid with four men on a reconnoitring patrol that night. The news at first inspired in him the customary feeling of gloomy foreboding, but in a short while he was cheered by the thought that this might be an opportunity to secure the Distinguished Conduct Medal, for the patrol was to be an important one, and when midnight came, the hour at which they were to start, he was in high spirits. They crowded out of the trench, Captain Duguid slightly in advance, and passed through an opening in the barbed wire to no-man's-land. Slowly and with great circumspection they approached the German line. When a Very light soared over them they lay immobile till the light should die. But Merriman made the mistake of lying on his side and keeping his eyes on the flaring brightness, so that when it sank into the darkness he was momentarily blind. The Captain whispered 'Come on!' Merriman, lurching forward on his belly,

thrust his bayonet stiffly ahead of him and heard a muffled cry
of pain.

'What's the matter?' he asked.

Another muted whimper answered him first, and a moment
later one of the patrol, in the broad untroubled accents of
Buchan, said hoarsely, 'Michty God, you've fair ruined the
Captain. You've stuck your bayonet clean up his airse!'

Corporal Merriman's response was to roll on his back and
let fly a great ringing shout of laughter. The Captain cried
petulantly, 'Be quiet, you fool!' The nearest private clapped a
muddy hand on his mouth. But the damage was done, and after
a brief interval of silence – as though the world were shocked
at this noise so irreverent in the midst of war – machine-guns
opened their iron stutter, star-shells lit the sky, and grenades
burst dully in the neighbouring soil. For half an hour the patrol
lay in acute danger and discomfort, and then crept miserably
back to their own lines with three men wounded in addition to
the Captain.

Corporal Merriman had his stripes removed for conduct
prejudicial to the maintenance of order and military discipline,
his vision of a be-medalled tunic vanished like a rainbow, and
Captain Duguid went home on a stretcher, face-downwards.
Some months later, on the Somme, Merriman himself was
wounded in the shoulder during a brief but hurried retreat,
and having recuperated very pleasantly in a volunteer hospital,
applied for and received a commission. He was then sent to
Mesopotamia, and after considerable service in conditions of
torrid heat, fever, and monotony, was ordered to join the force
organized by Major-General Dunsterville for service in Persia.
This fortunate adventure had a most important influence on his
subsequent career.

He remained with Dunsterville's small army throughout its
romantic existence, and journeyed with it into Southern Russia.
In the retreat from Baku he so distinguished himself that he
was recommended for the Military Cross, but his perverse
fate still unhappily pursued him. In the dull green calm of the
Caspian Sea he made his first acquaintance with vodka, and
such was its inflammatory influence that he defied all restraint
and led a deputation of three to the Commander-in-Chief with
an impolitic suggestion to return and launch an immediate
counter-attack, that would give him a chance to win a bar for

his promised medal. The resulting court martial behaved with laudable clemency, and balanced his impropriety by cancelling the recommendation for a Military Cross.

Peace being at last concluded, Merriman left the army with none of the decorations he had coveted, but only the service medals that indicated an undistinguished though useful capacity to survive or elude the perils and rigours of campaigning in the twentieth century.

(*from* Magnus Merriman)

Hugh MacDiarmid
1892–1978

In response to a request from George Ogilvie, his old mentor at Broughton in Edinburgh, MacDiarmid sent him his short story 'Casualties' in June 1919. It had been written as a result of the heavy losses sustained by both sides during the Battle of the Somme in 1916 and it was first published in the Summer 1919 issue of the *Broughton Magazine*. Throughout his war service MacDiarmid kept up a lively correspondence with Ogilvie in which he discussed political matters and his own literary aspirations. The unsigned letter of Christmas 1917 was published in the *Broughton Magazine* as part of a series from former pupils under the title, 'Letters from the Front'. See also p 63.

Sources: Alan Bold (ed.), *The Thistle Rises: An Anthology of Poetry and Prose by Hugh MacDiarmid*, London: Hamish Hamilton, 1984;
Catherine Kerrigan (ed.), *The Hugh MacDiarmid-George Ogilvie Letters*, Aberdeen: Aberdeen University Press, 1988

Casualties

For three weeks the working hours of the unit had been sixteen out of every twenty-four, and at length, in the centre of that sloppy and muddy field, appeared what was to be known to the Army as the Nth Casualty Clearing Station.

Tired enough from the strain of continued and unremitting road-making, tent-pitching, and the innumerable heart-breaking tasks incidental to the shifting of stoves and equipment, and the improvisation of those diversely essential things which cannot be secured except by indents which take many weeks to circulate through the chain of offices, the unit disposed itself, as units do, to snatch some sleep before the first rush should begin.

None too soon, it shortly appeared, for as we stumbled to the Fall-In, headlights began to appear on the road from Albert, a long trail of ambulance cars stretching back into the rainy dampness which hid the tremendous business so casually referred to as 'The Big Push.' The turn of the first car into the little road found a quietly active camp, for hasty preparations had been carried out in just such improbable corner-grounds many times before.

Here, as always in the track of armies in the Somme region, the salient element was mud – thick, deep, insistent and clinging mud that the strongest will could not treat as negligible. There it was and it made the smallest errand an exacting fatigue. The cars manoeuvred through it with the casual air that comes of much experience. Even London taxi-drivers might have learned something from the dexterous and undelaying way in which Red Cross cars were juggled over that boggy land. One by one the cases were slid out by stretcher-bearers working deftly and surely with a sort of tired ease. Car after car rolled up – just the price of 'strengthening the line and solidifying positions in the neighbourhood of —', as it would appear from the day's official report. Men of all units, tired, pale and dirty, were carried into the hut that a party of engineers had finished feverishly that very day. Their khaki barely showed through the encrusting mud save where it had been slit to rags to allow of temporary dressings being put on at Field Ambulances and First Aid Posts and now showing in curious patterns of white and red. Among them were some to whom this station would be something more than a wayside resting-place, men to whom the doctors up the line, working in dugouts where immediate attention to all could not be given, had given a desperate last chance. They died on the way or slipped off without fuss in the Receiving Room, but one or two were pulled through by efforts and methods that would stagger civilian practice.

All night the slow heavy labour of stretcher-bearing went on. And great grey cars pulled up with loads of less seriously wounded who straggled brokenly into the room, muddied and shivering, hatless and coatless often, and with that complete apathy of look and bearing which tells of strain that has gone beyond endurance.

The detached onlooker might have found it moving enough, but here, fortunately, there were not detached onlookers. Lady friends, of the type we all know, were compelled to find stimulants for their sentiment somewhat further down. But, here, a man who had been shovelling mud from the road during a back-breaking afternoon was now booking particulars of the arrivals. But some stared blankly through the interrogator, deaf and speechless, shaking and quivering, and that matter-of-fact fellow entered them as 'Shell-shock. – No particulars available', and they were led off in that new world of theirs to a mattress, and ultimately who shall say to what strange and undesirable destiny.

The slightest cases walked or limped casually up to the keen deft-handed doctor and his alert assistants with the air of men to whom this was but one more incalculable phase of a business whose immensity made all impressions unseizable. To them, indeed, it had been overwhelming, and many of them were so youthful that one felt that the first instinct of their mothers, could they have seen them, would have been to reprove them for being out without overcoats on such a night!

The lashed rows of marquees that had been dignified by the name of 'wards' received these exhausted men on straw palliasses and blankets, and even, for serious cases, cot-beds. Casualty Clearing Stations belong not to any particular division but to an army, and therefore hither came representatives of most of the troops of an Army – Canadian, New Zealanders and South Africans, as well as famous British regiments and new raised battalions, and sick from locally quartered West Indians, Artillery, Engineers, and billeted troops. And there were men in mud-stained grey, stoical as our own, who somehow seemed mere ordinary men again and enemies no longer!

Serious cases speedily filled every available cot and an overflow lay around on stretchers. From all sides came the accustomed moaning for water and the close and heavy breathing of those past even moaning. A strapping sergeant of New Zealanders, gasping out his last unconscious moments, was the first to go. There was no more than time for a quick laying-out (with the boot which was hanging so unnaturally to one side, the foot came off too, despite bandages). His transit must have been a desperate gamble from the start – a wrapping in a rough blanket with scrawled particulars attached, and the big fellow who had travelled so far to his fate was taken on a stretcher to the marquee that served as a mortuary.

Many joined him that night. With these hopeless ones there was no time even to stop to watch by the ebbing life, so many bedside fights there were where a forlorn hope still remained. Work went on without respite, changeless save for the occasional sudden appearance of officers who would leave a few hasty directions for the special treatment of cases which had just left their hands in the operation theatre. Those worst hours before the dawn passed in hectic attendance – the tiredness of the body had perforce to be treated merely as a clogging dream – and the day-staff came to the relief of worn-out men.

The peaceful dawn-wind smote the workers as they stooped to pass through the low canvas doorways and the first faint flush of red showed behind a tree on a far ridge.

Up to that ridge wandered the indescribable waste of the countryside, trenched and pitted and ploughed until it had become a fantastic and nightmarish wilderness. On this dreary tract nothing remained of the gifts once showered by nature. But the grim legacies of man at war were countless – chaotic and half-buried heaps of his machinery, munitions and equipment, and the remains of his hasty meals. And he himself lay there, shattered in thousands, to give a lurking horror to a treacherous and violent surface of mud and slime and unlovely litter. The very weeds which might have graced the desolation refused such holding-ground.

Pale now beside the compelling splendour of the reddening day showed the yellow stabs of our guns, flashes that had lit the sky in the night watches, and only the long road, never varying, told that the unspeakable harvest on the Somme was still being gathered in.

Letters from Salonika and France

While serving in Salonika Grieve kept up a regular correspondence with George Ogilvie. The 'flu epidemic' refers to the Spanish influenza epidemic of 1918 which claimed 17,575 lives in Scotland. Although John Buchan admired Grieve's Salonika poems these were never published in one volume. The Kerr referred to in the last letter is Roderick Watson Kerr (see p 52).

Dear Mr ———— ,

Camped on a high and airy promontory jutting out into the blue Aegean, across which, a day's sail away, my usual station is on a very clear day dimly discernible on a further coast. I am at present enjoying a rest-cure and write in a holiday mood for the first time in close on fifteen months.

A recent recurrence of malignant malaria left me deplorably reduced in physique and stamina and, noting my debility, the authorities took compassion on me and sent me hither to this 'change of air camp' for a ten-days' spell, of which four or five days have still to run.

There are caller air[s] which would revive me more speedily and thoroughly, I know, but failing these yet awhile (the wheels of the chariots of Mars stand badly in need of oiling), the change here is doing me a world of good – I feel a different fellow already – and by the time my holiday is over I should be quite built up again for the winter. Now that the colder weather is setting in I need fear no further recurrence of the fever till next summer by which time I hope to have shaken the dust of Macedon off my Army Pattern boots finally and forever – but one never can tell.

In the meantime, however, I have little to do but eat, sleep, bathe and remember old friends. The bathing is splendid, along a long sweep of beach (reached by a break-neck goats' track down steep cliffs) in waters clear to a great depth and with a fine smooth, sandy bottom. On walking along the shore one may see some quaint native fisheries, with two rickety ladder erections sticking up out of the water like the skeletons of stupendous cranes. From seats on the top of these the fishermen can see their prey entering their nets some distance out. They then haul up the nets until they go out and secure their yield in a primitive old boat. Red mullet, for the most part, and an eel-like fish with silver belly and bright green back, and curious thin sword-like mouths, like a snipe's bill.

More curious still is a chance encounter with a lonely but well-contented Scots highlander, line-fishing with an old cod-hook, baited with the entrails of mussels (with which the adjacent rocks are plentifully bestruck). He has a true highland knack of casting – power to his elbow! – and is doing great damage to a school of pink-and-silvery, flounder-like fish. But as he says, no doubt he'd be 'nane the waur o' a wheen worms'.

But mostly I lie on the cliff-top – the climb back from the beach liking me not – lie in the sunshine on almost bentless terrain, watching the crafts go up and down the shining waterways. All kinds and conditions of vessels are here. Modern men-of-war and motor-craft: old-fashioned sailing-ships and native boats, Trireme and Submarine, galleon and collier, schooner and motor-yacht pass and repass in striking epitomes of naval history.

Behind, the ground rolls endlessly in almost desert stretches. Scarcely a tree is to be seen. But all that Masefield in his *Gallipoli* says of Mudros and the Dardanelles, and the magic colours, which the powerful sunlight draws out of the rocky bareness there, is true also of my present location – and even Masefield's pen has not done full justice to the subtle wonders of these unsuspected colours that make it seem as if the wizardry of the slanting rays of the sun turned grey stone and brown clay into gold and silver and ruby and emerald.

And in such settings I lie and dream.

Your old pupil,
C. M. Grieve.

Somewhere in France [Dieppe?]

11 November 1918

Dear Mr Ogilvie,

It is some time now since I wrote you: but you will understand that I have had a somewhat busy time of late. I called down to see you at Broughton when I was on final leave but you were off ill and I had not time to come to your house. Shortly afterwards I was transported hither – to a great malaria concentration camp for a further course of treatment so-called. Conditions are somewhat rough and we are kept pretty well at it. Still I am A1, or rather B1. What leisure I do get I am devoting to giving courses of lectures on 'Political and Commercial Geography' and 'Civics and Town Planning' under the Army Educational Scheme. These monopolise three nights a week. I had little thought to return to teaching but the work is absorbing and I think greatly worth while.

News came today of the cessation of hostilities. It was taken very very quietly – incalculable relief but no mafficking. Technically we are still invalids and may be sent home and demobilised all the sooner on that ground. Anyhow it is splendid knowing that the duration is over and that one is at last actually on the last lap.

My plans for after the war are all cut and dried – I am ready and eager for a time of systematic production. But I shall hope to talk all my plans over with you and I know that whatever I write you will give me the benefit of your advice and experience.

My present address is:– 64020 Sergt C. M. Grieve, RAMC, No. 3 Group, Reception Camp, No. 2 L of C Area, BEF, France.

I hope your home has escaped the ravages of the 'flu epidemic and that you soon recovered from the indisposition you were suffering from when I was last in Edinr.

Please give my kindest regards to Mrs Ogilvie and the children. I hope this will find you all well in health and spirits.

With all good wishes.

Chris.

Somewhere in France

24 November 1918

Dear Mr Ogilvie:-

Your delightful letter to hand! It redeemed for me the
unspeakable unprofitableness of a cold dull Sunday forenoon
when I was vainly and with a stultifying sense of unworthiness
endeavouring to mitigate my bleak untidy boredom by
perusing the current issues of *La Vie Parisienne* and *Le
Rire*. Forthwith, as a sign of my gratitude, I am going
to scribble some sort of a return, for the inadequacy of
which please blame my cramping comfortless circumstances.
I am half-recumbent on damp and muddy tentboards, with
blankets, slarried over with mud, wrapped round ice-cold
feet, and unobliging vertebrae dove-tailing unevenly into
the humps and hollows of a stack of miscellaneous kit,
while a woodfire in a biscuit-tin brazier flames and smokes
unequally and disconcertingly in the mouth of the tent. Some
setting!

I was greatly interested in what you say of the termination
of hostilities and the future you forecast. I myself believe that
we have lost this war – in everything but actuality! When
I see scores of sheep go to a slaughter house I do not feel
constrained to admire their resignation. Nor do I believe that
the majority of soldiers killed were sufficiently actuated by
ideals or capable of entertaining ideas to justify such terms
as 'supreme self-sacrifice, etc'. I have been oppressed by
my perception of the wide-spread automatism – fortuity –
of these great movements and holocausts. A painter covers
a canvas with a number of rapid brush marks – a critic
comes along and writes it up at inordinate length, seeing
in it all manner of technical and aesthetic qualities which the
painter had probably not even the mentality to comprehend.
So with 'patriotism' – 'a war of ideas' – 'democracy versus
autocracy' etc. I more and more incline to the belief that
human intelligence is a mere by-product of little account – that
the purpose and destiny of the human race is something quite
apart from it – that religion, civilisation and so forth are mere
'trimmings', irrelevant to the central issues. However I cannot

justly present these opinions here nor have I the space or time
to show what has led to my forming them. Only, more and
more, with Matthew Arnold, do I believe in the necessity for
'keeping aloof from what is called the practical view of things.
To try and approach truth from one side after another, not to
strive or cry, nor to persist in pressing forward, on any one
side, with violence or self-will – it is only thus, it seems to me,
that mortals may hope to gain any vision of the mysterious
Goddess, whom we shall never see except in outline but only
thus even in outline.'

In saying in my last letter that all my plans for the future
are cut and dried I should have qualified myself. What I meant
was that my life-work is really done – that various books exist
complete and unchangeable in my mind – what remains is
only to do the actual writing. But alas in real affairs I must
condescend to the practical view. It will be necessary for me
to do my writing in what leisure and suitable atmosphere will
be allowed to me by bread-and-butter employment – and my
first duty will be to secure such employment as rapidly as
possible in some suitable place. What an odious problem! I
do not suppose for a moment that anything really suitable or
adequately lucrative will turn up. Fortunately the fact that I
am now married does not complicate these difficulties. But
we will see in due course.

Did I tell you, by the way, that Colonel John Buchan
expressed himself in very laudatory terms concerning my
Salonika poems?

Where and how is Kerr? I have not yet contrived to see any
of his stuff. Is he still active? I am greatly hoping to meet him
in the not-too-distant future.

Please give my kindest regards to Mrs Ogilvie and the
children. I hope they are all well and have successfully dodged
the 'flu epidemic which has according to the papers been so
bad in Edinburgh.

I hope you have completely recovered from your own
indisposition.

You were, by the way, wrong in fearing that I had had a
relapse of malaria. The phrase which led to the assumption
was 'wrot sarcastick'. I am afraid that, the Censorship being
still unabated, I cannot make the matter clearer in the
meantime. But I am really feeling marvellously fit although

conditions here are in every way conducive to an opposite condition.

Hoping to hear from you soon again – and ever with the kindest regards.

Yours,
C. M. Grieve.

Compton Mackenzie
1883–1972

Edward Montague Compton Mackenzie was born in West
Hartlepool, the son of a theatrical impresario. He was educated
at St Paul's School, London and Magdalen College, Oxford.
By the time that war was declared he had written a clutch
of bestselling novels including *Carnival* and the first volume
of *Sinister Street*. He applied for a commission in the Seaforth
Highlanders but was rebuffed by a War Office official who
told him, 'your job is to keep us amused by writing books.'
Nothing daunted, he used his contacts to find a place on the staff
of General Sir Ian Hamilton, (see also p 168) the commander
of the expeditionary force in the Dardanelles. Through Edward
Marsh, Churchill's private secretary, Mackenzie was gazetted a
lieutenant in the Royal Marines and he served in the Dardanelles
throughout the summer of 1915. During the landings at Cape
Helles he acted as official war correspondent and his reports
showed a clear understanding of the tactical situation which
confined the allied forces to their small beach-heads on the
Gallipoli Peninsula. Later in the war Mackenzie worked for
military intelligence in Athens, an experience that gave him the
material for his novel *Extremes Meet*. Although the overall tone
of his war memoirs is regret for the passing of the Edwardian
world, he was critical of the faulty planning and bad leadership
which brought about the failure of the Dardanelles operation.

Source: Compton Mackenzie, *Gallipoli Memories*, London: Cassell, 1929

The Dark Night of the Suvla Landing

*In August 1915 General Sir Ian Hamilton, the commander of the
British Expeditionary Force, made his second attempt to gain control
of the Gallipoli Peninsula. It was to involve a double strike against the
Turks at Ari Burnu (Anzac Cove) and a night attack on Chunuk Bair.
At the same time a new landing was made at Suvla Bay, a few miles to
the north. By the time the British assault went in the Turks had brought
up fresh reserves and the landings ended in failure. It was clear that the
Gallipoli operation had been a disaster and Hamilton was replaced by
General Sir Charles Munro who ordered a complete evacuation at the
end of the year. Of the characters mentioned by Mackenzie, Captain
C.F. Aspinall was to become the campaign's official historian, Major
Guy Dawnay was one of Hamilton's staff officers, Colonel Wyndham
Deedes was head of counter-intelligence and George Lloyd (later Lord
Lloyd) was a member of parliament engaged on counter-intelligence
duties.*

A t half-past three on the afternoon of the sixth of August
the thunder of the guns on Helles travelling across the
clear air to Kephalo proclaimed that the general attack ordered
there had begun. This was intended to occupy the Turks in the
Southern Zone and prevent their moving northward to reinforce
the defenders above Anzac, where the Australians and New
Zealanders launched their attack at half-past five. The gunfire
pulsated on the still air, and by seven o'clock the whole length
of the long line of tawny cliffs was twinkling with starry shells.
All through the afternoon the troops of the Eleventh Division
had been embarking in the new armour-plated motor-lighters
that from their appearance were known as beetles. Ten thousand
troops embarked at Imbros; six thousand were on their way
from Mudros. From Mytilene four thousand more were steering
northward into the unknown out of the unknowable, for half
an hour after the last trawler had left Port Iero *Canopus* had
deliberately fouled the cable so that no news of their departure
could be signalled from enemy agents in Lesbos.

The evening was brilliantly clear: the sea was calm. About
half-past seven I stood above the GHQ camp and looked down
across the waters of Kephalo to where on the level land beyond
K beach hundreds of evacuated tents clustered like ghosts in the

twilight. The roadstead was thronged with shipping; and the smoke of many funnels belching into the clear air and making turbid a sky slashed with the crimson of a long slow sunset suggested the glimpse of a manufacturing town in a hollow of the Black Country beheld from some Staffordshire height. One after another the ships moved out of the harbour: great liners like the *Minneapolis* with the newspaper correspondents on board, destroyers, trawlers, beetles, battleships, and many others. By half-past seven the roadstead was empty. The metallic blues and greens and blood-reds in the water had turned to a cold dull grey. Eastward the ever increasing surge and thunder of the guns: here an almost horrible quiet. At ten o'clock the new landing was due to begin. Hardly anybody spoke at dinner. Jan Smith had gone over to Suvla, so George Lloyd, Deedes and I drew lots for the three shifts of sitting up for Intelligence signals. Lloyd drew ten to one, Deedes four to seven, and I to my great pleasure the middle shift from one to four. This was the time, we reckoned, when we should be hearing of important events at Suvla. By now the heavy presentiment of failure had vanished. I was feeling positive that during my shift great news would come through which I should remember to my dying day. I was too much excited to go to bed, and from ten to twelve I worked on that absurd memorandum on the Müller family in Mytilene, and my proposed scheme for their elimination. At midnight I went across with George Lloyd to the O tent where we drank cocoa. No news of any kind had yet arrived; but we told ourselves that we really must not expect any quite as soon as this. Lloyd was listless and downhearted. I urged him to go to bed, such a headache had he, and as I walked with him to his tent he told me how much he hated being here and doing nothing while the push was on.

'I'm no good at GHQ to anybody,' he said bitterly. 'If I were with my regiment I should feel more respect for myself.'

It was difficult to reassure George Lloyd when he succumbed to these self-searching moods of despair. I left him and walked the back to the O tent after telling the orderly in I to bring across any telegrams. By one o'clock there was nobody left in the O tent except Guy Dawnay, Cecil Aspinall, Barttelot and the Cipher-major Orlo Williams with his code books. Sir Walter Barttelot was a Coldstreamer who had joined the staff while I was at Mytilene. He was a quiet attractive man, the head of one of the most ancient families in England. His father had been killed in South Africa: he himself was to be killed in 1918. I felt that depression was setting in here under the strain of waiting for news, and I tried to amuse them by enacting a series of imaginary scenes between various members of the General Staff. Apparently I was successful in being funny, for Orlo Williams told me the other day that one of his memories of Suvla night was trying not to laugh, because in the bruised condition of his bones after falling from his horse two days before every laugh was an agony. However, I could not go on being funny indefinitely, and we were soon sitting anxiously waiting for news.

Two o'clock went by without further news. Guy Dawnay and I walked out to listen for firing northward. The night was utterly still. General Birrell had gone back to his disturbed sleep. Over the Peninsula the blood-red horn of the waning moon just risen was clawing up at the sky. A rocket flamed on the horizon. A ship was hooting mournfully while it waited to be allowed in through the Kephalo boom. At half-past two somebody in O tent produced a bottle of Horlick's Malted Milk Lozenges, and we all started sucking them in a melancholy. Aspinall must have drawn forty ladies by now, each one becoming a little more wooden than her predecessor. I tried to cheer up things by reading out my scheme for kidnapping the Müller family. Guy Dawnay suggested that I should submit a scheme for kidnapping some of the Brigadiers of the new Divisions.

'Good God!' Aspinall rapped out suddenly. 'They must be ashore by now.'

A telegram came in to say that the fouled cable had been mended. That brigade and a half from Mytilene should be nearly off Suvla at this moment.

At half-past three I went outside again to listen for gunfire. The moon, clear of the mirk of the Peninsula heights by now, was shining very yellow in the eastern sky. But there was no news yet of the Ninth Army Corps, though the first grey of dawn was perceptible.

Then at ten minutes to four an orderly came in with a signal.

'At last,' cried Aspinall, tearing open the envelope. Then 'Damn!' he groaned, tossing the piece of paper down.

'*Bamboozled 800 punctured,*' said the message.

It was only a code message for the Quartermaster-General's

department; but it sounded as if some mocking demon had chosen those two words to tell us that the Suvla Landing had failed.

'But they must be ashore by now,' said Aspinall miserably.

It was now four o'clock and time to wake Deedes for the shift from four to seven. But before I woke him I ran down under the paling sky to the Signals tent and asked the sergeant in desperation if there was still no news from Suvla.

'Only this, sir,' he said, 'from the signaller on the New Landing. It was in reply to us, for it seemed so funny not hearing anything from over there.'

He wrote out on a form that the signaller of the New Landing reported he could now hear hot musketry and the sound of bursting shells behind him.

I hurried back with this message to the O tent.

'Well, they've landed anyway,' said Guy Dawnay grimly.

'Yes, they've landed,' Aspinall agreed. 'But this is what we ought to have heard three hours ago.'

I left him to discuss for the twentieth time what could have been holding up the operation, and went along to wake Deedes, whose tent was at the top of the Lines. The moon was now much higher, a frail silver slip of a moon turning to ivory in the pale eastern sky. The little wind of dawn was lisping through the withered herbage and ruffling the sand here and there with cat's-paws. The guns had started to growl again. I found Deedes already in his dressing-gown, and as he moved nattily about his tent he would stop from time to time to listen if the kettle on his spirit-lamp was beginning to boil. In the glimmering twilight of dawn he looked more than ever like a pious church-worker getting up to attend early Service. I told him about the disappointments of the night. He made no comment but advised down me to get off to bed. So I left him and walked down through the rows of tents which stood out against the wan air of dawn as black as the night fast receding into the west.

It was a long time before I fell sound asleep, for I kept waking to clutch at phantoms. There was no vestige of hope left in my mind that the Suvla Landing could now succeed. I felt as if I had watched a system crack to pieces before my eyes, as if I had stood by the deathbed of an old order. The guns I could hear might have been a growling that foretold the murderous folly of the Somme. The war would last now until we had all turned ourselves into Germans to win it. An absurd phrase went singing through my head. *We have lost our amateur status to-night.* It was foolish for me who had been old enough to appreciate the muddle of the South African War to go on believing in the practical value of the public-school system. I had really for long mistrusted it, but since coming out here I had fallen once more under its spell as I might have fallen under the spell of a story by Rudyard Kipling. Yes, the War would go on now. I must remember to write home to-morrow for more woollen under-clothes. We should be here indefinitely now. Queer that a man like Sir Ian Hamilton so perfectly cut out to ride into Constantinople at the head of a victorious army should be thwarted of his hope. He would appear so Wellingtonian, charging up Achi Baba on a black horse and looking over his shoulder to wave on . . . the picture faded as I woke up again fully . . . and then I trembled once more upon the verge of sleep with a vision of Sir Ian Hamilton standing beside a drum, the smoke of battle beyond his slim eager form, a field marshal's baton grasped tightly in one hand, the injured hand by his side lending an added dignity to his appearance like Nelson's missing arm . . . the smoke of battle . . . and along the horizon the domes and minarets of Constantinople. People years hence would stare at the heroic picture and never know what the man himself would have suffered before he could stand proudly up like that as a conqueror . . . once more I was fully awake, and that heroic battle-piece had faded. There were no domes and minarets along the horizon. There was only the long line of tawny cliffs and the sun fast overtaking a frail moon in the bland sky of morning. There were only the flies wandering over my mosquito-net, and an overwhelming desire to sleep while the day was still cool. Last night must somehow be separated from any other night by sleep, It had been too profoundly moving an experience to melt inevitably into another dusty day. It must be enshrined in sleep and remembered all the rest of my life as a dream in which I had beheld so many other people's dreams topple over and crash. And away in London they would be getting up presently, unaware that during the night the old London had vanished.

(*from* Gallipoli Memories)

John Maclean
1879–1923

John Maclean was born in Glasgow but his father's roots were
in the island of Mull. He was educated at Pollok Academy and
worked as a student teacher before becoming a part-time student
at Glasgow University. After graduating in 1904 he immersed
himself in the work of the Marxist Social Democratic Federation
and in 1916 he was partly responsible for the establishment
of the Scottish Labour College. During the First World War
Maclean advocated a termination of hostilities and the ending
of capitalism; he was dismissed as a schoolteacher by the Govan
School Board and he took an active part in the Glasgow
rent strikes of 1915. (See also John Buchan, *Mr Standfast*,
p 146.) As an opponent of conscription and a supporter of
industrial unrest, Maclean was arrested in 1916 and sentenced
to three years' penal servitude in Perth and Peterhead prisons.
Released in 1917 he was re-arrested the following year and
spent three further periods in prison before his final release
in October 1922. Maclean's position as a socialist nationalist
is unrivalled in Scottish political history and his achievements
in workers' education are important, but his health and political
stance were weakened by these long periods of imprisonment.
The journals, to which he contributed his anti-conscription
articles, *The Vanguard* and *Forward*, were suppressed early in
1916.

Source: Nan Milton (ed.), *John Maclean: In the Rapids of Revolution; Essays,
Articles and Letters 1902-1923*, London: Allison and Busby, 1978

The Clyde Unrest

The situation in the Clyde area is just as interesting as it was recently in South Wales, and as it is presently in Dublin where the transport workers have paralysed work at the docks. Unrest and dissatisfaction manifest themselves in many directions, but principally in opposition to the Munitions Act, the raising of rents, and the threat of conscription. We think it necessary to deal with these in the order mentioned.

Since the introduction of the infamous Munitions Act, in the output of which the leaders of the trade unions have played their treacherous part, the workers of the Clyde have found themselves bullied and ordered about by foremen and managers as never before. Men, seeking to leave one factory for another, have found themselves detained to suit the interests of the employers. Others, wishing to stay, have been dismissed without a clearance card and have thus been kept six weeks out of work to satisfy the desire for revenge of some vicious foremen or managers . . ..

In such circumstances, the men stop work and, of course, in due course become victims under the vile Slavery Act. Penalty after penalty, always against the workers, has convinced the workers on the Clyde that the purport of the Munitions Act was not increased supplies to the soldiers, but the crushing of trade unionism. In that we think the workers right . . ..

The capitalist class seized on the Marshall case to demonstrate that the men were doing their utmost to hold back production, and the presiding Sheriff gave a savage sentence to frighten others who might be thought guilty of the ca' canny policy, although Marshall was simply charged with an ordinary assault.

Things did not turn out as the silly old Sheriff and his class expected. The Beardmore workers, aroused by this vile spleen, rallied round Marshall and his family. At the same time they prepared to strike if he was not liberated. He was liberated.

This Marshall case revived the unofficial committee of shop-stewards in the engineering works, and as luck would have it the Fairfield Shipwrights' case arose as the Marshall one faded away.

The unofficial committee decided to widen its borders so as to include unofficial representatives from all allied trades in the engineering and shipbuilding shops. Now railwaymen and miners are admitted – and even a teacher [MacLean] – to show the solidarity of brawn and brain workers.

This wise provision entitled and enabled the committee to consider the Fairfield case and decide upon action, if need be . . . .

A move began among the Fairfield and other Govan workers to prepare a strike for the release of the three brave and good men.

The unofficial committee also roused itself to the occasion, and resolved that if the shipwrights and other workers in Fairfield struck the whole Clyde area would be paralysed . . . .

It is no surprise, then, to learn that the three men were released on Wednesday, 27 October, after three weeks in prison, the fine having been paid. We know the imprisoned men did not pay the fine and did not consent to its payment. Either the official gang or the government did it to save their dirt-stained faces . . . .

Grey is a fossil who has bungled his department; Asquith can only 'wait and see' while the Germans spread themselves around; Lloyd George is a good jumping-jack, and most of his other colleagues would do very well in a Berlin Museum. It is men of this kidney who would make criminals of our class.

It is up to the unofficial committee now to forge ahead, refusing to recognise officials who have betrayed the workers (as Highland chiefs and Indian princes have betrayed their peoples in the past to the English), and are equally ready to again do the trick. The withdrawal of the charge against our comrade Bridges, of Weir's, by the Minister of Munitions, shows that fear of a strike is the only thing recognised by the Russo-Prussians who rule this country. The very fact that Bridges was summoned because, as shop steward, he approached a man to join the union is further proof that the attempt is to crush the unions and to continue the stupid methods of irritation started under the protection of the Munitions Act.

Unless the Clyde men act quickly, determinedly, and with a clear object in view they are going to be tied up in a knot. We know that the Glasgow press was threatened with the Defence of the Realm Act should it make mention of strike had one broken out. We know that the military authorities had engineers and allied workers in the army at home ready to draft into the Clyde works in the event of a strike. We know also that, despite the clamour for munitions, young men are being dismissed from all the Clyde works in order to force them into the army. When the occasion arises they will be reinstated in their old jobs, but now as military slaves – worse even than munition slaves. Quick and firm action is needed if slavery is going to be abolished and conscription defeated. We must now fight boldly for the common ownership of all industries in Britain.

(The Vanguard, *November 1915*)

Rent Victories

Through the tireless energy of Mr McBride, secretary of the Labour Party's Housing Committee, and ardent support of the Women's Housing Committee, an agitation was started in the early summer against rent increases in the munition areas of Glasgow and district. Evening and midday work-gate meetings soon stimulated the active workers in all the large shipyards and the engineering shops.

Emboldened, the organisers by demonstration and deputation tried to commit the Town Council to action against increases. As it acts as the executive committee of the propertied class, the Council shirked the responsibility of curbing the greed and rapacity of the factors and house-owners.

Enraged, the workers agitated more and more until the government intervened by the appointment of a commission of inquiry – Dr Hunter and Professor Scott. This was the signal for all the factors in the city to give notices of increase in rent. They anticipated that this united front would influence the commissioners (as it did), and that the government would compromise the situation by allowing half the demands to be made legal.

They all calculated without consideration of the awakened anger of the whole working class. People in the previously unaffected areas saw no objection to munition workers paying more, but when they themselves became liable to increased rent they adopted the aggressive. Encouraged by the universal working-class support, and irritated by the operation of the infamous Munitions Act, the Clyde workers were ready to strike. This several yards did when eighteen of their comrades appeared before Sheriff Lee. Beardmore's workers at Dalmuir sent a big deputation to tell the Sheriff that if he gave an adverse decision they would at once down tools. We have been favoured with a report of the proceedings in the Sheriff's room from the principal spokesman. It is intensely interesting as described by one of the spokesmen. In the circumstances the Sheriff wisely decided against the factors' demand for an increase. We state the cause of triumph in these terms advisedly, for it really was due to joint action and not to the justice of the case (and there could be no juster) that success came to our side.

The strike having taken place, the workers were bent on letting the government know that out they would come again unless it restored rents to their pre-war level. It now transpires that a Rent Bill will be passed, forcing all factors of houses, rented at £21 and under (£30 in London), to reduce the rents to the levels prevailing immediately prior to the outbreak of the Great Slaughter Competition . . ..

It should be noted that the rent strike on the Clyde is the first step towards the political strike, so frequently resorted to on the Continent in times past. We rest assured that our comrades in the various works will incessantly urge this aspect on their workmates, and so prepare the ground for the next great countermove of our class in the raging class warfare – raging more than even during the Great Unrest period of three or four years ago.

Bear in mind that, although the government has yielded to enormous pressure, it must do something to balance the victory. Remember how Lloyd George came out with the Munitions Act as a reply to the victory of the striking Clyde engineers, and let that put us all on our guard . . ..

It is up to the workers to be ready, and resist with a might never exerted before. Whether the Clyde Workers' Committee as constituted today is able or willing to cope with the situation is doubtful; but it is just as well to give it a further chance with the added support of miners and railwaymen. However, just as this unofficial committee views with suspicion the official committees of the various unions and attempts to act as a driving force, we warn our comrades that they ought to adopt the same attitude towards the unofficial committee and see that it pushes ahead. If it still clings on to academic discussions and futile proposals, it is their business to take the initiative into their own hands as they did in the case of the recent rent strike. Remember that the only way to fight the class war is by accepting every challenge of the master class and throwing down more challenges ourselves. Every determined fight binds the workers together more and more, clears the heads of our class to their robbed and enslaved conditions, and so prepares them for the acceptance of our full gospel of socialism, and the full development of the class war to the end of establishing socialism.

A victory at football, draughts, or chess, is the result of many moves and countermoves. We do not lie down and cry when our side loses a goal. No; we buckle up our sleeves and spit on our hands, determined to get two goals in return, or more. So is the game of life. It advances from move to move, ever on grander and grander scale. Prepare, then, for the enemy's counterstroke to our victory on the rent question!

(The Vanguard, *December 1915*)

The Conscription Menace

This war was declared to be a war of freedom. We socialists considered that a deliberate lie, because the promoters of the statement know quite well that the workers of the world are their slaves, and will continue to be their slaves no matter the issue of the war. It certainly is a war of freedom for one national section or other of the robbing propertied class to corner for itself the whole, or the greater part, of the surplus wrung from the wage-slave class. Obviously, that is no concern of the workers one way or the other.

We have repeatedly expressed our perfect willingness to let those who benefit by capitalism enter the war, and slaughter one another to their heart's content. That is their affair, not ours. Their mutual extermination might, in fact, smooth the path leading to socialism, so that even many socialists might be excused if they departed from the policy of indifference and became active recruiting agents amongst the propertied class, urging them with fiery eloquence to defend *their* king and *their* country.

We have furthermore refrained from the attempt to prevent workers enlisting if they sincerely believed that Britain was entitled to enter the war. In fact, we usually insisted on them enlisting as the only logical outcome of their beliefs.

It is an entirely different matter when an attempt to force conscription on us is threatened. We socialists, who believe that the only war worth fighting is the class war against robbery and slavery for the workers, do not mean to lay down our lives for British or any other capitalism. If we die, we shall die here defending the few rights our forefathers died for. To us it is nobler to die for our own class than for the class which has robbed, ruled, despised, and imprisoned us.

They dare not murder us, for that would lift the veil of cant they have blinded the eyes of neutrals with . . .. They also had better not enlist us, for we will prove more dangerous with arms than without them. A reign of terror would certainly ensue. History backs us up in that assertion, for the mass of the men who refuse now to enlist do so on principle and not through fear . . ..

So far as mere trade unionists are concerned, we warn them that conscription means the bringing of all young men under the control of the military authorities, whether they be in the field of battle or in the factory and workshop. Every controlled factory comes directly under military discipline as well, and thus the old as well as the young will be bound hand and foot to Mr William Weir and his capitalist friends. Military conscription implies industrial conscription, the most abject form of slavery the world has ever known . . ..

To the old, as to the young, we appeal for stern opposition to conscription . . ..

The only way to retain our freedom – the small shred of it we now possess – is by solid combination as a class. The only weapon we can use today is the strike. We urge our comrades to be ready to use that weapon to prevent the coming of absolute chattel slavery.

Do not be paralysed by academic quack socialists, who insist that the only occasion justifying the strike is for the establishment of socialism. These men admit that the masses are still far from socialism. That means we must defer the strike to the remote future. See how absurd the position is, and act accordingly.

(The Vanguard, *December 1915*)

James Leslie Mitchell
1901–1935

James Leslie Mitchell was born at Auchterless in Aberdeenshire where his father was a farmer. When he was eight the family moved to the Howe of the Mearns and Mitchell was educated at Arbuthnott Village School and Mackie Academy, Stonehaven. Leaving school early, Mitchell worked as a journalist in Aberdeen and Glasgow before joining the army in August 1919. With the Royal Army Service Corps he served in Mesopotamia, Palestine and Egypt and he was discharged in 1923. Unable to find work he enlisted in the Royal Air Force and served with them in various bases in England until 1929. Although Mitchell disliked intensely the squalor and brutality of the barrack-room, his time with the services brought him into contact with veterans of the First World War and their experiences figure strongly in his autobiographical novel *The Thirteenth Disciple*. During the war his fictional hero Malcom Maudslay finds that his naïve socialist faith is destroyed amidst the carnage on the Western Front. The meeting with his brother Robert is an echo of Ewan Tavendale's incomprehension – this leads to his execution – in *Sunset Song* which was published under Mitchell's pen-name, Lewis Grassic Gibbon. (See also p 160.)

Source: James Leslie Mitchell, *The Thirteenth Disciple*, London: Jarrolds, 1931; Edinburgh: Paul Harris Publishing (Scottish Fiction Reprint Library), 1981

The Defile of the Beast

Subchapter i

He spent over two years in France; he was not once wounded or gassed or fever-stricken; he became a corporal and then a sergeant; he was twice pressed to accept a commission, declined like Metaxa, and was victimized in consequence; he grew to regard unclean equipment and unpolished buttons with a passionate disfavour; he robbed a German prisoner of three hundred American dollars and then shot that prisoner as the man turned on him threateningly; he sat three days in a shell-hole at Bois Louange, he and two others, marooned in a maelstrom of retreat and advance; he found a rat-eaten woman's corpse in the depths of a staff dug-out in the Hindenburg Line; he commandeered an abandoned Leyland lorry in the Spring retreat of 1918 and drove a score of men for thirty miles, and fell asleep, and awoke still driving them; he lived a life so fantastic that his memory was to refuse to treat it seriously, or, in self-defence, became deliberately treacherous.

He never spent a 'first day in the trenches.' They massed in emplacements and sunken roads in front of the gun-clamour of that July 16th and then went forward into a draggled, copse-strewn waste, a-vomit in sudden volcanic eruptions, drifting long clouds of gas. They jumped the last bank of the sunken road and yelled and went forward at a stumbling run. The air was filled with a whispering rush of bullets – Malcom was to remember that whispering sound first heard, like the sound of exhausted hail. The forward sky flickered and winked with gun-flashes; behind, the sound of the British barrage leapt forward and forward on their backs, like the leaping of pursuing dinosaurs. The upper air was populous and filled with an insane racket, while from copses to left and right arose a whoop-whoop presently merging into the whoop-oo-oor of gun-belts . . .. Malcom found himself plunging forward, an interested automaton, above the rhythmic play of his army boots. His company commander raced three paces in front of him, sobbing a foolish chant: 'Oh, you bloody bloody bloody – oh, you bloody bloody SWINE!' Suddenly his hat vanished

and with it the roof of his skull. He swayed and fell. Malcom
tripped over him, stumbled, recovered, with vision below his
eyes of a thing like an archaic cranium filled with a seething mess
of dun-coloured jelly . . ..

He was in 'A' company, 'B' was at its heels. Sergeant-Major
Metaxa, grinning, a knobkerrie in his hand, raced past. By
then the smoke-mist so patched ground that they lost direction
and found themselves enfiladed from the right. The battalion's
attack was north of the Bois de Trones and south of Longueval.
From the trees to the right, lines of echeloned machine-guns
raved at them. Men beyond Malcom doubled and crumpled and
sprawled – he saw one man impale himself on his own bayonet
– and suddenly a shell burst brightly against the infernal wood
and the gun-flashes. Unharmed, Malcom ran forward through
a raining spray of metal, saw Metaxa and a few others, joined
them, and was presently fighting and falling and scrambling into
the pits of the machine-gunners.

Then something happened which he was never to see recorded.
The machine-gunners, as Metaxa's company leapt amongst then,
cheered and laughed, as though it was some game. Malcom
stabbed one of those laughing gunners through the stomach,
and fell on top of him in an attempt to retrieve his bayonet, and
was trampled underfoot by the others. When he struggled up
again his hand and tunic were soaked with blood and his mouth
and throat sick with the smell of excrement . . ..

Nine officers and four hundred and eighty other ranks of the
battalion failed to answer that night, and were provisionally
posted 'missing' until when and if their exact fate could be
ascertained. The most of them had died like bogged flies in
the spider's web of trenches and cellars which guarded the riven
lands of Waterlot Farm.

Malcom spent most of the night in a captured trench, an
acting-corporal, and, overcome by his queasy stomach, again
and again very sick indeed because of the smell of his own
body.

Subchapter ii

Delville Wood, Trones Wood, Longueval, Ginchy – they
marched and counter-marched, took and re-took, stormed and
fell back amid those immense names for three weeks. Then they

were relieved and marched out and gave place to battalions of felt-hatted Australians who were to die in the mud and rains and futility of the Ancre. Thirty miles behind the lines, in rest-camp, the depleted Norsex were joined by drafts from England and set again to marching and training under an idiot colonel who believed in the imminence of open warfare. Malcom changed his tunic and acquired one that was unstained and had stripes sewn on it. He became smart and attentive in the presence of officers and blasphemous and capable in the presence of those who lacked both stripes and commissions. Metaxa organized vigorous football matches and Corporal Maudslay, battalion heavyweight, became a centre-forward of considerable proficiency.

Indeed, the battalion Soccer team acquired a reputation. It would go miles in lorries to play rival division teams. In one away-match Malcom tripped over and sat on a sturdy half-back who was blunt and blasphemous and Scotch.

It was his brother Robert.

He had joined the Seaforth Highlanders, but was then in training as a gunner for the Tanks. Amazed strangers, they sat either side of a packing case in the barn of Robert's company, and looked at each other uncertainly and unconvincedly. Robert tried to break through the veils of unreality.

'Christ – Malcom, little Malcom. A corporal – an . . . d'ye mind when I smacked ye for stealin oat-cakes? . . . Never sent me that six pounds, never wrote. Ginchy? Christ, I was at Longueval. Why'd you never write hame? Auntie Ellen's dead. We heard you'd left Glasgow; Auld Ian was there an looked in to see ye, and you'd gane . . .. What'd you join an English regiment for?'

'What do you think of it all, Robert?'

'It's jist fair hell.' He sighed. 'Though I dinna say onything . . .. Have ye ever seen a German?'

Malcom nodded. Robert smoothed his short, brindled hair. 'Never seen ane o them. The daft B's. Why the hell did they start it? Mebbe they didna. We're as daft as they are.' He sighed again. 'God, I'd like richt weel a plate o new bannocks and warm milk, and then go ower the brae by Tocherty and see the Leekan lichts below. Mind them, Malcom?' He suddenly grew shy. 'I was married afore I cam oot. Ane o the Murray lassies.' He had a flash of the old, whimsical arrogance. 'Jean, the bonniest ane.'

'Jean was the bonniest,' Malcom said, gently. Robert kindled, his kind eyes shining.

'You mind her? I wantit you there for my best man. She's kept a piece of the cake for you. I'll write an tell her to send it . . .. She's lonely there, up in the cotter hoose at Pittaulds. A weet summer, she says, but the corn comin fine. The clover'll stand thick and bonny below the Stane Muir at Chapel – mind the lang field?' He glanced out below the barn eaves and muttered to himself. 'They'll be bringin hame the kye the noo.'

And suddenly all that was peasant in Malcom wept for his brother, this strayed, lost peasant. He sat and gripped his hands in his pockets and held himself from speaking, and went out to the darkness and the homeward journey with his heart wrung in a passion of pity and rage.

Ten days later, in the attack on Thiepval, he saw his brother, thrusting his gasping face from the port-hole of a Tank, go by into the hell of bright fires and smashed entanglements where the Wurtembergers had died. He caught sight of Malcom, shouted something, and passed, a man in a dream.

Malcom never saw him again.

(*from* The Thirteenth Disciple)

Naomi Mitchison
b. 1897

Naomi Haldane was born in Edinburgh and educated at the Dragon School, Oxford. Her brother was the scientist J. B. S. Haldane and an uncle was R. B. Haldane, the Secretary of State for War who was responsible for the formation of the Territorial Army in 1908. Shortly after war broke out Naomi Haldane became engaged to Richard ('Dick') Mitchison, a barrister, who was serving with the Queen's Bays, a yeomanry regiment. While he served in France she worked as a VAD (Voluntary Aid Detachment) nurse at St Thomas's Hospital in London. After their marriage in 1916 he was badly injured in a motor-bike accident in France while serving with the Royal Signals. With her father-in-law, whom she did not particularly like, Naomi Mitchison crossed over to France to be with Dick and she kept a diary of the experience which was published in the second volume of her autobiography.

Source: Naomi Mitchison, *All Change Here: Girlhood and Marriage*, London: The Bodley Head, 1975

Bad News from France

Naomi Mitchison received the news of her husband's injury while staying with her parents-in-law in London. With her brother Jack – at home on leave – she had just attended a matinée, starring the Bing Boys and Gaby Dislys. Her husband, Dick, was suffering from a fractured skull and he was being treated at the Le Tréport military hospital near Boulogne.

We went back in high spirits to the Mitchison house on the Embankment and there was a telegram. Dick had gone on his motor-bike on some errand for the Signals mess. At Gamache crossroads a French army car ran into him and left him for dead with the motor-bike on top and burning him. A British car which was following them picked him up unconscious and took him to the base hospital at Le Tréport. Here they found he had a fractured skull. The administrative wheels began to turn. I as next-of-kin was sent for; this was done in that way when possible for seriously wounded cases. His father came with me; it should have been a chance for him and me to get to know one another, but it didn't work out that way, which was a pity and mostly my fault. I kept a diary for this period which somewhat shows me up. It is written in pencil on a flimsy block of paper which I must have bought at Le Tréport, but is quite legible.

When I started it I was already extremely impatient with Dick's parents and yet felt guilty about my feelings towards them. The diary is very competently written with sharp and intelligent descriptions of people and places, and knowledge of myself trying to keep calm by thinking that now I knew how the heroine of a novel, which I was already trying to write, was going to feel. This habit of taking notes on one's own behaviour in periods of emotional stress is rather dangerous if people catch you at it.

At the beginning I was getting my main support from Jack (still called 'Boy' throughout). Here it starts, as we came back from the theatre to the house on the Embankment. When I was going back upstairs, my father-in-law

'. . . caught me by the wrist and half dragging me up to the stairs, said in a harsh and painful whisper "We've had a telegram. Dick is hurt." Then I, "How badly, my God, how badly?" "Very dangerous." I thought suddenly that he was breaking it to me that Dick was killed. "Give me the telegram. Where is he hurt?" "The head. Dangerously." I was in the dining-room by this time; Mrs M was sitting on a chair; she got up and kissed me and I thought to myself – the skull; probably he's dead now. And tried to remember about the respiratory centre and the vagus – suddenly all reality was sucked away from things and there was no way of telling whether I was dreaming or not. "Let me tell Boy," I said, but Mr M went to tell him leaving me and Mrs M in the dining room: I still had the tune of one of the songs tinkling somewhere back in my mind; but the rest was completely a dream. I wanted Boy very badly. Mrs M was crying; she was all shrunk up and her emotion was catching at mine and breaking down my self-control. I looked at the telegram – dangerously ill – they wouldn't say that unless it was very bad indeed . . . Mr M came in, he was looking very old and both of them almost hopeless . . . I thought I should never see Dick again . . . Boy came in, and he was very calm and strong, but a little white and already thinking what to do . . . I felt very sick and clutched at the edge of the table and choked . . . I was being shaken by the certainty that Dick was dead; every few minutes I felt that suddenly and bit my hand but couldn't stop myself crying . . . the day went by and I can't remember exactly, only some things isolated . . . Boy alone with me in the dining-room when the crest of one of these waves of fear and longing for Dick caught me and I clutched at his arm with both hands and he was so perfectly and splendidly sane and spoke fairly sharply like cold water . . . and the queer feeling that I was acting and must do the thing expected of me in my part . . . '

Then there were all the arrangements to make and clearly I became reasonably calm and efficient and annoyed at the general assumption that I must be looked after. The night before we left, ' I dreamt that it would be all right and woke wondering whether that would be a good sign.' Good bye to Jack and would I see him again before the end of the War – or then? We went down to Folkestone in a Pullman car – I for the first time – then embarkation, 'beautifully smoothly worked'. I looked about me.

'The lower deck of the boat was thick with soldiers, sitting or standing about, with their equipment and a haversack full of things. On the upper deck were officers – a lot of red tabs, and some French, sitting on ship's chairs, and a few like us, civvies, anxious looking. Everyone wore life belts, uncomfortable as they could be, but looking less stupid over khaki than over mufti . . . We started in half an hour or so, with a faint and not inspiring burst of cheering. A little spray came onto the decks; below a few of the men were singing *Michigan* and *Tipperary* spasmodically and with no great heart . . . I had recovered my *aequanimitas*, saying to myself: we shall find Dick better; in a little I shall be laughing at my fear now and wishing I had known that it was going to be all right, so as to be able to enjoy this crossing; therefore let me enjoy it now. I was also saying: if Dick is dead, what shall I do? I must have some plan; I think I shall take Greats or be a doctor . . . But still I was a little stunned and the clock of reality seemed to have stopped twenty hours before.

At Boulogne Dick's poor father fussed and tried to hurry things 'which was of course no earthly use. There was a crowd of RAMC people, a sturdy little woman, a canteen worker, very much pleased with her khaki, a tall, gaunt lady in black, dishevelled from the voyage, also trying to hurry her papers through . . . It was all very simple though; our things were not even looked at in the *douane*; an officer herded us through; we went off to a hotel in a car, Mr M hurrying me on when I wanted to change my money and then being late himself.'

By that time I had made friends with Mrs Johnstone, the dishevelled lady in black, whose boy was wounded in the leg and arm in hospital at Abbeville; she lent me a motor veil; one needed them in those days. Lunch was served by VADs in uniform – no doubt older than me, as one wasn't allowed out of the country until at least over twenty. The RAMC captain saw us into an official car and off we went through the cobbled streets of Boulogne, past a sentry onto a road with barley growing at each side, while the lady with the wounded son and I talked together, finding we were fellow Scots; the son was only twenty-one.

'I thought the harvest seemed very thin and poor; there were few boundaries and cattle grazed tethered . . . sometimes a girl, straight bodiced and barefoot, driving a cow; a few gleaners, old men and women, each with a ragged bundle of corn . . . villages with straggling houses, painted white or blue and usually an *estaminet* with the French soldiers in their pretty and unfamiliar horizon blue standing about. Along one stretch every village was full of zouaves, bronzed and handsome people with red fezes and baggy knickerbockers, who grinned at us as we went past bumping on the *pavé*, hooting wildly before corners . . .'

For we were driving at the unprecedented pace of fifty miles an hour with the wind beating and booming in our faces and ears.

After two tyre bursts, and my admiration for the RAMC chauffeur who changed wheels so quickly, we got to Abbeville and found the hospital where Mrs Johnstone's boy was, and waited.

'After a time the chauffeur came out saying, "That lady's had bad news; they say her son won't live." It depressed Mr M visibly but I thought it might be the natural delight in horrors – even after two years in France at war – of that class. And so it was, for after a long time she came out, more than ever dishevelled with her eyes bright, but saying he might have to have a leg off but would live. We left her things at the YMCA building in a little courtyard . . . It came on to rain, torrents all in a minute beating along the streets . . . we put up our canvas hood; I noticed how very many house pipes leaked.'

But by now I was worrying and wondering as we got nearer Le Tréport. I had

'. . . a picture in my mind: a long ward, just getting dark, a few yellowish lights along the walls, the evening grey

outside; rows of white beds, a grave sister; red screens
and two round one bed; inside a little light, on the pillow
a head bandaged; eyes shut; perhaps a little muttering or a
vague toss about of hands, not conscious life. I elaborate
the picture; put in a basin or two on a locker by the bed –
ice in a flannel bag – hear myself ask the sister how it goes
– the watch through the night –'

About this time I began taking omens from the magpies in
the fields. But Dick's father had no such irrational consolation.
We got to Le Tréport and I put down every detail of the
place. 'Suddenly I feel very Queer.' We pulled up in front
of the hospital, I jumped out and ran up the steps, asking
the cheerful-looking RAMC sentry for Lieutenant Mitchison
– Queen's Bays. 'Surely he would have known if there had
been a death among the officers.' Then the doctor came, quite
young, nice-looking, speaking to Mr Mitchison who seemed
more upset than ever and couldn't speak. 'How is he?' I said.
'You are the wife, aren't you?' I nodded. He explained that Dick
was slightly better, but the condition was still very dangerous.
We went up three flights of white stone stairs, which I was to
know very well. The hospital had been a grand hotel, as I write
later 'the sort of hotel one has never been to oneself, bathrooms
to every bedroom and landings one could dance on'.

'I wait outside, while Sister goes in, leaving the door ajar.
Suddenly a voice, so strong and familiar I can hardly
believe it. "What, my wife? Bring her in at once, Sister."
I go in. It is a small white cheerful room, a bed with a
silk quilt. Dick, looking very well and normal, but for a
very unshaved chin: "Hullo Nou!" Sister leaves us for a
few minutes. I try not to talk or let him but he, talking
rather too loud, asks questions, is very cheerful, moves
his head about, is sorry he is such a wretched sight but
he can't get his shaving things. There is a slight smell of
paraldehyde . . .'

After that his father and I settled into the Hotel des Bains,

'a quaint place with a twisty stair . . . my room is small but
has three windows that swing open like doors. One looks

towards the *place* and the harbour with grey-sailed fishing boats, the other two on to a narrow street, very crowded in the evenings with poilus and their girls. I expect Mr M is writing letters in the salon or reading the Continental *Daily Mail* – a bad paper but with good news. His letters take three times as long to write as mine.'

At this point, we were going up to the hospital twice a day though only I was allowed in.

'I see him every day for an hour or two . . . his head aches of course, very badly . . . I think it's a great pity they don't tell him more; as it is he is always trying to get up, even when I am there, and when I prevent him calls me all kinds of stupid fool, which I'm sure I am, but not for that. Mostly he is quite sensible, and even when delirious very rational, arranging a dinner party, talking about the Signal Troop or leave; he even wrote out a telegram to the Paris Hotel . . . The usual thing is five minutes normal though in pain, talking sensibly and not very restless; then a few minutes while the pain comes on, very restless,, perhaps trying to get up, with his body and arms rigid, mouth open and eyes shut, cursing his headache or complaining of the pain, calling on himself to stop it, and then five minutes lying back, quite exhausted, often with one arm thrown over his forehead . . . His date memory has stopped the day of the accident; sometimes he asks how old I am . . . hearing all right, though eyes are not yet.'

I give a run–down on the doctors, who sound efficient and on the whole cheering, but my real praise is for Sister Holbeach, charming and sympathetic, 'not un-necessarily professional . . . as becomes a nurse, optimist'. I had told her about my nursing experience at St Thomas's and she said that she had spoken to Matron and I would be allowed to nurse Dick more of the time. What I don't say in the diary, and yet now I remember most vividly, is that, at the first interview, the doctor said he would probably not live, but conceded that he was in very good condition and might recover. I know I dug my toes in about this; it was just not going to happen; that is why I didn't put it into the diary. When it didn't happen I was told that he would probably never recover intellectually and might live in a somewhat crippled condition. I expect they were quite sorry for this eighteen-year-old, faced with a life sentence of this kind. But again, I refused to believe it and that is why it isn't in the diary. I was fighting to win, as Janet fought for Tam Lin.

Meanwhile I was taking in Le Tréport. By this time I was reasonably fluent in French, and, from looking at a notebook I kept for years with quotations in it, it is clear that I normally read quite a lot of French poetry. So now I looked about me:

'The blue French soldiers in the streets are slightly more untidy than their English *confrères* – a step nearer the battlefield – many of them wearing one or two medals. I never can tell the ranks apart. Some very fine horses . . . and there is khaki among the blue, officers mostly, either RAMC or from the regiments near here – come in mostly as far as I can see for a drink and a bath, possibly for a little distracting society . . . the ladies of the place are mostly bourgeoisie – a quantity of flappers, less obvious and more subtle than the same type at, say, Bournemouth . . . short skirts, bright coloured blouses and caps or veils tied over their hair.'

There were families staying at the hotel.

'A very nice French colonel with grey moustache and grey kind eyes; he has a boy of seventeen and one of about eight, delicate looking, both of them . . . a young mother and a charming little girl of five or six with masses of yellow hair, blue jersey and shorts and long bare legs . . . a good lady with hair in a tight knob who has a horrid snivelling son in a tight brown suit whom she is always looking after very carefully; I think French boys of that sort of age are particularly horrible. . . . at the *table d'hôte* a group of VADs in their blue caps, cheerful and English, sometimes a single lady in a velvet tamoshanter and a short coat edged with fur who looks incomplete without an officer . . . the hotel people are charming and friendly . . . but I find everybody's nice to me.'

We walked to the hospital every day through the middle of the market, and sometimes I bought a few flowers. There were

385 steps to the cliff top. 'We probably meet Mr and Mrs Sassoon, very Jewish, friendly and good folk, but somehow one cannot imagine her pearl necklace, which is probably extremely valuable, to be anything but rather a bad sham.' We filled in the day somehow; I read a lot of Guy de Maupassant at this time. But I daren't buy a copy of the *Vie Parisienne*, because Dick's father would be shocked. Clearly we get on dreadfully badly, and I realise that it is largely the generation gap, but that didn't help.

'He's very English (doesn't shake hands when I, as a Scot, would) and when some of Dick's superior officers came to find out how he was . . . he was very formal and a little nervous and, when one of Dick's Signal troop came to find out too, he tipped most adequately, but it was I who did the talking . . . I wonder how much I misjudge him and myself; it's partly shyness with him; I'm not shy in the same way.'

It was early September and sometimes there was a storm which made bathing more exciting. I bathed usually in the early mornings when there was no crowd and one could run down from the hotel.

'There are long flat shadows on sea and sand; the sun is bright but not hot and when one is knee-deep in the smooth grey water, rhythmically stirred by long slow ripples, it makes a pathway; but there is no one to go with. I have a comic French bathing-dress with scarlet trimmings and two blue anchors on the collar.'

There was shopping, trying to get some silk to make silk pyjamas for Dick. 'Sometime perhaps, I shall go into Eu, or walk along the beach to the rocks, but one wants someone to go with who will enjoy it in the same way.' But the days went by. Dick saw another specialist, Gordon Holmes and was said to be out of danger. But the fight had to go on and was sometimes curious.

'Today for instance he didn't even know me. In the morning he had a long talk with me, calling me Lindsay

– a Signalling Officer. I think he enjoyed it very much, for, by a curious coincidence, this Lindsay knew many people at Oxford, Willie for instance, and Joseph. He had known Heath [Heath had been killed earlier that year] and on his saying that he was the finest man he had known, he and Dick gripped hands. Dick also told him about his "missus" and her family and finally they shook hands and Lindsay went away promising to come back soon. A few minutes after, Dick called Sister to ask me to go to him, and when I was there told me what a nice man was this "Lindsay" – poor Lindsay who only existed for ten minutes. Then in the afternoon, after a sleep, Dick woke up to say that he was going off at once to East Hertford to contest the seat with Pemberton Billing. He sat up and was not put off long by my saying there was no need for him to go for a fortnight. Then, for I didn't want him to struggle to get up, I tried to make him remember where he was. "No," he said, "I'm in hospital at Bethnal Green; I must telephone to the other hospital; how did I get here? Please fetch my clothes, I must go to Hertford." I reminded him of who I was, but he was politely incredulous, a little surprised at my wearing his wife's rings. "Admit, nurse, that you have stolen them!" and utterly shocked – the picture of virtue! – at this strange nurse kissing him! "My good girl, I've never met you before; I quite like you, but I wish you'd go away." I couldn't stop him getting up, so I called the orderly and finally Sister who managed to quiet him, taking his orders about telephoning to Hertford with the greatest calm. Then, as she was going away, Dick remarked, "Oh Sister, will you please ask this nurse to go; I don't know her," implying that she wasn't a credit to any hospital. Exit me!'

Once we went up to the hospital and found a big convoy had come in and there was a correspondingly big evacuation of patients well enough to go back to Blighty.

'We found all the back part of the hall covered with stretchers, on each an officer in a brown blanket, a woolly cap, and labelled. Most of the MOs were there, giving orders, looking at the labels, bending over to talk to their

patients. The Sassoon boy was there, also Major Cripps.
A long string of ambulances, all driven by women, came
up to the door, one by one. The first row was picked
up one after another, two orderlies to a stretcher, with
sometimes a man in front shifted so that they could get
one out from behind, like a great game of patience. It all
went wonderfully smoothly . . . The next day the Sassons
and Miss Cripps left, which I'm sorry for. We used to see
the Sassoons every day up at the hospital . . . once I went
in to see the boy – a typical young Eton Jew, who will
probably get on in the world very well.'

But could this have been Siegfried?
I had gone swimming and walking with Miss Cripps; we said
'*bon soir*' but disengaged ourselves from the poilus. Often there
were a few officers in for two-day leave from the division near
us.

'Two evenings ago, after dinner in the salon, Mr M was
reading, I was playing patience. We heard three or four
officers come in and begin talking to Madame . . . they
wanted to know about bathing; then they began to talk
to one another about some particular incident at Delville
Wood. Finally I chucked my patience, got up and said I was
going to give them chocolates; Mr M seemed somewhat
surprised and said it would embarrass them. However I ran
upstairs and came down with my chocolates and offered
them; they were really pleased and began talking to me,
all at once, and before Mr M came out of the salon – very
shy – I knew their names and some of their histories, where
they'd come from, what they'd been doing, and how very
particularly pleased they were to get back to real dinners
and beds and bathing . . . They were KSLI 5th Battalion
. . . Last night about half a dozen came into the salon
and started a conversation as soon as they possibly could.
They were awful TGs[1] mostly, but they'd just come from
fighting the Boche in Delville Wood . . . we had a long talk
about Syndicalism . . .'

[1] Temporary Gentlemen – who remembers that bit of class-slang?

244 IN FLANDERS FIELDS

Another was an Australian ranker, who told me about holding a trench for thirty hours in an advanced position; he was recommended for the Military Cross.

I try to type them.

'They're all conscientious fatalists and they all try to talk about England or after the war, but always after a little you get back to shop. There was a Major and several others, also a nice little Canadian doctor up at the Hospital, whom we had seen several times before, and he was quite drunk; I think he often is: not a good thing for a doctor . . . Here am I, sitting on a table in the middle of the stuffy salon of a third-rate French hotel, being as charming as I can to an audience of TGs, all to give them the memory of a pleasant evening to take back to the trenches by Givenchy; that's why I wear pretty frocks and hats and do my hair just not anyhow, but to look nice; it's probably as much worth doing now as it ever will be again in my life. I would give a lot to be able to sing.'

At this time another specialist, Meyers, saw Dick, said he was to go to Netley Hospital, where most people with brain damage went, and apparently thought that ultimate mental recovery was only a matter of time. But, as I write, 'It's certainly rather disconcerting that he's still just as bad mentally.' I describe another incident:

'He gets violently angry with both me and the orderly when we stop him, calling us both dirty cads and damned liars; he also hits out like anything, and when the orderly has gone reproaches me bitterly for having called him, saying it's the sort of low thing I would do and often, which of course is the best thing, turning over and being offended till he falls asleep. But often I leave him to the orderly, particularly when he says *"Enlevez cette femme là, c'est la mienne, mais enlevez la."* And then as a parting shot when I'm going out "I don't ever want to see you again." He forgets all about it by next time, but I'm so afraid it will stay in some sort of distorted image in his subconscious memory. Yesterday morning he told me how the doctors

and orderlies had lured him to an opium den and nearly
killed him, but how he had fought them all.'

Clearly this was fairly exhausting, especially as one could not
be quite certain about ultimate recovery. But I had a last evening
with two VAD nurses, Miss Duval and Miss Tozer.

'We went off in a car to the Forêt d'Eu . . . the most
lovely evening . . . the Forêt still full of wild flowers
and very green . . . long stretches of slim tall beech trees,
sudden rises among birch and chestnut with a steep white
bank at the roadside, trailed over with honeysuckle, small
roads under an arch of beeches and a deer leaping across,
a clearing with a reaped cornfield and back through high
woods of straight thin trees and the pink sunset blinking
behind the stems like jewels. I don't know whether they
were lovelier when it was growing dark or before, when
you get broken patches of sunlight lying across the road
and clear, sudden greens, almost spring-like. We stopped
at a little farm, in the middle of the wood like a fairy tale,
a square court-yard, an orchard of apple trees covered with
small red fruit and the forest closing in all round. In the
quiet of the wood we heard twigs snapping, a bird, a dog
far off, and then listening closer, every few seconds a thud,
less sound than vibration, as if the earth were snorting a
long way under, and that is the guns. When the wind is
right they are quite loud and on dark nights they see, from
the hospital, the horizon all lit with flashes.
'We had a perfect French dinner, omelette, chicken,
haricot beans stewed in milk, cider, jelly and cream and
bowls of thick soft coffee. And we all told one another our
life histories and made friends and deplored the badness of
a girl's schooling and how hard it is for her to make her way
to any really educated work. Both the girls are scientists
. . . it seems an awful waste that they should be VADs
here in the position of privates under sisters who may or
may not be nice, but anyhow discourage questioning and
are very jealous. No chance of rising from the ranks or
learning any more than they know now. They work for a
twelve and a half hours' day, with three hours off and short
meal times; once in two months a week's leave. They're

both going to chuck it when their terms are up and I think they'll be quite right.

'They were telling me one thing which must be particularly annoying to Miss Tozer, who was doing brain research before the war – that there are any amount of splendid head cases here which die, and it would be the chance of a century if there was anyone here to note symptoms and do a PM. Of course if she were to suggest such a thing – which she could probably do perfectly – the authorities would first faint and then kick her out. But it is stupid.'

So there was the magic again, but also the proper concern of the scientist. Miss Tozer, Miss Tozer, what happened to you? I looked you up in *Who's Who* just in case, but as we agreed, it is so hard for a girl to get up to the top – if that *is* the top.

We left the next day. There had been no more forty-eight hour leave people. But plenty of rumours. I add, 'Poor old Dick will be sick if the cavalry, as seems likely, get through in three weeks.' So, apparently, we thought!

There the pencil diary ends, with only a few more guilt feelings about my father-in-law. Typically, I never managed to arrive at what to call either him or Dick's mother. I couldn't think of them as parents and they were the wrong generation for first names.

So there we were, waiting very anxiously in London, where it had somehow been arranged that, before going to Netley, Dick should come to the Clock House hospital. It seems odd that these private arrangements could have been not only possible, but were not disapproved of. One only asks oneself whether the treatment of wounded officers was very different from that given to ordinary private soldiers. That wasn't a question I had asked, so far. One took certain things for granted. But Dick's parents and I were all in a rather agitated state, totally unsure of how he would be.

But something very odd had happened. For three weeks Dick had been in a strange country, usually in a hurry with something important he had to do. Sometimes he met people he knew, but often he was alone, or chased by non-human entities. Then he was on a boat in mid-channel and there were creatures crawling about the decks, sea snakes and whatnot. Then 'something clicked', and he was back in the ordinary world, gradually realising where he was and why. And that was how he was when he came to us in London, very weak, but himself. He never quite recovered his sense of smell, though this is never strong with fairly heavy smokers as he was. But smell is supposed to come into taste, especially of wine, and this never left him. And quite soon he stopped being able to draw maps of the strange country.

(*from* All Change Here)

John Reith
1889–1971

John Charles Walsham Reith, the founding father of the BBC, was born in Stonehaven and educated at Glasgow Academy and Gresham's School, Norfolk. While training to be an engineer he enlisted in the Territorial Army and was commissioned into the 5th Scottish Rifles in 1911. At the outbreak of the war he was appointed the battalion's transport officer and crossed with them to France for service on the Western Front. Reith's prickly temperament led to quarrels with his commanding officer and adjutant on matters of discipline and dress – he insisted on wearing the wrong colour of shirt and ate in the sergeants mess – and shortly before the Battle of Loos in September 1915 he was transferred to the Royal Engineers. While serving with 1/2nd Highland Field Company RE he was badly wounded in the face and jaw. After convalescing Reith was put in charge of a new rifle factory near Philadelphia in the United States and between May 1918 and April 1919 he worked on an Admiralty project establishing a hydro-electric submarine barrage in the English Channel. Reith wrote his war memoirs during a three-week spell in 1937 but his friends warned him against publication, fearing that his outspoken views would prejudice his public position. Toned down, they were published a few years before his death.

Source: Lord Reith, *Wearing Spurs*, London: Hutchinson, 1966

Heaven Can Wait

O ur kits had turned up, and next morning after a few hours'
sleep I got into smart clothes for the first time, including
the light shirt and collar which had caused so much commotion
earlier, and very light coloured riding breeches. I went along to
visit the 5th SR, taking care that I was observed by the CO
and Adjutant, but of course without speaking to them. The 5th
had had no officer casualties and very few in the ranks. Then,
borrowing a horse from a friendly gunner, I rode for two and a
half miles to where the 5th SR Transport was quartered. What
a joy this was – to see Bob Wallace and all my old friends.

The same afternoon the Field Company moved to Cuinchy
and there, in 7 Harley Street, the officers were given quite
a comfortable billet about one thousand two hundred yards
behind the front line. The top storey had been shelled away
but on the ground floor we had a dining-room and three or
four rooms to sleep in. I discovered that these sappers had no
inconsiderable capacity for making themselves comfortable; we
all had, for instance, home-made beds to sleep on.

At 9 p.m. I went up with a complete section of the company
and the hundred attached infantry to wire along the Wiltshire
front – 58th Brigade. This was the nastiest job I had been on;
it was by the Cuinchy brickstacks and there was a great deal
of shelling and sniping. The infantry were in a rather unhappy
state and, with no wire in front of them to speak of and no
immediately visible means of support, one could not wonder.
We certainly gave them good entanglements and their officers
were very grateful. I was pleased with myself that night. This
was RE work, and we had made a whole Battalion happy –
anyhow much less unhappy than they had been. I made another
unwitting score; while superintending the erection of the barbed
wire I was suddenly 'taken short'. I had forgotten to take my
usual dose of chlorodine that morning – necessary since my
feat with the manure water. Instead of going back to the trench
and enquiring if they had a latrine handy, I went about twenty
yards further out into No Man's Land. I was not conscious of
doing anything foolhardy; as a matter of fact I did not know
if the Germans were a hundred or a thousand yards off. But it
was general knowledge in the Field Company next day. I got

in about 1.30a.m. and found the major waiting up. All that I record is: 'I had a very funny scene with him.' To my joy a mail had arrived – the first letters I had had.

When I rose next morning there was a roaring fire in the dining room. Eggs and bacon and toast all piping hot were brought in for me from the back regions. The other officers came later. This was going to be a good life; I thought I might get on all right with the major when he had gotten accustomed to me. In the evening I had a similar task to that of the night before – this time for the Cheshires; but it was much livelier. To their relief I sent the infantry carrying party home as soon as they had deposited their loads by the front line. There was no doubt about the proximity of the enemy lines on this occasion. Two trench mortars added to the general discomfort, and a little further along, where we had been working the previous night, it was reported that an aerial torpedo had buried a whole platoon. We saw it land; a fearsome instrument of war. I was glad when this job of work was satisfactorily completed. My sappers were excellent fellows; but it makes a lot of difference to men's form on a hazardous task like this on which side of the wire their officer stands or walks in the course of his supervision. There were some particularly vulnerable bits on this Cheshire front so I said we would bring them up ten big *chevaux de frise* next night. These creations were too bulky to be carried conveniently along communication trenches, so I made a survey of the ground for an overland route and we had no casualties and much less bother. The weather was bad; I asked my mother to get my big war umbrella sent out.

At one in the morning I was awakened by a terrific fusillade; the captain came into my room to ask what I thought should be done. It certainly sounded as if the Germans were coming through but there was nothing we could do – except to go to sleep again. We had our horses up next morning and the captain and I rode to our Transport about three miles back. I told him about Sailaway and he said she must be fetched at once; he would tell the major about it. In the afternoon I took some men to repair the bridge over the La Bassée canal by Cuinchy station – to strengthen it up for heavier traffic than it could previously carry. It had been shelled, and there was little of it left. This was a real RE job of work. In the evening I took up more gear to the Cheshires and on returning to the billet finished my record of the day: 'I am feeling in fine form and really enjoying life thoroughly'. The captain woke me up at 3.00a.m. to hear shells arriving close by. But what is the point of listening to shells; I went to sleep again. Next morning came an official communication from Irwin stating that 'the bay mare belonging to you has now recovered and is ready to be moved'. The captain had found the major unexpectedly and unreasonably opposed to my sending for her; he had argued him round and we made arrangements to despatch a corporal and a man to fetch her from Hamhock just north of Poperinghe where the mobile section now was. We worked out distances on the map; they were to start two days later, October 7th and I notified Irwin accordingly. They never started at all.

October 5th and 6th passed in normal fashion. In a letter to my mother on the morning of the 6th I told her of the forthcoming joyous reunion with Sailaway. 'This is a tremendously interesting life', I wrote, 'and I am very well and very happy.' To my father that night I wrote (No 20 since returning to France) that another officer had turned up making us one over strength with five subalterns; I had clearly been sent to the wrong Field Company. (Later it turned out that the 2/2nd had been expecting me.) I told him the RE knew how to live comfortably; that I was in excellent health and thoroughly enjoying myself; I had been out most of every night since I came, and was going out again tonight; I would finish the letter in the morning.

The major was, as expected, changing his attitude to me. He told me he had been hearing all sorts of stories about what I did on wiring jobs, and that the men were talking about it. He asked me if I were never afraid. It was he who, in a sense, finished the letter to my father. I was 'a most charming fellow and a most excellent officer'. And three weeks later he wrote me: 'I can understand your being very angry as you were so very keen on the work. I know I have lost an exceedingly good officer and one who in a short time had inspired great confidence in the men. I could *well* do with you again. I regret only the little unpleasantness of our beginning owing to misunderstanding on my part. We could have got on very well together and I shall try hard to get you back. I can still hear your voice: "Is the major there?" You made me feel like your father and I could do so little. I don't mind telling you that it took me days to get over it all.'

My next direct communication home was a telegram from Wimereux hospital; it was sent on October 10th: 'Crossing tonight. Doing well but angry. John.' And I managed to write a letter that day: 'I'm more disgusted than I can say. I was getting on so well and enjoying the work and everything. Of course it was a narrow shave and they tell me I am very lucky. I'm very hungry as I can't open my mouth to eat anything. And I've spoilt my best uniform.'

Five days later I wrote from a London hospital. On arrival they had said I was likely to stay for about two months and had talked about silver plates and graftings and all sorts of awful things; but later had decided that nothing was required at all and that the wound healed as they watched it. This is what I wrote to my father: 'I very much want to go back to the Front and as quickly as possible. A good staff job *might* keep me at home if sufficiently busy and with real responsibility. But I'm not at all sure. I really want to go to France again.'

They had had a shock at home, of course: an official telegram that I was badly wounded had arrived just as my father was leaving the house to speak at some big public meeting; days of anxious waiting. They both wanted to come to London but I telegraphed that it was quite unnecessary and that I should soon be home. My sister, who had deplored being unable to fight herself or even do the nurse's work for which she was so well qualified, wrote that she wished she could look after me herself; no one would do it so well; she was about to undergo a serious operation.

My father had also received a letter from the Deputy Chaplain General who had come upon me lying on a stretcher on the floor of a school house – a thorough bad looking case, head bandaged and only one eye showing. This eye was open so he knelt on the floor and asked if I was in much pain. 'I'm very angry,' I whispered back, 'and I've spoilt a new tunic.' He turned to his ADC; it was obviously a case of delirium. 'Dr Sims,' I said, 'I should be very grateful if you would write to my father and tell him I'm all right. Dr Reith of Glasgow.' He duly wrote, repeating the answer I had given to his first enquiry.

As a matter of fact I was in some pain – despite a heavy injection of morphia – and had lost an appalling amount of blood. Eventually a stretcher had come along and I had been lifted on to it; but the trench was narrow and twisting and I

was very long. To the amazement of those in attendance I had
called to them to stop and put me down; I had then walked for
about half a mile, but when we came to an overhead trolley
arrangement I was glad to get back on the stretcher. At an
underground dressing station the doctor was surprised that I was
conscious. A second or two later I was sorry myself for, with a
wound on the side of one's face five inches by three inches, the
application of iodine with a swab brush is harrowing. He was a
kind doctor and there was a kind RAMC sergeant whose hand
I must have hurt as I held it during the iodine applications.

At the Field Ambulance they found other wounds but they
were not serious. Proper dressings were put on and I was told
that that would be the end of the war for me. I enquired why.
Apart from anything else, the Doctor asked, could I see out of
my left eye. Yes I could. I asked if I should have a mark on my
face. 'A mark!' he said. It was he who told me the size of it; and a
good bit of the bone shot away. How odd, I reflected, that I shall
look different from now on. I lay on the floor for two hours and
by the time I got to Choques in a motor ambulance I was very
cold. They put three hot bottles in my bed; I was hungry but
for several days I could only take liquid food because I could not
open my mouth. This also was annoying. I gave them a surprise
by getting out of bed and saying I wanted to go 'round the
corner'. But that night I had my first and only war nightmare:
I was caught on the wire and the Germans had a searchlight and
a machine-gun trained on me.

And this was how it happened – completely banal. I had had a
hard time of it and had gone to bed in the early hours of October
7th. I would have the next morning off and ride back to my old
Transport. I got up about 9a.m., had a lovely hot bath in a tub
and dressed in my best tunic and riding breeches and light shirt
and generally felt that all was very well indeed. I breakfasted
alone with the major 'who by this time seems to have a high
opinion of me and to like to have me around.' To my surprise
he announced that he thought of going up the line to look at
some redoubts. I thought he would see a lot more if I went with
him than if he went alone, and there were more important things
than redoubts to look at. I had heard that a mine had blown up
and I might as well see the damage with a view to making it good
that night. I said I would come too and he was very pleased. Of
course I should have changed into trench-going uniform but did

not. I realised that, rigged as I was, I was pretty conspicuous, but I could not be bothered changing. I registered a determination not to get dirty, however. There was a jam in the narrow and deep communication trench so I climbed up and walked overground, inviting him to do likewise. He stayed where he was pushing his way slowly past the outgoing troops; when he was clear of them I jumped down again. Presently we came to the front line and I enquired where the mine trouble was: a hundred yards or so along to the right. There was plenty of work to be done; the trench was in an awful state, the parapet in several places being blown away. There seemed to be few troops about and the German line was close at this part. And now the mine explosion was round the next traverse. I was very interested and was pushing on ahead of the major.

One evening when walking past the cricket nets at school, I was hit on the side of the head by a straight drive down the pitch over the bowler's head. But that was not the explanation of the singing in my ears and the crack on the head I had just received. The Germans wouldn't heave a cricket ball at me. What could it be? *Blast it*, I've been hit. I wonder what by. Couldn't have been a shell as there was no explosion. Must have been a bullet. *Damnation*, look at the blood pouring down on to my new tunic. I've been hit in the head. Has it gone through and smashed up my teeth. No, they were all there. Was the bullet in my head? If so this was the end. Meantime I had better lie down. Apart from anything else I was standing in exposed ground and if hit once could be hit again and there was no point in that. It would be nice to have a few minutes to collect myself. I stepped back a pace or two behind the parapet and lay down. I suppose this had occupied in all about four seconds, but the processes of thought and action were definite and sequential. I became aware of other people. A Wiltshire sergeant appeared; I heard him say something about a sniper in a brickstack forty yards away. He lifted up the skirt of my tunic to get my 'first field dressing'. Of course I had none on my good tunic and told him so. He was very agitated. (I wonder if he is still alive?) He tore off his own and tied it round my head but it did not seem to stop the flow of blood. I was looking straight up into the clear and cloudless blue of the sky. 'Is the major there?' I said. 'Here I am, Reith,' he replied in a trembling voice. 'Can you give me a bit of paper?' It was the Wiltshire sergeant who tore a sheet from

a little notebook and handed it to me. I got out my fountain pen
and in a very shaky hand wrote my mother's name and address,
and then: 'I'm all right.' I did not mean what the words would
obviously first suggest. But no one with such a wound as I had
would be so silly as to suggest he was 'all right' in the ordinary
sense. I hesitated and nearly wrote the few additional words
which would have made it clear; but I was sure my father and
mother would see in the message what I meant them to see. 'Can
you read it?' I asked the Wiltshire sergeant, for I could hardly see
it myself. He read it out. Then I thought I might write in Latin
the message I really wanted to send; but I let it go. I was tired
and wanted to look up at the sky again. The opening lines of a
children's hymn came to mind:

> 'Above the clear blue sky
> In Heaven's bright abode . . .'

Well, very soon now the supreme mystery would be solved, I
was completely content and at peace. All was well . . ..

I heard the Wiltshire sergeant say that I had another wound
in my shoulder. Oh had I indeed. Well, as I was facing in the
direction from which the bullet had come it couldn't have hit
my shoulder first. So it wasn't my head, and all this soliloquising
about Heaven was premature. I wasn't going to die. I was only
badly wounded. I felt rather foolish. And then very angry. I was
so happy; I had only had three weeks of the RE after all the fuss
to get there. But in after years I have often wished that I could
contemplate the blue of eternity with such equanimity as then.

(*from* Wearing Spurs)

David Rorie
1867–1946

David Rorie was born of Aberdeenshire parents in Edinburgh where he trained to be a doctor. After graduating he worked for a time as a medical officer at the Bowhill Colliery in Fife where he developed a life-long interest in folk culture. In 1905 he returned to his native north-east of Scotland to become a general practitioner in Cults on Lower Deeside where he was to remain for the rest of his life. Although he was 47 at the time, he enlisted at the outbreak of war and served with the Field Ambulance, RAMC, attached to the 51st (Highland) Division. A field ambulance was responsible for collecting, treating and evacuating casualties and Rorie was to say of the men under his command that, 'none was stouter-hearted than the stretcher-bearer; none carried out his job more steadily and efficiently during the campaign.' After the war Rorie continued his interest in military matters by becoming President of the Aberdeen Branch of the Royal British Legion. He also started writing poems in Scots, of which 'The Lum Hat wantin' the Croon' is the best known. The extract from his war memoirs describes the aftermath of the 51st (Highland) Division's successful assault on the Beaumont Hamel Ridge in November 1916.

Source: David Rorie, *A Medico's Luck in the War*, Aberdeen: Milne and Hutchison, 1929

The Pity of War

*The attack on the Beaumont Hamel Ridge on 13 November 1916
was the last great battle of the Somme which had begun four-and-a-half
months earlier. Most of the men who took part in it were New Army –
Kitchener battalions, Territorials and troops from Canada, Australia,
New Zealand, India and South Africa. Amongst their number were
men of the 51st (Highland) Division which had been assessed by
German military intelligence as the most formidable formation in the
British Army. Four days later, after some fierce hand-to-hand fighting,
the Scots had taken the heavily defended German positions in Y ravine
below the ridge. They suffered 2,200 casualties. In the aftermath of
battles fought during the First World War RAMC personnel of the
Field Ambulances treated both German and British casualties.*

A nd now came the inevitable stage of clearing up the
battlefield and searching all possible places where wounded,
either British or Boche, who had not been picked up in the actual
battle, might have sought shelter. At daybreak an MO and a
party were sent to work from Y Ravine towards White City;
while another party, including two Jocks with rifles (as the
dug-outs with which Beaumont Hamel was tunnelled were not
yet clear of whole-skinned Huns), worked across to meet him, an
officer of the 6th Seaforths acting as guide. A further object was
to search for a wonderful legendary underground Hun dressing
station of the Arabian Nights variety, which, incidentally, we
failed to locate.

It was drizzling wet and vilely cold, the trenches in places
thigh deep in clay and an awful mess of smashed barbed wire,
mud, disintegrated German dead and debris of all sorts. In one
trench our occupation for half an hour was hauling each other
out of the tenacious and bloodstained mud; and during our
mutual salvage operations we had evidently made ourselves too
visible, as the enemy started shelling. There was nothing for it
but to take to the open and make for another trench, which we
promptly did: doing a hundred yards in rather good time.

Now, the Jocks and I were of the Julius Caesar, Napoleon and
Lord Roberts type of physique, while our guide was a tall man,
whose greatcoat – which for some obscure reason he had put on

before starting – blew out as he led us, doubled up on account of the *phut-phut* of bullets, across the open; and it struck me with a great feeling of irritation as we ran that we must be providing excellent comic effect for any of the enemy observing us through glasses, by suggesting an alarmed hen and three chickens on the run. (I had the opportunity of being in a gunner's OP, near Cambrai in 1918 and seeing four Germans doing a sprint under similar conditions. For once I felt a definite kinship to the Hun; I, too, had been at the wrong end of the telescope.) In the next trench we again set about searching the dug-outs and placarding them, to catch the eye of the stretcher-bearers who would follow, as containing so many wounded for removal; but again the Hun gunners got on to us in an exposed place and we had a second sprint across the open for another trench, where we had to stay below in a *sous-terrain* for an hour till things got quieter.

This dug-out was typical of the many with which Beaumont Hamel was honeycombed. On descending about forty steps one was in a large floored and timbered chamber some fifty feet long; and at the further end a second set of steps led to a similar chamber, one side of each being lined with a double layer of bunks filled with dead and wounded Germans, the majority of whom had become casualties early on the morning of the 13th.

The place was, of course, in utter darkness; and, when we flashed our lights on and the wounded saw our escort with rifles ready, there was an outbreak of '*Kamarad!*' while a big bevy of rats squeaked and scuttled away from their feast on the dead bodies on the floor. The stench was indescribably abominable: for many of the cases were gas-gangrenous. Any food or drink they had possessed was used up, and our water bottles were soon emptied amongst them. After we had gone over the upper chamber and separated the living from the dead, we went to the lower one where the gas curtain was let down and fastened. Tearing it aside and going through with a light, I got a momentary jump when I caught a glimpse in the upper bunk of a man, naked to the waist, and with his right hand raised above his head. But the poor beggar was far past mischief – stark and stiff with a smashed pelvis. Some twenty other dead Germans lay about, at the disposal of the rat hordes. The romance of war had worn somewhat thin here.

When the shelling had eased up and we quitted the place, the wounded firmly believed they were being left for good; although we had repeatedly assured them that in a short time they would all be taken to hospital. But to the end of the campaign the wounded Boche could never understand that he was not going to be treated with the same brutality as he had meted out to others at the outset of war; so it was amidst a chorus of shrieks, wails and supplications that we made for the welcome open air, ticketed the dug-out as containing fourteen wounded for removal, and renewed our search in similar surroundings for fresh casualties.

One other memory of Beaumont Hamel is still vivid. Parallel to Wagon Road, and on its Auchonvillers side, ran a *chemin creux* in which were several dug-outs where we – and the Division on our left – had Battalion RAP's. It had been severely shelled and the sides of the road had fallen in, reducing the cart track to a foot-path knee deep in mud. Going up it one morning soon after daybreak, I saw a headless corpse lying on a stretcher at the path side. From the neck a trickle of blood ran to the feet of a man outside a dug-out who was calmly frying some ham in his canteen lid over an improvised oil-can stove. His mate – fag in mouth – was watching him. What was beside them had ceased to be worth comment. They were surfeited with evil sights. And they were hungry.

On the 16th, Tenderloin in White City became our HQ for forward evacuation; and there with two MOs and a hundred and twenty bearers we stayed until the 19th, searching all possible locations in the field for any cases possibly missed, and clearing a large quantity of wounded for the Division on our left, who were stunting and whose RAPs could not be cleared without our help. All this time White City and the roads into Beaumont Hamel were distinctly unhealthy, and the weather was vile; while the atmosphere inside our dug-outs – one long chamber with over a hundred and twenty occupants – was almost palpable. A wash was an unknown luxury, of course; but though lousy we were cheerful – even tuneful at times, thanks to the corporal's penny whistle and a veteran gramophone – as our job was nearly done.

By the 22nd our unit had still twenty-four bearers in the RAPS at Beaumont Hamel, twenty-four at Tenderloin, thirty-six in reserve at Auchonvillers, and a tent sub-division at the ADS at Mailly-Maillet; while, in addition, we were running the MDS at Forceville, handed over to us by the 3rd HFA, which had left for Puchevillers; so our hands were fairly full. But, on the 23rd, we handed over, and started overhauling equipment in view of our next move.

What Field Ambulance officer does not recall overhauling equipment after a push? The counting of stretchers, blankets, wheeled carriers, etc., etc.; the exploring of Field Medical and Surgical panniers to check missing 'unexpendables'; and the inevitable and unanimous finding of all concerned that what couldn't be found had certainly been destroyed by shell-fire! However, on this occasion we had increased and multiplied exceedingly; for we came away from Beaumont Hamel outstandingly to the good in the essential matters of blankets, stretchers, and especially wheeled stretcher carriers; so that the soul of the ADMS rejoiced within him, until at the first DDMS conference he had to meet his suffering and blood-thirsty colleagues who had been on our right and left flanks.

Four days later we moved from Forceville to Senlis, and took over a set of hutments on top of a windswept hill above the village from a Canadian Field Ambulance, finding the place – to be quite honest – in a most unholy mess. He was a good man, the Canuck, right enough, and a 'bonny fechter': but he had a way of his own all through the campaign. Our advance party officer was taken round the show by a Canadian *confrère* (in shirt sleeves, breeches and gum-boots) who, on giving an order to a sergeant *en passant*, received the reply: –

'You go to ——, John!'

The officer's only comment was a grieved: –

'Well, now! He shouldn't say that, should he?' – and the matter apparently ended!

Here, then, we stayed for several uncomfortable cold and wet weeks while the Division was in the line at Courcelette; thence for some weeks of severe frost to the Buigny-St Maclou area near Abbeville, where we were not far from historic Crecy. Later, we were once more at the hutments of Haute Avesnes: and marched thence to Caucourt, on the other side of DHQ at Villers Chatel, to run a Divisional Rest Station and prepare the forward medical posts for the next push, the famous Vimy Ridge battle, where the 51st were on the right of the Canadians.

(*from* A Medico's Luck in the War)

Charles Hamilton Sorley
1895–1915

Sorley was an avid writer of letters and his correspondence, both before the war and during it, was collected for publication by his father. His other correspondents were two school friends Arthur Hopkinson and Alan Hutchinson, and Arthur Watts, a self-taught lecturer whom he had met in Jena. (See also p 118.)

Source: Charles Hamilton Sorley, *The Letters of Charles Sorley*, Cambridge: Cambridge University Press, 1919;
Hilda D. Spear (ed.): *The Poems and Selected Letters of Charles Hamilton Sorley*, Dundee; Blackness Press, 1978

Letters from an Infantry Officer

To: A. E. Hutchinson   10 (?) August 1914
                                        Cambridge

. . . Having proved my identity at home as distinct from the
gardener's, I investigated my (a–hem!) 'papers' and found, among
the old receipts for college clothes and such like, a lovely piece
of paper, which I daresay you have got too, which dismissed me
from the corps. Only mine had EXCELLENT written (in the
Major's hand) for my General Efficiency. Yours can have had,
at very most 'very good'. I took this down to a man of sorts
and said '*Mit Gott für Kaiser und Vaterland*, I mean *für König und
Mutterland*: what can I do to have some reasonable answer to give
to my acquaintances when they ask me "What are *you* doing?" ' He
looked me up and down and said, 'Send in for a commission in the
Territorials. You may get something there. You'll get an answer in
a fortnight's time, not before.' Compromise as usual. Not heroic
enough to do the really straight thing and join the regulars as a
Tommy, I have made a stupid compromise [with] my conscience
and applied for a commission in the Terriers where no new officers
are wanted. In a month's time I shall probably get the beastly thing:
and spend the next twelve months binding the corn, guarding
the bridges, frightening the birds away, and otherwise assisting
in Home Defence. So I think you were sensible to prefer your
last term at Marlborough. Only I wish you could come and join
the beastly battalion of Cambridgeshire clerks to which I shall be
tacked on: and we could sow the corn and think we were soldiers
together.

But isn't all this bloody? I am full of mute and burning rage and
annoyance and sulkiness about it. I could wager that out of twelve
million eventual combatants there aren't twelve who really want
it. And 'serving one's country' is so unpicturesque and unheroic
when it comes to the point. Spending a year in a beastly Territorial
camp guarding telegraph wires has nothing poetical about it: nor
very useful as far as I can see. Besides the Germans are so nice, but
I suppose the best thing that could happen to them would be their
defeat . . .

To: A. J. Hopkinson   October (?) 1914
                                              Shorncliffe

. . . The two great sins people impute to Germany are that
she says that might is right and bullies the little dogs. But I
don't think that she means might *qua* might is right, but that
confidence of superiority is right, and by superiority she means
spiritual superiority. She said to Belgium, 'We enlightened
thinkers see that it is necessary to the world that all opposition
to Deutsche Kultur should be crushed. As citizens of the world
you must assist us in our object and assert those higher ideas of
world-citizenship which are not bound by treaties. But if you
oppose us, we have one alternative.' That, at least, is what the
best of them would have said; only the diplomats put it rather
more brusquely. She was going on a missionary voyage with all
the zest of Faust –

> *Er wandle so den Erdentag entlang;*
> *Wenn Geister spuken, geh' er seinen Gang;*
> *Im Weiterschreiten find' er Qual und Glück,*
> *Er, unbefriedigt jeden Augenblick!*

– and missionaries know no law. As Uncle Alder says, her
Kultur (in its widest sense) is the best in the world: so she must
scatter it broadcast through the world perforce, saying like the
schoolmaster or the dentist 'though it hurts at present, it'll do
you no end of good afterwards'. (Perhaps she will even have to
add at the end of the war 'and it's hurt me more than it's hurt
you'.)
   So it seems to me that Germany's only fault (and I think
you often commented on it in those you met) is a lack of real
insight and sympathy with those who differ from her. We are
not fighting a bully, but a bigot. They are a young nation and
don't yet see that what they consider is being done for the good
of the world may be really being done for self-gratification – like
X who, under pretence of informing the form, dropped into
the habit of parading his own knowledge. X incidentally did
the form a service by creating great amusement for it, and so
is Germany incidentally doing the world a service (though not
in the way it meant) by giving them something to live and die
for, which no country but Germany had before. If the bigot

264 IN FLANDERS FIELDS

conquers he will learn in time his mistaken methods (for it is only of the methods and not of the goal of Germany that one can disapprove) – just as the early Christian bigots conquered by bigotry and grew larger in sympathy and tolerance after conquest. I regard the war as one between sisters, between Martha and Mary, the efficient and intolerant against the casual and sympathetic. Each side has a virtue for which it is fighting, and each that virtue's supplementary vice. And I hope that whatever the material result of the conflict, it will purge these two virtues of their vices, and efficiency and tolerance will no longer be incompatible.

But I think that tolerance is the larger virtue of the two, and efficiency must be her servant. So I am quite glad to fight this rebellious servant. In fact I look at it this way. Suppose my platoon were the world. Then my platoon-sergeant would represent efficiency and I would represent tolerance. And I always take the sternest measures to keep my platoon-sergeant in check! I fully appreciate the wisdom of the War Office when they put inefficient officers to rule sergeants . . ..

To: Mrs Sorley   March 1915
                                                      Aldershot

We are off for a wild game this weekend under the eyes of Kitchener. But going out still remains an uncertainty as to time, and has become a matter of the indifferent future to most of us. If we had gone out earlier we would have gone out with a thrill in poetic-martial vein: now most of us have become by habit soldiers, at least in so far that we take such things as a matter of course and a part of our day's work that our own anticipations can neither quicken nor delay.

I talked a lot (in her native tongue) to the hostess with whom I was billeted, and her sensible German attitude was like a cold bath. She saw the thing, as German *hausfraus* would, directly and humanly and righteously. Especially sensible was she in her remarks against the kind ladies who told her she ought to be proud and glad to give her sons to fight. After all, war in this century is inexcusable: and all parties engaged in it must take an equal share in the blame for its occurrence. If only the English from Grey downwards would cease from rubbing in that, in the days that set all the fuel ablaze, they worked for peace honestly and with all their hearts! We know they did; but in the past their lack of openness and trust in their diplomatic relationships helped to pile the fuel to which Germany applied the torch.

I do wish also that people would not deceive themselves by talk of a just war. There is no such thing as a just war. What we are doing is casting out Satan by Satan. When once war was declared the damage was done: and we, in whom that particular Satan was perhaps less strong than in our foes, had only one course, namely to cast out the far greater Satan by means of him: and he must be fought to the bitter end. But that doesn't alter the fact that long ago there should have been an understanding in Europe that any country that wanted *Weltmacht* might have it. The Allies may yet score a victory over Germany. But by last August they had thrown away their chances of a true victory. I remember you once on the Ellerby moors telling us the story of Bishop What's-his-name and John-Val-John from *Les Misérables*. And now, although we failed then of the highest, we might have fought, regarding the war – not, as we do regard it, as a candle to shed light upon our unselfishness and love of freedom, but – as a punishment for our past presumptuousness. We had the silver candlesticks and brandished them ever proudly as our own, won by our own valour. Germany must be crushed for her wicked and selfish aspiration to be mistress of the world: but the country that, when mistress of the world, failed to set her an example of unworldliness and renunciation should take to herself half the blame of the blood expended in the crushing.

To: Mrs Sorley
28 April 1915
Aldershot

I saw Rupert Brooke's death in *The Morning Post*. *The Morning Post*, which has always hitherto disapproved of him, is now loud in his praises because he has conformed to their stupid axiom of literary criticism that the only stuff of poetry is violent physical experience, by dying on active service. I think Brooke's earlier poems – especially notably 'The Fish' and 'Grantchester', which you can find in *Georgian Poetry* – are his best. That last sonnet-sequence of his, of which you sent me the review in the *Times Lit. Sup.*, and which has been so praised, I find (with the exception of that beginning 'These hearts were woven of human joys and cares, Washed marvellously with sorrow' which is not about himself) overpraised. He is far too obsessed with his own sacrifice, regarding the going to war of himself (and others) as a highly intense, remarkable and sacrificial exploit, whereas it is merely the conduct demanded of him (and others) by the turn of circumstances, where non-compliance with this demand would have made life intolerable. It was not that 'they' gave up anything of that list he gives in one sonnet: but that the essence of these things had been endangered by circumstances over which he had no control, and he must fight to recapture them. He has clothed his attitude in fine words: but he has taken the sentimental attitude . . ..

To: Arthur Watts   1 June 1915
                                                              (France)

. . . But this is perfect. The other officers have heard the heavy guns and perhaps I shall soon. They make perfect cider in this valley: still, like them. There are clouds of dust along the roads, and in the leaves: but the dust here is native and caressing and pure, not like the dust of Aldershot, gritted and fouled by motors and thousands of feet. 'Tis a very Limbo lake: set between the tireless railways behind and, twenty miles in front, the fighting. Drink its cider and paddle in its rushy streams: and see if you care whether you die tomorrow. It brings out a new part of one's self, the loiterer, neither scorning nor desiring delights, gliding listlessly through the minutes from meal-time to meal-time, like the stream through the rushes: or stagnant and smooth like their cider, unfathomably gold: beautiful and calm without mental fear. And in four-score hours we will pull up our braces and fight. These hours will have slipped over me, and I shall march hotly to the firing-line, by turn critic, actor, hero, coward and soldier of fortune: perhaps even for a moment Christian humble, with 'Thy will be done.' Then shock, combustion, the emergence of one of these: death or life: and then return to the old rigmarole. I imagine that this, while it may or may not knock about your body, will make very little difference to you otherwise . . . .

To: Mrs Sorley   10 July 1915
                                      (France)

We have taken over a new lot of trenches and have been having a busy time this past week: our exertions have been those of the navvy rather than those of the soldier. And – without at all 'fraternizing' – we refrain from interfering with brother Boche seventy yards away, as long as he is kind to us. So all day there is trench duty broken by feverish letter censoring. No amount of work will break the men's epistolary spirit: I am qualifying for the position of either navvy or post-office clerk after the war. During the night a little excitement is provided by patrolling the enemy's wire. Our chief enemy is nettles and mosquitoes. All patrols – English and German – are much averse to the death and glory principle; so, on running up against one another in the long wet rustling clover, both pretend that they are Levites and the other is a Good Samaritan – and pass by on the other side, no word spoken. For either side to bomb the other would be a useless violation of the unwritten laws that govern the relations of combatants permanently within a hundred yards of distance of each other, who have found out that to provide discomfort for the other is but a roundabout way of providing it for themselves: until they have their heads banged forcibly together by the red-capped powers behind them, whom neither attempts to understand. Meanwhile weather is 'no *bon*': food, 'plenty *bon*': temper, fair: sleep, *jamais*.

Such is 'attrition', that last resort of paralysed strategy of which we hear so much.

I hate the growing tendency to think that every man drops overboard his individuality between Folkestone and Boulogne, and becomes on landing either 'Tommy' with a character like a nice big fighting pet bear and an incurable yearning and whining for mouth-organs and cheap cigarettes: or the Young Officer with a face like a hero and a silly habit of giggling in the face of death. The kind of man who writes leading articles in *The Morning Post*, and fills the sadly huge gaps in his arguments by stating that the men at the front either all want conscription or think that Haldane should be hanged, is one step worse than [the people] who think that our letters concern our profession and not our interests. 'I hate a fool.'

To: Professor Sorley   15 July 1915
                                                         (France)

. . . It is now almost dark: come out and see the fireworks. While waiting for them to begin you can notice how pale and white the corn is in the summer twilight: no wonder with all this whooping-cough about. And the motor-cycles: notice how all these races have at least a hundred entries: there is never a single cycle going. And why are there no birds coming back to roost? Where is the lark? I haven't heard him all today. He must have got whooping-cough as well, or be staying at home through fear of the cow. I think it will rain to-morrow, but there have been no swallows circling low, stroking their breasts on the full ears of corn. Anyhow, it is night now, but the circus does not close till twelve. Look! there is the first of them! The fireworks are beginning. Red flares shooting up high into the night, or skimming low over the ground, like the swallows that are not: and rockets bursting into stars. See how they illumine that patch of ground a mile in front. See it, it is deadly pale in their searching light: ghastly, I think, and featureless except for two big lines of eyebrows ashy white, parallel along it, raised a little from its surface. Eyebrows. Where are the eyes? Hush, there are no eyes. What those shooting flares illumine is a mole. A long thin mole. Burrowing by day, and shoving a timorous enquiring snout above the ground by night. Look, did you see it? No, you cannot see it from here. But were you a good deal nearer, you would see behind that snout a long and endless row of sharp shining teeth. The rockets catch the light from these teeth and the teeth glitter: they are silently removed from the poison-spitting gums of the mole. For the mole's gums spit fire and, they say, send something more concrete than fire darting into the night. Even when its teeth are off. But you cannot see all this from here: you can only see the rockets and then for a moment the pale ground beneath. But it is quite dark now.

And now for the fun of the fair! You will hear soon the riding-master crack his whip – why, there it is. Listen, a thousand whips are cracking, whipping the horses round the ring. At last! The fun of the circus is begun. For the motor-cycle team race has started off again: and the whips are cracking all: and the waresman starts again, beating his loud tin tray to attract the customers: and the cows in the cattle-show start coughing,

coughing: and the firework display is at its best: and the circus specials come one after another bearing the merry-makers back to town, all to the inevitable crash, the inevitable accident. It can't last long: these accidents are so frequent, they'll all get soon killed off, I hope. Yes, it is diminishing. The train service is cancelled (and time too): the cows have stopped coughing: and the cycle race is done. Only the kids who have bought new whips at the fair continue to crack them: and unused rockets that lie about the ground are still sent up occasionally. But now the children are being driven off to bed: only an occasional whip-crack now (perhaps the child is now the sufferer): and the tired showmen going over the ground pick up the rocket-sticks and dead flares. At least I suppose this is what must be happening: for occasionally they still find one that has not yet gone off and send it up out of mere perversity. Else what silence!

To: Arthur Watts   26 August 1915
                                                         (France)

Health – and I don't know what ill-health is – invites you so much to smooth and shallow ways: where a happiness may only be found by renouncing the other happiness of which one set out in search. Yet here there is enough to stay the bubbling surface stream. Looking into the future one sees a holocaust somewhere: and at present there is – thank God – enough of 'experience' to keep the wits edged (a callous way of putting it, perhaps). But out in front at night in that no-man's land and long graveyard there is a freedom and a spur. Rustling of the grasses and grave tap-tapping of distant workers: the tension and silence of encounter, when one struggles in the dark for moral victory over the enemy patrol: the wail of the exploded bomb and the animal cries of wounded men. Then death and the horrible thankfulness when one sees that the next man is dead: 'We won't have to *carry* him in under fire, thank God: dragging will do': hauling in of the great resistless body in the dark, the smashed head rattling: the relief, the relief that the thing has ceased to groan: that the bullet or bomb that made the man an animal has now made the animal a corpse. One is hardened by now: purged of all false pity: perhaps more selfish than before. The spiritual and the animal get so much more sharply divided

in hours of encounter, taking possession of the body by swift
turns . . ..

To: Arthur Watts   5 October 1915
                                                          (France)

Just a line – albeit on military ruled paper. It is the eve of our
crowning hour.

I am bleached with chalk and grown hairy. And I think
exultantly and sweetly of the one or two or three outstandingly
admirable meals of my life. One in Yorkshire, in an inn upon
the moors, with a fire of logs and ale and tea and every sort
of Yorkshire bakery, especially bears me company. And yet
another in Mecklenburg-Schwerin (where they are very English)
in a farm-house utterly at peace in broad fields sloping to the sea.
I remember a tureen of champagne in the middle of the table, to
which we helped ourselves with ladles! I remember my hunger
after three hours' ride over the country: and the fishing-town of
Wismar lying like an English town on the sea. In that great old
farm-house where I dined at 3 p.m. as the May day began to cool,
fruit of sea and of land joined hands together, fish fresh caught
and ducks fresh killed: it was a wedding of the elements. It was
perhaps the greatest meal I have had ever, for everything we ate
had been alive that morning – the champagne was alive yet. We
feasted like kings till the sun sank, for it was impossible to overeat.
'Twas Homeric and its memory fills many hungry hours.

I was interested in your tale of meeting Wells. Yet a man
to whom every private incident is legitimate 'copy' I cannot
understand.

I can see you amongst your staff of warrior non-combatants: and
(with you) both wish you, and wish you not, rid of them. To
be able to prove oneself no coward to oneself, will be great, if it
comes off: but suppose one finds oneself fail in the test? I dread
my own censorious self in the coming conflict – I also have great
physical dread of pain. Still, a good edge is given to the sword
here. And one learns to be a servant. The soul is disciplined. So
much for me. But the good it would do in your case is that it
would discipline your liver. The first need of man is health. And
I wish it you for your happiness, though somehow I seem to know
you more closely when you are fighting a well-fought battle with
ill-health.

Adieu! or (chances three to one in favour of the pleasanter alternative) *Auf Wiedersehen*! Pray that I ride my frisky nerves with a cool and steady hand when the time arrives. And you don't know how much I long for our next meeting – more even than for the aforementioned meal!

To: Professor Sorley   5 October 1915
                                                              (France)

Many thanks for the letters which arrived with the rations this morning. We are now embarked on a very different kind of life; whether one considers it preferable or otherwise to the previous, depending on one's mood. It is going to be a very slow business, but I hope a steady one. There is absolutely no doubt that the Boche is now on his way home, though it is a long way and he will have many halts by the wayside. That 'the war may end any year now' is the latest joke, which sums up the situation . . ..

You will have seen that we have suffered by the loss of our chief: also that our battalion has lost its finest officer – otherwise commissioned ranks have been extraordinarily lucky. For the present, rain and dirt and damp cold. O for a bath! Much love to all.

Further Reading

SCOTTISH LITERATURE

Bold, Alan, *Modern Scottish Literature*, London: Longman, 1983

Craig, Cairns, (ed.), *The History of Scottish Literature*, vol. IV, Aberdeen: AUP, 1987

Hart, Francis Russell, *The Scottish Novel: A Critical Survey*, London: John Murray, 1978

Harvie, Christopher, *No Gods and Precious Few Heroes, Scotland 1914-1980*, London: Edward Arnold, 1981

Lindsay, Maurice, *History of Scottish Literature*, London: Robert Hale, 1977

Royle, Trevor, *Macmillan Companion to Scottish Literature*, London: Macmillan, 1983

Smout, T. C. *A Century of the Scottish People 1830-1950*, London: William Collins, 1986

Thomson, Derick, *An Introduction to Gaelic Poetry*, London: Gollancz, 1974

Watson, Roderick, *The Literature of Scotland*, London: Macmillan, 1984

LITERATURE OF THE FIRST WORLD WAR

Bergonzi, Bernard, *Heroes' Twilight*, London: Constable, 1965

Cross, Tim, *The Lost Voices of World War I*, London: Bloomsbury, 1988

Fussell, Paul, *The Great War and Modern Memory*, Oxford: OUP, 1975

Gardner, Brian (ed.), *Up the Line to Death*, London: Methuen 1964

Giddings, Robert (ed.), *The War Poets*, London: Bloomsbury, 1988

Johnston, John H., *English Poetry of the First World War*, Oxford: OUP, 1964

Parsons, Ian, *Men Who March Away: Poems of the First World War*, London: Chatto & Windus, 1964

Silkin, Jon, *Out of Battle*, Oxford: OUP, 1972; (ed.), *The Penguin Book of First World War Poetry*, London: Penguin, 1979; (ed., with Jon Glover), *The Penguin Book of First World War Prose*, London: Viking, 1989